CALLED TO CONTR✡VERSY

THE UNLIKELY
STORY OF
MOISHE ROSEN
AND THE
FOUNDING OF
JEWS FOR
JESUS

RUTH ROSEN

THOMAS NELSON
Since 1798

NASHVILLE   DALLAS   MEXICO CITY   RIO DE JANEIRO

For those who still wonder . . .

Published in Nashville, Tennessee, by Thomas Nelson. Thomas Nelson is a registered trademark of Thomas Nelson, Inc.

Thomas Nelson, Inc., titles may be purchased in bulk for educational, business, fund-raising, or sales promotional use. For information, please e-mail SpecialMarkets@ThomasNelson.com.

Unless otherwise noted, Scripture quotations are taken from THE NEW KING JAMES VERSION. © 1982 by Thomas Nelson, Inc. Used by permission. All rights reserved.

Scripture quotations marked KJV are from KING JAMES VERSION.

Library of Congress Cataloging-in-Publication Data

Rosen, Ruth, 1956-
    Called to controversy : the unlikely story of Moishe Rosen and the founding of Jews for Jesus / Ruth Rosen.
        pages cm
    Includes bibliographical references.
    ISBN 978-1-59555-491-8
    1. Rosen, Moishe. 2. Christian converts from Judaism—Biography. 3. Jews for Jesus.
4. Missions to Jews. I. Title.
    BV2623.R58R68 2012
    289.9—dc23
    [B]

                                                                                        2011048513

Printed in the United States of America

12 13 14 15 16 QGF 6 5 4 3 2 1

CONTENTS

PREFACE

I was only seven years old when it occurred to me that my father might be famous. I considered this a possibility because people that I didn't really know or care about sometimes told me how lucky I was to have him for my father. I also knew that Dad often traveled to speaking engagements, which could mean that crowds of people were listening to him. My curiosity about the extent of his importance beyond our small family grew.

Which led me to ask my mother, "Is Daddy famous?"

Mom—who in 1963 resembled a Jewish Donna Reed with (I thought) a twist of Jackie Kennedy—wanted to know what I meant by "famous."

I thought a moment and replied, "Do lots of people know who he is and think he is important?"

"I suppose you could say that," Mom replied. She was guarded about anything that might lead a family member to get what she termed "a big head." "He *is* well known in certain circles," she cautiously added.

"Mom," I said, "is Daddy famous like Billy Graham?"

"No," she firmly replied. "Nowhere nearly as famous as Billy Graham."

My curiosity was satisfied, and I didn't think about Dad being famous for a long time. Years later, when he became a keynote speaker at a Christian festival at the Felt Forum in Madison Square Garden, I barely noticed. Later still, when strangers I met on my own speaking engagements characterized my father as "a Jewish Billy Graham," I smiled and changed the subject. To this day, when people ask me what it was like being Moishe Rosen's daughter, I usually reply, "Compared to what? I've never been anyone else's daughter." But every now and then, I let myself think about how some would call him famous, others, infamous.

My father, Moishe Rosen, is probably best known as the founder of Jews for Jesus, a high-profile evangelistic agency that, in the words of its mission statement, "exists to make the messiahship of Jesus an unavoidable issue to our Jewish people worldwide." This in itself makes him a hero to some people, a villain to others.

Every author has a bias and an agenda and I will state mine here.

My bias: first, I share my father's belief in Jesus as the Jewish Messiah and Savior of the world. But while I hope this book provides insight, my purpose is not to push his or my beliefs on readers who might not share them.

Second, I love and respect my father.

Third, I believe I know and care for him well enough to portray him honestly without overlooking his weak points and even his failures. Athough he did not live to see this book completed, he saw and vetted most of the chapters. My mother vetted the rest on his behalf. No doubt some readers will be delighted to see some of Moishe Rosen's weaknesses or failings recorded, while others will be surprised and perhaps disappointed. I believe shortcomings are part of every real story. The Bible is remarkable inasmuch as it portrays many men and women of faith who knew God intimately—and it shows them as real people with ordinary feelings and failings.

I speak of my father in the company of these men and women, not to elevate him, but because their lives uncover clues about my father's life, just as they uncover truths about any life that has had a great impact. My father joined me in the hope that his biography would encourage others to see how God uses imperfect people to bring about great things.

So much for bias. Now for agenda. First, my father did, said, and thought things that many people found interesting and valuable. A record of his life and thoughts will resonate with some readers, perhaps helping them on their own faith journeys.

Second, since he is a controversial man, I want to nail down some facts that otherwise might fly away on wings of speculation.

Third, I want to present a more personal and detailed portrait than would be possible by a writer less acquainted with him than I am, or one with less access to him and those who knew him. My research included many hours spent taping interviews with my father, so you'll hear him explaining much of his life in his own words. Phone interviews and e-mail exchanges with friends, colleagues, and former colleagues bring their voices into the mix; and I include thoughts and memories from other family members as well as drawing from old correspondence and various documents recording his thoughts.

But I've also included my own firsthand observations and reflections, which I hope will prove insightful. My father found them to be so and told me that he learned some things about himself through reading this manuscript.

I hope the combination of narrative, dialogue, quotes, and commentary will give you more than the usual *whats* and *whens*, but will also show more of the *who* and *why*. Most of my footnotes elaborate on the main text and are separated out for those who want to delve.

Fourth, my father tried hard to communicate certain philosophies and principles. One of his great concerns was that they would be lost after he was gone. Many of Moishe Rosen's philosophies and principles are woven throughout this book because they are inseparable from his life story.

You, the reader, will decide how well and truly I've presented my father's life and thoughts. I offer the story of a man who has had a profound impact on many people, and I cannot help hoping that you will appreciate him on some level—as well as catch glimpses of the God he could not ignore.

Notes to reader: There are a few first person observations in some of the early notes, but most first person references come in later chapters, when my experiences and observations come into play. Also I refer to my father as "Moishe" almost exclusively up till the point in the story when I was born, then I use "Moishe" interchangeably with "Dad" or "my father." During the time he was executive director he preferred his daughters to refer to him as Moishe so that was not unnatural for me and referring to my mother as Ceil came just as easily. At home he was the consummate dad, and in many situations he enjoyed the role of proud papa—but once he became our boss, he did not want to show partiality so we addressed him the same way everyone else did.

INTRODUCTION

It didn't surprise Moishe Rosen that no friends or family members came to Denver's Stapleton Airport to greet him. He squeezed himself into a rental car and headed straight to General Rose Memorial Hospital, named for Maurice Rose, a Jewish war hero. Many of the patients were Jewish, including the one he had come all the way from New York to visit.

Moishe parked the car, squared his shoulders, and strode through the large glass double doors. He turned down the hall to the elevators. He hated hospitals. The smells made him queasy, and he disliked hardening himself to the moans of strangers as he walked down the corridors. But if he didn't steel himself, he would be too depressed to be of any use to his dying mother. What an awful phrase: "dying mother." She was so much more to him than that, yet as he'd observed, death dominates the identity of those whom it is about to claim. Still, as long as she had breath in her body, he would continue to hope.

The elevator door opened, and he stepped in. He prayed silently for his mother and for courage. Once again the door slid open. He stepped out of the elevator and walked down the long corridor to her room.

His father, brother, and sister-in-law were talking in the hall. They acknowledged him but did not say much. He entered the room and swallowed hard as he saw her lying there, looking small and weak. She had been such a strong woman. "Ma?" She turned to look at him. Though she was too spent to manage much expression, he felt she was glad to see him. "Hi, Ma." He mustered a weak smile and would have kissed her forehead or maybe her cheek, but he knew that sort of thing embarrassed her. He sat in the chair next to her bed, as close as he could get, and searched her face, hoping for a sign that there would be something he could say or do for her. No one from the medical staff or from the family had told his mother that she was dying, but she was an intelligent woman. She met his gaze, and he saw comprehension in her eyes. She knew why he had come. She understood that she would never see the other side of those big glass doors. She began to cry, a quiet, childlike whimper: "I don't want to die."

Ma, I don't want you to die either! he groaned, but not out loud.

Still whimpering, she repeated, as though it were a song, "I don't want to die. I want to live. I want to live." Just like in the movies.

He saw her, frightened, as she faced death and it was one of the worst things he'd ever witnessed. He would never forgive himself if he did not at least try to offer her the hope that he'd found. The moment hung before him, daunting and inevitable.

He patted her arm lightly, hoping the touch would bring some comfort. "Ma," he said, feeling almost as though he was listening to someone else's voice say the words carefully and calmly, "you don't have to be afraid . . .you really *can* live forever . . ."

That was as far as he got. Rose Rosen sat up, her gray-blue eyes suddenly wide, alert, and flashing with anger. With a strength that belied her condition she spat out the last words he ever heard from her lips: "If you've come to tell me about Jesus, you can go to hell!"

———

One might wonder why Moishe Rosen did it. Not why did he distress his dying mother by trying to tell her about Jesus. He had no choice about that because he firmly believed that Jesus could bring her peace, quiet her fears, and give her the hope of heaven.

Yet one might wonder why he ever allowed himself to consider Jesus as an option fifteen years earlier. Hadn't he realized it would lead to a moment like this? And why had he brought shame on his family by becoming a missionary? Why did he accept that it was his lot in life to be called *meshumad* (traitor) or in more sterile terms, *apostate*?

At times, unsolicited answers to these and other questions have been suggested by some who opposed his efforts. Remarks during his lifetime ranged from "He's not really Jewish" to "He did it for the money" to "He did it to win the approval of the goyim" (Gentiles) to "He's evil." One of the more interesting explanations was: "He's a self-hating Jew." Various rabbis and Jewish community leaders have made these remarks in newspaper and magazine articles, and many of their opinions and accusations trickled down to the public.

Moishe never took those remarks personally. Such statements concerning his faith and profession were like buttresses on the buildings of a status quo skyline—constructed to support the assertion that there's no good or wholesome reason for a Jew to believe and proclaim that Jesus is the Jewish Messiah. That assertion is so concrete that many see it as foundational for Jewish identity. After all, very few "givens" remain when it comes to describing what it means to be Jewish.

On the whole, the Jewish people are not likely to agree anytime soon on a set of beliefs and behaviors that make up one's Jewish identity. While a significant sector of the Jewish community is devoutly committed to a set of traditional beliefs, many others are far more subjective about what it means to be a Jew, often relying on what one cannot believe or do in order to set boundaries around their Jewishness. And the "cannots" become fewer all the time. Assimilation and intermarriage make it desirable to exclude as few as possible from the Jewish fold. Jewish Buddhists, agnostics, and Unitarians abound, and all may find their place within the community. And so the question arises, Where do we draw the line?

It often comes down to the following assertion: You cannot be Jewish and have a Christian belief in Jesus, because being Jewish and Christian are mutually exclusive. To many, this assertion is considered not only self-evident, but crucial to Jewish survival, almost the lynchpin of Jewish identity. The certainty that Jesus is not for Jews has kept collective heads above water in a sea that roils with relativism, secularism, and many other isms that have little to do with the God of Abraham, Isaac, and Jacob.

What has all this to do with a man whose beloved mother suggested that he go to hell rather than tell her about Jesus? Just this. Moishe Rosen grew up with the same set of assumptions and nonnegotiables regarding his identity as the rest of his Jewish family and friends—yet his life took a radically different turn.

Most people find it painful to part with lifelong assumptions. In this, Moishe was like anyone else. He often said that he was an ordinary person who would have been content to go on living an ordinary life based on ordinary assumptions—assumptions that excluded Jesus. Yet his life did not remain ordinary. Whether one lauds or loathes Moishe Rosen's mission in life, he became an extraordinary force, causing countless people to question age-old assumptions about being Jewish and believing in Jesus.

Here is how it happened . . .

PART ONE

The Early Years

ONE

I was born in Kansas City, but raised in Denver.
So far as I knew, I would never leave my home town.
—MOISHE ROSEN

Ben Rosen was seeing Kansas City through different eyes now that it was his home. As a child, he'd been there often—whenever he and his brother, Dave, visited their married sister, Annie Singer. Sadly, they were more welcome at her house than in the Denver home that had once been theirs. Within a year from the day the boys' mother, Dora, died of diabetic complications, their father, Edel, had taken a new wife. She seemed to resent the fact that her three youngest stepchildren, Ben, Dave, and Ida, were too small to fend for themselves. Edel did not resist his new wife's insistence that his children make way for her own five, all daughters.

Annie took in Ida, the youngest sibling, and helped the boys whenever she could. Dave and Ben took turns visiting her in Kansas City. The one who stayed in Denver did chores by day and curled up to sleep in the unheated shed at night.

With maternal love barely a memory and a father who was not known for treating his children affectionately,* it's no wonder that Ben grew up tough and proud of it. Perhaps for a time he was a little too tough. He always remained true to his father, even covering for Edel in the matter of some bad checks. When Ben found himself on the wrong side of the law, he gritted his teeth and took it rather than implicate his father. After that incident, Ben decided the best way to turn his life around was to leave Denver. With Annie and Ida in Kansas City, he headed for Missouri.

Finding a job wasn't difficult. Tall and strong, Ben had a quiet confidence and was not afraid of hard work. As he strode down Troost Avenue one sunny

---

* When I asked Moishe about his grandfather, he simply said, "He was not a nice person," with a look that conveyed far more than his brief statement. I surmise that my great-grandfather may have disciplined his sons quite roughly, and my grandfather may have done the same with his boys. I also believe family honor kept my *zayda* (grandfather) from speaking ill of his father. Moishe, while not wanting to paint a false picture, was also reluctant to speak ill of his grandfather.

3

day in 1928, Ben had reason to be optimistic—and hungry. The smell of food brought him into the local bakery / delicatessen, and the sight of a lovely young woman behind the counter kept him coming back. Ben watched with admiration as Rose Baker deftly carved corned beef and lox into thin slices, demonstrating a strong, steady hand as well as a pretty face and figure. He began to flirt.

Rose might have blushed inwardly, but she accepted his attentions with outward composure. She mentioned that she had just bought a tennis outfit, and Ben quickly offered to teach her, though he knew nothing about the game. After Rose agreed to go out with him, Ben explained that he was "just kidding" about the tennis lessons. He had a wide, easy grin and eyes that telegraphed his mirth even when he tried to keep a straight face. Rose smiled back. The rest, as they say, is history. Rose's sister Esther had a man of her own, Sam Cohen, and so the Baker sisters made it a double wedding.

––––––

Were it not for this love story, Moishe Rosen, and subsequently Jews for Jesus, probably would not exist. Nor is it likely that it would have come about if the Bakers and the Rosens had settled far from one another. Unlike so many Jewish immigrants who struggled to build new lives near other Jews in the enclaves of Manhattan's Lower East Side or Brooklyn, these two families chose less populated, yet robust Jewish communities farther west. Though completely unknown to one another, one day two of their offspring would meet and marry and produce two sons. One of those sons would revolutionize Christian missionary efforts among Jewish people in what many would consider a shocking turn of events.

Who can predict the effects of seemingly unrelated circumstances? When Jacob Baker and his family left Austria, they were not fleeing anti-Semitism; they were taking a brisk walk away from it. Hitler and his black-booted terror troops were not yet on the horizon, and under the reign of Franz Joseph, Jews were treated relatively well. Unhindered by many restrictions that confronted Jews throughout Europe, the Bakers lived rather comfortably. Jacob was a carpenter who built especially fine cabinetry and had developed a formula for furniture polishes. His skills were highly respected and suitably rewarded by the Franz Joseph regime via a commission in the military.

However, when the Bakers' oldest son, Arthur, was ready to train for his chosen profession, the family discovered that Austrian equality did not extend quite far enough to admit Jews into medical school. Jacob decided to move his entire family to America where the young man's dreams might be fulfilled. Jacob was willing to sacrifice the status and connections he enjoyed for his son to become a doctor—but the young man was not accepted to medical school in America, either. Yet Papa Baker did not want to turn back. Had he not pressed on in his new life, who can say what would have become of him and his family in Austria? No one knew the horrors that awaited European Jews when the Bakers made their way to Kansas City to join their cousins, the Beisers, who had previously emigrated.

Jacob, his wife, Dora, and their sons Arthur, Joe, and Ben, along with their daughter, Esther, found their places in a Jewish community and settled into a way of life that would later be termed Reform—even though the synagogues they attended were Orthodox and later Conservative. Certainly they believed in God, and the heart of the family beat with an unequivocally Jewish rhythm, cycling through celebrations and sorrows shared by Jews everywhere. But they were more ethnically than religiously oriented. Into this setting the last two Baker children—Rose, and a younger brother, Milton—were born.

Edel Rosen left his Eastern European homeland under less sanguine circumstances as Russian persecution against Jews was prevalent and pointed. While details remain unknown, family lore has it that if the persecution itself had not been reason enough for the family to flee to America, Edel, through some act of vengeance against the persecutors, had become a fugitive from the law. One of Edel's uncles had made the voyage two years earlier; when officials at Ellis Island noted his lung condition, they sent him to Denver, Colorado. There the air was therapeutic, and he would find treatment to help him regain his health and become a productive citizen. Edel joined him.

The Rosens were not as affluent as the Bakers nor was Papa Rosen as benevolent a father to his sons as Papa Baker was to his sons. But if Ben had received all the encouragement and affection the most accomplished father could give or even if his stepmother had been able to create a loving environment, Ben might never have come to Kansas City, and he might never have met his bride.

Ben and Rose's first son, Martin Meyer Rosen,* was born on April 12, 1932,

---

* Moishe stopped using the name Martin in the 1970s and made his Yiddish name his legal and permanent appellation.

in Kansas City's Menorah Hospital. Martin was given the Hebrew name "Moshe" at his circumcision, but his grandfather Edel called him Moysheleh, the Yiddish derivative. In 1934 the family moved to Denver, where Moishe's brother, Don, was born.

Moishe's earliest memory was that of asking for more to eat—and being told there was no more. He must have been around four years old at the time. He never forgot that gnawing sensation or the ubiquitous oatmeal for breakfast, lunch, and dinner when the family could not afford better. He maintained an aversion to oatmeal for the rest of his life. The amount and variety of good, fresh food that eventually became available doubled as one of his chief enjoyments and most perilous problems.

The Great Depression years deeply affected those who lived through any part of them. The thirties, Moishe's childhood years, were lean for most people. Ben's sister Ida had married Sam Freedberg, who worked in a produce store and later a fish store. That meant the Freedbergs had extra food to share, and whenever they could, they'd give some to Ben and Rose and the boys.

When Moishe was nine years old, his mother became ill. No one told him the nature of her sickness, but he remembered radiation treatments, so it was most likely some form of cancer. Rose was generally hearty and strong, but she became greatly weakened, unable to cook or clean house. Moishe's father taught him to prepare meals, and with help from his brother, Don, Moishe took over that responsibility for a while. The boys also washed and dried the dishes, and Moishe scrubbed the kitchen floor on hands and knees.

He never questioned his extra responsibilities because he knew that family takes care of its own; when one is weak, others take up the slack. This value was deeply embedded in his childhood and remained with him always.

When things got better, Moishe's mother tried to encourage him to pursue a part of childhood he'd missed. "Go out and play with other children," she'd urge him. But he tended to be a loner and a daydreamer.

Though the family struggled, they managed to live with dignity—and to live as Jews. It cost a dollar a week to go to *cheder* (Hebrew school, also known as Talmud Torah). Some weeks Ben could pay the *melamed* (teacher), and other weeks he taught his sons Jewish traditions and prayers at home. As family finances improved, the boys were able to attend cheder regularly.

Grandfather Edel Rosen maintained strict adherence to Jewish holidays, traditions, and dietary rules. Following his grandfather's death, Moishe's family continued the affiliation with the Orthodox synagogue for special events, but their home life was just plain Jewish.

A certain amount of religious activity was expected in order to show loyalty to the Jewish people, but as is often the case, those activities neither stemmed from nor inspired deeply held spiritual convictions in the Rosen home. Moishe's father maintained that "all religion is a racket," and his mother, while not sharing her husband's cynicism, did not seem interested in religion. It would be fair to say that Moishe's childhood was strongly shaped by Jewish values, but not by Jewish faith.

Moishe was also strongly influenced by the regard his parents demonstrated for each other. He said about his parents' relationship, "There was a lot of romance there. I can still remember how my father would take us out for Sunday rides with my mother beside him in the front seat and us boys in the back. As my father drove along, he would sing love songs to her. He always told us how terrific our mother was, in front of her."*

This was one of many childhood lessons that carried over to Moishe's adult life. Accordingly, the next few chapters provide a look at Moishe's childhood, beginning with an emphasis on his mother and her influence on him.

---

* Moishe passed on this lesson by frequently telling people that an effective way to affirm someone is to speak appreciatively of his or her good qualities to a spouse or a parent.

TWO

As a Jew, I grew up being alternately fascinated and angry with
Christmas. I had no idea that thousands of miles away, a little Jewish
girl from a far stricter background than my own was hearing Christmas
carols, wondering why the one they spoke of was not for her.

—MOISHE ROSEN

The radio was playing songs about a jolly old man, and it was easy for five-year-old Moishe to imagine that man with his white beard and red suit. He knew that Santa was somehow able to figure out who was naughty or nice. This in itself was not especially interesting to a five-year-old, but there was the promise of a present for nice children. Santa understood about presents because he had a big sack filled with toys.

Toys! Like most kids, Moishe made playthings out of anything at hand. Cardboard boxes became cars and boats. Once he got hold of some wonderful wooden blocks, left over from carpentry repairs. But all too soon, they disappeared into the fiery maw of the coal stove. When you're very young, it's hard to understand that firewood is more necessary than toys.

Moishe began singing along with the radio: "Santa Claus is coming to town." *Is Santa listening?* he wondered. Even if he wasn't, the bouncy song was fun to sing.

His mother turned quickly, surprised to hear her son singing what she considered a Christian song. Ironically, Rose liked Christmas music, and as her son put it years later, "No one held it against her." If there was a hint of a double standard, it was probably because as an adult, she was fully educated about the need for Jews to reject the Christian religion. She could therefore enjoy a few of its harmless trappings. But a five-year-old boy had to be taught the difference between what was Jewish and belonged to "us" and what, as part of someone else's religion, must be relegated to "them."* So she called out: "Moishe, it's nice

---

*Moishe was conscientious about maintaining those distinctions. He recalled, "One year our teacher was handing out candy canes to the whole class. She told us they were for Christmas. Of course I wanted the candy, but still I told her, 'I don't get one. I'm Jewish.'" The exclusion from anything connected with Christmas was entirely self-imposed as a matter of loyalty. (The teacher, who did not want any child to feel excluded, smiled and said, "'That's all right. You can have yours for Hanukkah.'")

that you're singing, but that song . . ." She paused. It wouldn't do to have him singing it when Ben got home. And if the boy's Zayda Edel ever heard it, that would be far worse.

"Is it a bad song?" Moishe didn't recall any naughty words in the song.

"Well, if your father or grandfather heard you singing that song, it would make them unhappy. Anyhow, Santa Claus isn't coming to our house."

"Why not?" he wanted to know. He couldn't see that there was anything wrong with his house, nor did it seem to him that other boys and girls were noticeably nicer than he.

"Because we're Jewish, and Santa Claus doesn't come to Jewish homes," his mother explained patiently. Then, partly because she did not want him to think that Santa Claus was among those who disliked Jews, and partly because she was a very truthful person, Rose explained that actually Santa didn't come to anybody's home because he was not real. She compared him to a character in a fairy tale. But that didn't satisfy Moishe.

So Rose very carefully began to separate childish fiction from the realities of life. As Moishe listened, he began to accept that some things he'd heard about or imagined did not exist. For the first time, he began to wonder about other realities he had taken for granted. His thoughts turned to a special Someone Else that people talked about, Someone from whom people seemed to expect good things and who mysteriously knew everything about everyone. Okay, so Santa was made up. "But, Ma," he asked, "is there a God?"

Rose paused thoughtfully, and then, as though answering the question as much for herself as for him, she said, not quite as emphatically as he would have liked, "I'm pretty sure there is."

———

That was the first conversation Moishe recalled regarding the existence of God. Rose did not often talk about such things, but she held certain beliefs that showed through in her outlook.

Moishe said, "My mother believed in rectitude, that God saw everything and would ultimately make sure justice was served. I know that she believed in hell. She was certain that Hitler was there. But she never exactly said if she believed in heaven."

While his mother's concept of God was rather remote, her vision of right and wrong was close at hand and very practical. Moishe remembered her saying, "You may be forced to lie to an outsider, but never lie to yourself. If you're doing wrong and you tell yourself it's right, even when you want to do right, you'll continue doing wrong. But if you can admit to yourself that you're wrong, then you stand a chance of someday changing and doing right." Moishe never forgot that lesson: know right from wrong, and remember that right and wrong involve truth.

His mother spoke in aphorisms such as, "The person who lies to himself is the biggest liar in the world." Some of her sayings seemed cynical, such as, "Advertising is all lies," but that was her way of protecting herself and her family—because she didn't merely mean the advertising of shopkeepers and other merchants. She meant people who would "advertise" their own good qualities. She was fond of saying, "I'm from Missouri. You have to show me." Moishe once said, "My mother was an antiperfectionist. She thought something was authentic if she could see the flaws in it." Some of Rose's ideas of good and bad, right and wrong, may have been subjective, but there in the middle of it all, the focal point was honesty.

Rose was never insincere. She cared nothing for the good opinion of someone she didn't like. And she was a profound friend to her friends, among whom her reputation was not so much as a woman of manners, but as one who was kind-hearted, generous, and loyal.

Rose Rosen was an intelligent woman with a highly inquisitive nature. An overflow of her enthusiastic pursuit of knowledge was her love of sharing information, and it was a way of relating, an indication of fondness for those with whom she exchanged facts or points of view.

She also related to people by feeding them. She was known to all her friends and family as an excellent cook, and as the economy improved, she exercised her culinary talents with gusto. During the high holidays,* her kitchen became something of a strudel factory. She'd make large quantities to give away, and still there was plenty for the family. To her, Jewish holidays were not so much religious events as occasions to cook and have company.

She was not tremendously demonstrative when it came to physical affection, yet Moishe always knew her as a very affectionate and loving person. He recalled, "On rare occasions, she would kiss us [his brother or him] on the cheek, and she didn't ordinarily hug us. But when I was a little kid, when I hurt myself, my mother would hug me and rock me. And then she'd look at me

---

* Rosh Hashanah and Yom Kippur

and say: 'Did that help the hurt go away?' To my mother, being loved caused healing."

Rare as those outward demonstrations may have been, the love that inspired them was constant, and Moishe always knew that his mother cared for him. He also knew that his father cared about him, though dynamics between fathers and sons are bound to be different—perhaps more complex—than those between sons and mothers. Likewise, the influence of Jewish religion and identity on Moishe was strong, but complex. To that latter influence we will now turn.

THREE

To a little child, there's not much difference between a star and a
streetlight. My world was so small that, for all I knew, the moon could
have been a decoration on the wall of the sky. But as I began to gain a
larger view of the universe, my sense of awe over God grew.

—MOISHE ROSEN

April 12, 1945, was not a good day. Moishe felt somewhat numb as he processed the news that Franklin Delano Roosevelt, the thirty-second president of the United States, was dead. He had arrived at cheder as usual and immediately noticed that something was amiss. His teacher, Mr. Lerman, was looking down at his old hardwood desk. He waited until the whole class was seated to look up and then, with great effort, said, "Boys, I have something terrible to tell you. . . ." He paused, struggling to compose himself, but his voice was still choked with emotion as he announced, "President Roosevelt died today. He was the best friend the Jews ever had! All of you who know how to say *kaddish* [A prayer recited in daily synagogue services and also by those mourning the recent death of a close relative.] can join with me now." He began to sing the ancient Aramaic chant: "Yisgadal, v'yiskadash, sh'may rabboh . . ."

Later that evening, Moishe and his family huddled by the radio. They were torn between grief over the president and fear of what his death might mean for the country, for the war, and for the whole free world.

"Hitler can't hold out much longer," Ben said in a low voice.

But what about the Japanese? Moishe thought. *They got one of our destroyers today.*

Meanwhile, the radio commentator was reminding sorrow-stricken Americans of Roosevelt's achievements. And then came the voice of the dead president, repeating those famous words from his first inaugural address: "The only thing we have to fear is fear itself." The president was sixty-three years old when he died.

Fifty years older than me, Moishe thought. *I'm never going to be that old.**

---

* For whatever reason, he never expected to have a very long life.

Sixty-three years meant sixty-three birthdays. Moishe wondered if any of FDR's birthdays had been real clinkers. He wasn't sure which year was supposed to be special for the *goyim* (Gentiles). For Jewish boys, it was definitely the thirteenth year. That was the big birthday, the one that meant he could be bar mitzvah,* no longer a boy but a man.

Moishe would always remember *his* thirteenth birthday and how it would forever be associated with the passing of a United States president. It was a sad and dreary day; the entire country was in mourning and celebration of any kind would feel strange and unseemly.

Still, now that he was 13, he was to be bar mitzvah—and so the following Thursday he went to a small neighborhood synagogue to perform the proper rituals.

"How come I don't get to do it on Saturday, like the other guys?" Moishe had asked when his father first broached the subject.

"You do it on Saturday and the whole shul** is there. Everyone expects a big party after."

"Yeah," Moishe nodded. "I know." He didn't mention that he'd worked hard at learning the Hebrew and wanted to celebrate his accomplishment, or that a nice reception afterwards would show that his dad was proud of him.

"You want a big party?" Ben frowned. His son did not usually ask for such things.

"Sure. Why not? It's a big deal, a bar mitzvah, right?"

"You know how much a party like that costs?"

Moishe looked down. He knew his family didn't have a lot of extra money to spread around, but he didn't think they were that poor. Not anymore.

Then a painful thought occurred to him. Maybe his dad wasn't proud of him and didn't want the whole shul to witness his bar mitzvah. Moishe knew that he sang off key. One might think that singing the scriptures to the appropriate minor key melodies would make it easier to remember the Hebrew words, but not for Moishe. Somehow the elusive notes would not stick in his head the way they were supposed to. Singing only seemed to make it harder. Not only that, but he had a bit of a stammer and that was bound to come out if he tried merely speaking the words.

---

* *Bar mitzvah*, literally "son of the commandment," refers to the boy who undergoes the rite of passage, but it also refers to the ceremony itself. Traditionally, the bar mitzvah recites the Hebrew prayers and reads from the Torah during the weekly worship service.

** Shul is a Yiddish word for synagogue.

So he sighed in resignation. Maybe doing it on Thursday wasn't such a bad thing after all. He certainly would not be the first bar mitzvah to enter into manhood through the downstairs classroom of the synagogue instead of the upstairs sanctuary.

Every Thursday morning a *minyan* (quorum of ten Jewish men needed for prayer) met at the synagogue to listen to the rabbi teach a Talmud class in Yiddish. On the designated day, father and son arrived at the synagogue and went directly downstairs where they joined twelve to fifteen older men sitting around a large table. Moishe knew many Yiddish words, but unlike his parents, he did not speak the language fluently. Consequently, it was difficult to concentrate on the lesson.

Finally the rabbi finished his remarks, and with no fanfare, the bar mitzvah proceeded. A couple of men placed the Torah scroll on the table, unrolling it to the text for the day. With a *yarmulke* (skullcap) on his head and *tallis* (prayer shawl) around his shoulders, Moishe approached the scroll and began the first blessing as best as he could: "Barachu et Adonai Ha-me-vorach."

The men around the table sang back to him, as per tradition: "Baruch Adonai ha-me-vorach le-olam va-ed."

Taking a breath, Moishe continued: "Baruch ata adonai, eloheinu melech ha olam asher bacher banu mi kol ha'amim, v'natan lanu et torato, baruch ata adonai notein ha torah. Amen."

One man stood beside the boy, holding a *yad* (literally hand). The long-handled silver pointer was a reminder that the Torah is sacred and not to be touched by human hands. Moishe was glad enough for the traditional helper to hold out the long pointer so that he could keep his place in the ocean of Hebrew words before him.

Moishe had not completely memorized his portion, but since he had learned how to read Hebrew, he thought he would recognize any words he did not know by heart. Unfortunately, the Hebrew he'd studied had vowel points, and the Torah scroll had none. This slowed him down considerably. As for the melody, Moishe chanted the Scripture portion in a singsong style that he could only hope sounded something like the appropriate chant.

When he finished, once again he recited the proper blessing. He looked half expectantly at the rabbi, who smiled and nodded, but did not ask him to give a speech. The other men likewise smiled and nodded, but offered no words of encouragement or congratulation. He returned to his seat.

Ben had brought two bottles of whiskey to make it a festive occasion for the *minyan*. But for Moishe, the bar mitzvah was a big nonevent.

———

Despite the disappointments over his bar mitzvah, Moishe always viewed his Jewish upbringing as a profound influence that afforded many invaluable life lessons. His early days in the synagogue and cheder taught him a sense of awe for God. Through Judaism, he began to learn about holiness and how some places, and some objects, were to be set apart and handled (or not handled) in a special way. That sense of setting things apart for God even affected how one dressed. Before the high holidays in the fall (Rosh Hashanah and Yom Kippur) when possible, his family bought new clothes for the special synagogue services. Likewise, in the spring, if they could afford them, they bought new clothes to wear for Passover.

Although religious objects—the tallis, phylacteries, and holy books—inspired a sense of awe in Moishe, his childhood concept of God was not confined to, or even most often experienced, through religious activities. Usually when he thought of God, it was in the context of a game, in which he regarded God as a companion. As a child, Moishe would jump over tires, trying not to let his foot touch rubber, and think, *I'm doing this for you, God.*

Consciously or not, Moishe learned the idea of setting things apart for God from the Jewish religion. Yet he did not develop confidence in the religion—not the way that he saw it practiced in his grandfather's house or even in his own house while his grandfather was still alive. There were so many rules, and the rules did not seem to provide understanding: they imposed fear and a continual anxiety lest they be broken.

Contrast this with Moishe dedicating his childish games to God, imagining that the Almighty would actually enjoy them. The desire to dedicate his efforts to God was probably rooted in religion. But the idea that they could be joyful or fun efforts probably came from an inner sense—more intuitive than religious—that God loved him and could relate to him.

Moishe's growing understanding of the vastness of the universe expanded his idea of God. He could not regard Judaism as the sole custodian of holy knowledge. Nor did he view the religion of Judaism as the final word on Jewish identity.

"Being Jewish always gave me a personal context of being," Moishe explained. "It told me, in part, who I was so far as the rest of the world was concerned. My sense of Jewishness was not derived from religious practice, though I did my share of rituals. My Jewishness was generated from an inner sense of mystery. I felt a sense of awe at our history."

Jewish identity was based not only on being part of one community, but also on being separate from another. That separation was often demanded rather forcefully from non-Jewish communities. Moishe recalled the first time he experienced such a demand. He was nine years old and wandered from his neighborhood (they lived at Fifteenth and Federal Boulevard). He said, "I wasn't particularly aware that the Jewish neighborhood only extended as far north as Eighteenth, and even if I had known, I probably still would have gone well past it. Then I turned down one of the side streets, and saw some boys playing in an empty lot."

The boys were digging a big hole, wide enough for all of them to get into it. Moishe recalled,

> Lacking in social graces, I thought if I just stood there they might invite me to join them. And so I came near, and looked at them, and smiled. The boy who was digging with a spade stopped and looked back at me. He said, "You're new around here. Where do you live?" I said, "Fifteen Ten Federal Boulevard." And another boy said, "That's Jew-Town, isn't it?" Another boy said, "Are you a Jew?" And I answered quite confidently, "Yes," with the unspoken assumption, "Isn't everybody?"
>
> One boy yelled, 'We don't want any Jews around here! Go away, you dirty Jew!' Well, anyone who looked at these boys could see that they'd been digging in the mud. And me? I wasn't dirty—at least not until one of them threw a spade full of mud at me. I hurried away, somewhat hurt and very puzzled."

Once home, he and his mother had a talk about what Moishe called "the Jewish facts of life." His mother said, "'Don't go out of the neighborhood. You'll just get into trouble. They [meaning non-Jews] are not like us, and they don't like us." According to Moishe, the rest of the discussion went like this:

> "But, Ma, how come they don't like us?" With patience, she explained, "Well, it has to do with their religion. They think that we killed their God."
> I said, "Well, did we?"

She said, "Do you think that anybody could kill God?"

As I thought it through, I realized it was a ridiculous idea. So I knew that we were right, and they were wrong, and we were smart, and they were, well, I didn't know all of them, but those I'd met that day seemed less than smart. After that, if anybody asked me if I were a Jew, I would say in a not especially friendly tone, "Why do you want to know?" And if they didn't have a good reason for asking, I could give them a good reason not to ask in the future.

This type of negative experience, which was to be repeated at various stages and with varying severity, galvanized Moishe's identity as a person who was part of a people who were separate from others. And why would he want to be part of those people who mocked and hated others whom they didn't even know? Yet somehow he knew that the separation went beyond the prejudices of those who would reject him for being Jewish. And he knew that his religion could not explain the separation. He'd learned that there was a difference between "us" and "them," but though he knew who "we" were, like many others who grew up Jewish, he did not exactly know *what* we were or why we were different.

"I never questioned that God chose the Jewish people, as we'd been taught from the Bible," he said.

At the same time, I never imagined that the rabbis—with their laws upon laws and their need to know almost everything about almost nothing— could really understand what an awesome people we Jews were. Somehow with all of their learning, I never felt they adequately explained what it meant to be Jewish.

Intuitively I knew that if being Jewish was something from God, it should not be so hard to understand. So many rules and procedures, and the not-so-subtle hints that much more study was required all seemed to obscure the issue: What does it mean to be a Jew?

Like his father, Moishe eventually grew cynical toward religion, but also like his father, he did not allow such feelings to compromise his Jewish identity. Ben Rosen was absolutely loyal to the Jewish community. He knew the prayers and made sure his sons knew them, too, because that was part of what it meant to be a Jew. Once he had the means, he contributed generously to Jewish causes, even to the synagogue that he only occasionally attended. Likewise, Moishe's assessment of the religion as inadequate in no way lessened his sense of Jewish identity or his loyalty to the community.

Part of that loyalty meant not trading his religion for another. Moishe had heard how Christians tried to convert Jews to their own religion—the very religion (he supposed) that caused people to hate Jews as Christ killers. He rehearsed over and over for the day when some Christian would try to lure him to "the other side." He would smile and say, "That's all right for you, if you want to believe that way," and then he would add in his best don't-mess-with-me voice, "But as for me, I'm a Jew."

Moishe recalled, "As Jews, we knew that we weren't regarded as being champions by non-Jews. But our attitude was, if they weren't going to like us, then we were going to like ourselves." He quickly learned to accept that part of his identity as a Jew was to be hated for no particular reason. Yet he always felt accepted and secure in his own community, the Jewish community. The fact that he was pretty much finished with the religion by the time he was thirteen was no reflection on his place in that community. In fact, it made him more like than unlike most Jews he knew, including his father, whose influence was considerable.

FOUR

I'm always amazed at how much I accepted my father's values on one hand and, on the other, how much I reacted against them.

—MOISHE ROSEN

The light of the long summer day was finally fading, but the lanky fourteen-year-old had not caught a single fish. He wasn't disappointed, though; he'd enjoyed the day immensely. He had long since honed habitual daydreaming into a fine art, and fishing was a generous patron of that art.

He'd heard enough radio shows and read enough to fill the big screen of his imagination with all kinds of stories. Sometimes Moishe starred in his own daydreams, but often he reconstructed famous characters. He knew a lot about superheroes and their powers from comic books, which he bought or borrowed whenever possible. If Captain America wasn't strong enough to handle a job Moishe dreamed up for him, well, he simply added in a quarter of Superman's abilities for good measure.

It made little difference to him that no fish were biting. That saved him a chore, after all. His mother's maxim was, "I cook fish; I don't clean them," and the subsequent warning was, "If you catch anything, it better be cleaned by the time you get it home." Thinking of fish caught or uncaught reminded Moishe that he was hungry, and he was glad when his father drove up. But before the boy could pack up his gear, his dad had jumped out of the truck and picked up the rod.

Nodding to his son, he asked, "Catch anything?"

"Nah," Moishe answered.

Ben said, "Let me show you how."

Moishe was pretty sure his father realized that he already knew how to fish. So he sighed, and silently wondered, *Why don't you just say you want to try for a while?* And he prepared for the inevitable. Sure enough, his dad soon reeled in a fish. Ben continued to fish, speaking slowly, amiably, about things his son already knew. The line jerked, and he pulled another fish off the hook.

Instructions that imparted no new information were bound to irritate the hungry adolescent. It didn't occur to him that while his dad liked to fish, he

19

might also want to spend time with his older son. Ben's way of relating to his boys was to teach them. When he wasn't teaching, he was teasing.

The son watched as his father caught another fish and another. He'd spent a whole afternoon without catching anything and had not felt the least bit inadequate. But now he heaved an audible sigh. "Uh, Dad? I'm pretty hungry. Can we go home?"

His dad shrugged. "Sure. But first I better clean these fish. You know how your mother feels about that."

———

Ben Rosen triumphed over the Great Depression years to become a successful businessman and a good provider. He began with buying and selling goods from a truck and eventually he and a partner, Izzy Weiss, opened R & W, a secondhand store. In the mid- to late-1940s, Ben started his first junkyard, Rosen Brothers, with his brother, Dave, his brother in-law Joe, and his nephew Louie (Annie Singer's husband and son). Ben poured every drop of sweat and smarts into his trade, eventually shaping it into a large and lucrative business. In 1956, Ben started Atlas Iron and Metal with his younger son, Don, and a couple of Don's in-laws.

Busy as he was, Ben set aside an hour or so each evening to teach his sons his philosophy of life. Moishe recalled this as "a combination of the Jewish sense of culture and achievement and his own brand of homey diligence." He said, "Dad periodically made sure we could recite our Hebrew prayers, and he stressed business principles that, had we written them down, would have made a valuable course in any business school. He taught us how to deal with people, how to determine the value of an item, and how to buy and sell."

Regarding the prayers, Ben never hid the fact that he did not think much of religion in general. Moishe knew that if his father believed in God at all, it was not the God of the Jewish religion. At one point he asked, "Dad, why do we say these prayers if you don't believe God is listening?"

"Sonny Boy," his father replied, "we say the Pledge of Allegiance to the flag because we are Americans. I don't think the flag can hear us, do you? We say the prayers because we are Jews. If we don't do these things, how else will people know we are Jews?"

And so Moishe learned from his father that the Jewish religion, though not necessarily to be believed in, was to be respected and practiced because it was part of what made people to be Jews.

These lessons were not relationship-building times, per se. "I never really thought of myself as having a relationship with him," Moishe explained. "At school I was supposed to learn from the teachers and at home I was supposed to learn from my father."

Ben was extremely devoted to his family, but he hadn't many clues from his own father when it came to drawing out his sons as individuals or providing one-on-one experiences they could enjoy together. Moishe's fondest memories of his dad were times when the entire family was together, around the supper table or out for a drive. He also remembered taking pride in watching his dad excel or receive acknowledgment in various public arenas. Their private father-son moments were not as satisfying—perhaps because those times afforded more possibilities and therefore greater potential for disappointment.

"He never took me to do anything that I wanted to do," Moishe recalled, not by way of complaint or accusation. "He took me along to do what he wanted to do." Then, correcting himself, he added, "I take that back. He took me to see *Snow White* when I was five years old. It was a big deal because at the time we were still very poor. . . . He hadn't chosen the movie for his own pleasure. He expected me to enjoy it, since the film was created for children."

Unfortunately, a pale, shaken little boy emerged from the theater, wide-eyed with horror. As he told the story seven decades later: "When that witch, with her big ugly face that filled the screen leered at poor Snow White, offering her that poisoned apple—it terrified me!"

Moishe may not have had a truckload of happy memories of moments spent with his father, but he certainly learned a great deal from him. He was decisive in pointing out the major influences: "I learned two important things from both my parents. First, I learned that you have to live by principles. It wasn't enough to do what was right; you had to understand why it was right. Second, I learned curiosity."

Ben worked hard and had a good reputation as a man to be trusted, and he transmitted these values to his sons. But at times, there seemed to be contradictions.

"There was a time when I was nine years old," Moishe recalled, and I was with my dad at his little secondhand store. . . . Somebody came in to buy a tool and when they named a price, my father said, "I paid that much for it myself." I knew that he had paid less than the amount stated, and thought he must have forgotten. So I corrected my father in front of the customer. He didn't say anything at the time, but later when we were alone, he referred back to the situation and said, "In business, you do things like that. There's truth for the family, then there's truth in business. And in business, sometimes you say things that aren't true."

He could see that I was puzzled, so he patiently put it in terms I could understand. "It's like a game—each side says something to try to win. If you, the seller, get your price, you've won. And if they buy it for their price, they've won."

To Ben, this was a common outlook that businesspeople understood and accepted.

Moishe accepted the explanation for a while, but within a few years, he concluded that employing such a tactic while making a sale was "not nearly as necessary as my father had indicated." Even before Moishe came to regard truth as something to be told because of its intrinsic value, he had already rejected the notion that sacrificing a small piece of it was a reasonable requirement for striking a good deal.

Despite the liberties he sometimes took in the interest of business, Ben paid what he owed, and he loved and provided for his family in every way that he knew how. He also insisted that both sons learn how to work, and so, at nine years of age, in addition to chores at home, Moishe had occasional chores in the family business. As he grew older, those chores expanded to a part-time job on the weekend. His pay was three dollars for a day's work, most of which he was expected to contribute to help with household expenses. At twelve, he was taking apart automobile motors at the junkyard, and by the time he was fourteen, he was swinging a sledgehammer to break cast iron. Most employees used twelve-pound sledgehammers, but Ben had Moishe using an eighteen- or twenty-pound sledgehammer to show that he was working harder than they did.

Moishe said, "It didn't occur to me that I had any choice until one day when I complained to my father about having to use a bigger sledgehammer than the grown men. His answer was, 'Well, if you want to get a job elsewhere, do it.'"

Ben had every reason to assume that both sons would eventually take over the business as partners. But it bothered Moishe that when he felt things should be done differently, he had no authority to make any changes. Instead, he decided that if he ever had a business to run, he would do things a certain way. So without realizing it, the "if ever" began to take him on a different path.

Moishe never could feel the way his father wanted him to feel about the family business. Added to the issues mentioned above was the simple fact that Moishe disliked being dirty.

"There was this mysterious difference between my father and me," he recalled. "My father would take a bath and he seemed to get perfectly clean, with nothing but hot water, lava soap and a scrub brush. But no matter how much I washed and no matter how hard I scrubbed, it seemed like I could never get the grease from the junkyard off my hands, and I could never get the dirt out from under my fingernails."

Moishe found much to admire in his father. His work ethic, determination to provide for his family, and unflagging love for his wife were all things Moishe learned to emulate. Ben had other talents and skills that Moishe appreciated, though he was unable to emulate them. But there were also areas where Moishe found that he differed from his dad, and as those areas solidified, he went his own way.

FIVE

If people around me were interested in something,
it was easy for me to become interested, too.
I enjoyed other people's enthusiasm for what they were doing.

—MOISHE ROSEN

It was Saturday afternoon, and Moishe was engrossed in a comic book.

"It's such a nice day. Why don't you go outside and enjoy it?" his mother suggested.

He shrugged. "Yeah, okay. Maybe I'll go see if Paul wants to do something." He whistled a tune through his upper front teeth as he walked up the long block of Federal Boulevard to where his friend lived. The houses here were a little bigger and nicer than they were on his block. Moishe was just about to walk up to Paul's front door when it opened and his friend came out. Paul was on his way to church, and he invited Moishe to come along.

Moishe asked, "How come you're goin' to church on Saturday? I thought you guys did all that church stuff on Sunday."

"That's for mass, but I hafta go for confession. It won't take long."

"What's confession?" Moishe asked as the two boys headed toward St. Dominic's Church.

"Every week I go and confess my sins. Then the priest pronounces forgiveness and tells me how many Hail Marys and Our Fathers I should say to show how sorry I am."

"Hail Marys and Our Fathers?" Moishe's nose wrinkled in confusion.

"Those are just the first few words of the prayers we say for penance," Paul explained patiently. He recited a prayer that didn't sound like any prayer Moishe had heard in the synagogue.

Moishe looked at his friend skeptically. "Paul," he said, "you're one of the nicest guys I know. I've never seen you sin. I don't see how you have something to tell that priest every week."

Paul laughed. "Maybe I don't do the really big sins," he said, "but everyone does stuff or says stuff that's wrong, and if nothing else, thinks stuff that's wrong—and every time you do that, it's a sin.'"

Soon they were at St. Dominic's. "It sure is fancier than our synagogue," Moishe observed. The building's conspicuous cross made him a little uncomfortable, but he didn't say anything.

Paul asked, "You wanna wait out here, or you wanna come in?"

"Are you sure they allow Jews inside?" Moishe asked doubtfully.

"Why wouldn't they?" Paul looked at him curiously.

Moishe thought it best not to mention how he and his friends had gotten into fights with other Catholic kids who called them "dirty Jews" and "Christ killers." Paul wasn't like that. But lots of other people were.

"Maybe I'll just wait out here," he said.

"Sure," Paul shrugged and quickly disappeared behind the big doors.

I wonder what it's like in there, Moishe thought. Finally, curiosity got the better of him, and he went inside.

The first thing he noticed was how all the stone columns and arches pointed toward the eighty-foot high ceiling of the inner room, or sanctuary. Something about that ceiling—probably the sheer height of it—made it nearly impossible not to look up.

The next thing he noticed was a collection of candles flickering, each in its own little jar, on a table in the foyer. This puzzled Moishe because it reminded him slightly of the Jewish tradition of *yahrzeit* candles, which were lit at home to memorialize the anniversary of a loved one's death. These church candles were smaller and didn't look as though they would last for twenty-four hours, the customary time for a yahrzeit candle to burn. It was very quiet in the church and a bit chilly, though it was warm and sunny outside. Statues of people were situated all around the sanctuary, and there in the front of the sanctuary, hanging from a cross, was a larger than life-sized statue of Jesus. *It must be ten feet tall*, Moishe thought. Unlike the other statues, this one was illuminated. The feet were at eye level, and red paint indicated blood where the huge nail sank in, affixing both feet to the cross.

For Moishe, the strangest thing about this statue was something like a window around the chest, where people could see a heart. But it didn't look like a real heart because it had no veins or arteries. It looked like something that belonged on a card for Valentine's Day. *But then*, he thought, *they think he's supposed to be God. And if God had a heart, I guess it could be any shape he wants.* These observations took less than a minute, but their overall effect on Moishe was a sense of eerie otherness. He stuffed his hands in his pockets and began to fidget with the contents, unconsciously pulling out his key ring. As he was fiddling with it, it dropped to the floor.

The clatter seemed to resound throughout the entire church. Moishe felt his cheeks burning as he bent down to retrieve it. He stood in time to see Paul emerging from a wooden closet-like structure. With great relief, Moishe headed toward the doors where he waited for his friend to join him.

Outside, the sunlight seemed to melt away all the strangeness of the experience.

They agreed to go downtown, even though Moishe had no money. Denver had several dime stores. Cap guns and comic books, boxes of crayons, and barrels full of penny candy were just a few of the items offered. They chose to go into Grant's. They walked up and down a few aisles until they got to a rack of sunglasses. Moishe removed a pair, then quickly looked around to see if anyone was watching. He peeled off the price sticker and stuffed the sunglasses into his pocket. "Okay," he said, grinning. "Let's go."

They were almost outside when a woman's stern voice stopped them in their tracks. "Just a minute, young man. I believe you're hiding a pair of our sunglasses," she said, "and I can only assume that you were planning to leave without paying for them."

"Huh?" Moishe said.

"I saw you put the merchandise in your pocket, and I've called the manager," she said, even more sternly than before.

The manager was there within seconds. "What seems to be the problem?" he asked.

"This boy was stealing a pair of sunglasses," the saleswoman explained.

"If you mean these," Moishe said, pulling the glasses from his pocket, "then you're right that they were your merchandise. But I bought them here a couple of weeks ago."

The manager examined them and then looked carefully at the boys' faces. Neither showed any sign of guilt or fear. Handing the glasses back to Moishe, the manager said to the boys, "Get along you two." Then he nodded to Moishe and added, "You, perhaps, would do well to do the rest of your, ah, shopping, elsewhere."

Moishe shrugged. "I guess, if you say so, sir." He and Paul left the store as casually as possible. When they were half a block away, Moishe gave a little whoop. "That was close!"

Paul shook his head sadly. "Stealing *and* lying," he lamented.

"Aw, don't worry about it," Moishe said, though he felt a little badly about distressing his friend. "Look, I don't do it very often. It's just a little adventure and it's not like it's stealing from a real person or hurting a family business. It's just some big company, and they've got way too much merchandise as it is. They expect people to take a few things here and there."

As Paul looked at him, his silent reproach spoke far louder than words.

"Well anyway," Moishe said, clapping his friend on the back, "thanks for not snitching."

"You know I'm no snitch."

"Yeah, I know," Moishe replied, and he silently resolved not to shoplift during future outings with Paul. For all he knew, the guy considered it a sin to watch someone else stealing. He didn't want his friend to have to say any more Our Fathers or Hail Marys on his account.

———

One of the paradoxes of Moishe Rosen's personality is that while he always considered himself a solitary person, he truly enjoyed getting to know and appreciate others. It's hard to say exactly how or when a boy finds people and things besides his parents to help shape his ideas and worldview. Everything from books to movies to friends and teachers help broaden one's perspective. This was as true for Moishe as for anyone and, in some regards, perhaps more. His inquisitiveness and his willingness to be influenced by others may be among the reasons why so many others were influenced by him.

Radio had a powerful influence on Moishe; before he learned to read, it was not only his main source of entertainment, but it also provided the most fuel for his imagination. Moishe once said, "Looking back, I feel we [children] were somewhat understimulated. People didn't talk to children as much in those days." Perhaps for this reason he was quickly riveted to whatever could entertain or absorb his attention or cause him to really think. The problem with radio shows was that when they ended, one had to wait another week for the next episode. Not so with books, which was one reason why Moishe loved to read. Action, adventure, and science fiction became favorites.

Despite his love of reading, school was somewhat problematic for him. Moishe recalled, "My body went to school, but my mind went elsewhere." In class, he sat absorbed in his own thoughts and imagination, paying just enough attention to pass. He found it difficult to listen to most teachers because, as he put it, "I just didn't have a sense that they were talking to me." (Years later, he wondered if he'd had attention deficit disorder.)

His lack of interest in distinguishing himself was not limited to the classroom. He had no interest in sports or other physical games.

As far as socializing, probably Moishe's earliest influences other than his parents were members of his extended family, his cousins. Moishe's cousin Donald was a year older, and in many ways Moishe looked up to him, often asking him about things he found perplexing. For example, there was the whole issue of Christmas. Moishe was not altogether satisfied with his mother's explanation of why the holiday was not for Jews. Donald explained, "Goyim have their own kind of *yomtov* [holiday] about this magical baby. The baby was magical because he was born without a regular father and he grew up and did magical things, like made sick people well, but if he got mad at anybody, he could kill them by magic. He was also magical because he couldn't be killed."

By the time Moishe was in the third grade, Donald was in fourth and they were past believing in magic, but they had not outgrown their ambivalence toward the "magical baby." Moishe's parents were able to move into a more Jewish neighborhood where the kids made fun of Christmas because, as Moishe recalled, "making jokes about it helped us feel as though we wouldn't have wanted to celebrate the holiday even if we could."

Moishe's friend Paul became Moishe's window to Christianity when he was eleven or twelve years old. Moishe enjoyed their discussions, and his friendship with Paul helped to dissolve some of his childhood misunderstandings and prejudices. Though Paul was a committed Catholic, Moishe did not feel the main difference between them was Catholic versus Jewish, but "very religious" versus "not so religious." The religion itself, as far as he was concerned, was predetermined. People stuck with the religion in which they'd been raised. The choice, it seemed to Moishe, was how serious one was about his or her religion. It wasn't so much Paul's religion itself that was interesting, but "mostly," Moishe explained, "I could see that his religion meant a lot more to him than Judaism meant to me. It was his devotion and commitment that I found interesting."

Most of Moishe's friends were Jewish and, like him, not so religious. There were about six guys approximately the same age who stuck together. Moishe recalled, "We used to say, 'The fewer people in the group, the fewer can snitch on you,' and snitching was a very big deal." It's not that "the gang" got in any serious trouble, but certainly they knew that some of their activities would get them punished if anyone knew what they were doing. For one thing, they would often play where they had no business being. Then there was the occasional petty thievery: stealing cherries off the neighbor's trees and occasional shoplifting.

From time to time, there would be a fight. These altercations were not over territory or drugs. Usually one guy would hit another, and then, in a semi-civilized manner the other would say, "You wanna fight? Okay, you get your guys and I'll get my guys and we'll meet in the empty lot on Knox Street."

Moishe did not recall any major injuries on either side. The fights normally lasted less than five minutes and ended when one side or the other ran home. But still, the boys might have done serious damage to one another. One of Moishe's teachers tried to persuade him to forgo these fights, but Moishe felt he'd be letting down the other guys if he didn't participate. Yet the teacher was a voice of moderation, and Moishe made a point of telling the other guys what the teacher had said. Although the fights didn't stop, they grew fewer and farther between. By the time junior high was over, the boys had pretty much outgrown them.

Around the same time that Moishe discovered science fiction, he began reading books that stimulated his intellect as well as his imagination. One book assigned in junior high school was by John Dewey, about which Moishe said, "It was definitely over my head and there was much that I didn't comprehend, but I understood enough to become very interested in thoughts—how people think, how people see things." The world of ideas presented a new kind of adventure that Moishe found captivating throughout his life.

Eventually Moishe drew conclusions diametrically opposed to Dewey's, particularly regarding metaphysics and the belief in God. Yet he recognized Dewey as a major influence in his early thinking; the book helped him to question thoughts and evaluate ideas critically.

As far as ideas and ideals, socialism was a strong influence in Moishe's youth. He recalled, "When I was growing up, most of the Jews on the west side of Denver were influenced by Marx and Engels. We looked forward to the day when all people would be free and would not be 'wage slaves.' There would be great equality. There was no talk of violent revolutions or world conquest—certainly none of the darkness of communism. What we shared was a kind of political optimism, believing that socialism would usher in a time when all people would have enough food and whatever else was necessary to live well."

As for Moishe's quality of life, it took quite a radical turn when, at fifteen, he began spending time with the person whom he credited with having had more influence on him than anyone else he'd ever met, before or since.

SIX

My girlfriend and wife is the most influential person in my life. She is someone of superior intellect and imagination, a very caring person.

—MOISHE ROSEN

Moishe adjusted his long strides to keep from outstripping the petite brunette beside him. Even as he slowed, she lengthened her short, brisk steps, and their initially awkward gait fell into a companionable rhythm. They headed toward Sloan's Lake on what was, at least for Moishe, their long-awaited first date.

When the attractive Boston-bred newcomer first moved into the neighborhood, all the guys had been eager to meet her. One day, fourteen-year-old Celia Starr—or Ceil, as she later preferred to be called—joined a group of teenagers who had congregated outside the house next door. The guys teased her, asking her to say *park* and *car* and *bottle*. Then they hooted gleefully and tried to imitate her as she pronounced the words *cah* and *pahk* and, best of all, *boh-ull* with no *t*.

Moishe watched and listened with interest. The new girl's exotic accent was almost as appealing as her pretty face, framed by long dark hair, and her very feminine figure. But Moishe saw something that had escaped the rest of the guys. The new girl was shy.

It had taken forever before Ceil had finally agreed to go out with him. He didn't know that the next-door neighbor girl, Paula, had given Ceil a "friendly warning" to ignore Moishe's attentions. "He's a nobody," she'd said, "and if you want to get to know the popular kids, you'd better stay away from him." Ceil had been grateful for the quick and convenient friendship with Paula and decided, at least for the time, to take her advice.

Over the next twelve or so months, Ceil often saw Moishe helping her mother carry groceries, and she smiled inwardly to think he was probably hoping for a chance to see her. One day Mrs. Starr reciprocated Moishe's kindness as he went door to door, selling glow-in-the-dark light pulls (to be attached to ceiling fixtures) and house numbers, and she bought light pulls.

When Moishe delivered the pulls a few days later, Ceil was at home. They struck up a conversation, and she agreed on a date to go rowboating at the nearby lake.

At the lake, Moishe secured the oars in the locks and deftly rowed out into deeper water. He didn't bother telling his date that he didn't know how to swim. The pair stayed on the water for two or three hours and never ran out of things to say. Her shyness melted as he encouraged her to talk. Moishe's questions flowed from genuine interest. It wasn't just that she was pretty; she was smart, *and* she'd been to places like New York City. He wanted to know what those places were like and was impressed by her ability to describe them. As he listened, he could almost see the Statue of Liberty and other famous landmarks he had only read about.

Ceil was what his parents considered a nice Jewish girl. Yet she was, by her own admission, "sick and tired" of religious rules and regulations that, to her, seemed old-fashioned and irrelevant. They tried to teach that sort of thing in Hebrew school as well as at home, but as a teenager, she wasn't having any of it. "I liked learning Hebrew," she said. "Languages are fun. But forget about all that other stuff."

"You were still in Hebrew school when you left Revere?" Moishe was surprised since most people he knew stopped going once they turned thirteen.

She explained that it was an upper division school, Hebrew Teacher's College in Roxbury. But she started cutting classes because it took an hour and a half travel by subway and streetcar each way—and she found the translation of minutia with no explanation as to its relevance boring.

"And what about your trip across the country?" he asked. "What was that like?" As he listened to her describing the sights, Moishe nodded and asked more questions and was happier than he could remember being in a long time.

She concluded, "It was night when we got close to Denver, so I couldn't see, but when I woke up, there were these big, beautiful mountains in the distance, all purplish-pink in the morning light. I'd never seen anything like it."

Moishe grinned, inexplicably proud that the Rocky Mountains—which seemed to spring up practically in his own backyard—had impressed this girl who had seen so much more than he had.

She smiled back, studying his face. There was that funny gap between his two upper front teeth—you couldn't help noticing it, but still, he had a nice wide grin. His light brown hair was brushed back, but a stubborn cowlick always flipped one lock of hair back over his forehead. His brown eyes were warm and friendly, he had a strong jaw, and his features were regular and actually kind of handsome. *Yes*, she thought, *if he wasn't so skinny, he would be handsome.* He was no weakling, though, she observed, as he continued to row the boat around the lake.

Then the sky began to cloud up, and it started to rain, so the two hurried ashore. Moishe walked Ceil to her door and mumbled something about hoping to see her again soon. She thanked him, perhaps a little primly, and said she'd had a nice time. While she was not exactly swept off her feet, she would not mind seeing this boy again.

At first, Ceil was mainly impressed by how impressed Moishe was with her. She recalled, "But as we began to get to know one another, I found him to be easygoing and very caring. He was never demanding and always willing to spend more on our dates than I thought he should, considering he didn't have very much money." She slowly grew to appreciate Moishe for his own qualities and eventually found herself returning all the romantic fervor of a first love.

Moishe was smitten from the start. "Anyone could understand why I would get a crush on this girl," he said.

She was very pretty and poised, and she had charm. I suppose those things might grow less impressive after a while if her personality had been dull. But she would tell me about things I never heard of before, and through her, new worlds opened up to me.

At fifteen, I'd only left Denver once, and that was on a train trip to Kansas City. It didn't occur to me that I could experience much beyond my hometown. . . . I figured I'd go into some small business or other. I had never been very ambitious, didn't want very much for myself. But I really wanted Ceil's company. So, in arranging social things, she'd take the lead. And that meant I was meeting new people, going places—even to a dance, though I felt awkward and wasn't much good at it. But I'd do more, try more, because of Ceil.

There were also a few things I discontinued because of her. For example, the occasional shoplifting stopped. I figured my girlfriend wouldn't like it, and I didn't want to have secrets from her. Caring for her good opinion made me want to be a better person.

She became the most significant person in my life. I knew that she was overconfident about some things, and maybe overly opinionated about others, but I liked her backbone. I didn't see myself as a particularly resolute person so I admired her decisiveness. . . . She'd learned to read early and had skipped first grade, so even though we were the same age, she was a year ahead of me in school. Of course I was attracted to her physically, but she also stimulated my mind.

Though Ceil was shy and somewhat reserved, she chose choral performance classes and sought out extracurricular activities that put her in touch with school life. Unlike Moishe, who didn't care much for sports, she appreciated the social aspects of attending their school's sporting events. She was thrilled when she got accepted into the Valkyries, North High School's somewhat elite all-girl pep club. Despite Moishe's disinterest in sports, he was more than willing to sit through a football game if it meant being with his girlfriend.

Moishe took Ceil to school functions because he wanted her company. In return, she went with him to air shows and listened to him talk about guns and airplanes and other military stuff that fascinated him, and for which she politely pretended interest. But mostly, they did things both could enjoy such as taking long walks by the lake or joining his family on outings when they'd all pile into his father's big Buick on a trip to the mountains or a picnic in the park.

Ceil gravitated more and more to the Rosens' house at the end of the block. There the atmosphere was far less controlling than the environment in which she'd been raised. Nevertheless, it took her a while to feel comfortable around Moishe's father. Ceil recalled, "His mother was always friendly, but his father scared me because he just sat in his big easy chair by the radio and never talked much. I thought he didn't like me."

Within less than a year, the couple had decided they were in love. And one day, when they were sixteen, Moishe asked Ceil, somewhat casually, "You wouldn't be interested in someday marrying a guy like me, would you?" She was surprised because they were still in high school—but it did seem to be a logical conclusion to the relationship. So after a moment's reflection, she replied, "Yeah, probably I would."

While it was not an official engagement, both of them considered that some kind of proposal had been made and accepted. From then on the couple took it for granted that one day they would marry. They fell into a weekly routine of Sunday afternoons at the movies. Every Sunday as they walked from the streetcar stop to the theater they passed a street preacher who stood at Sixteenth and Champa, in front of the big department store. He sang and recited Bible passages loudly enough to be heard half a block away.

Sunday after Sunday, the couple never stopped to listen or talk to the man. He might have seemed clownish to some, yet Moishe was deeply impressed by the man's courage and dignity. In a strange way, Moishe envied him. Once as they passed him, he told Ceil, "I wish *I* believed in something strongly enough that I'd be willing to stand up on the street corner and shout it."

Moishe had long since lost the sense that the Almighty took any real interest in his daily life. As far as religion went, Moishe had never really connected God and religion. To him, religion was always a human effort, not something delivered from or expected by God. Over time, Moishe's perception of religion and religious people took on a rather cynical perspective, not unlike his father's.

Through his teen years, Moishe had developed a more or less pantheistic view that God "is all and in all." But he wasn't ready to give up the idea that God had a mind and God had a will. He always believed that there was a First Cause that brought the world into existence, but following that, he figured that God might or might not know, care, or otherwise be involved in what was going on. Moishe later described this as "a weak deist view which, by the time I was sixteen or seventeen, was a cynical skepticism."

Whereas Moishe felt that one couldn't really know much about God and need not be too concerned about his existence, Ceil was quite outspoken about her view that God did not exist at all. As much as Moishe respected her intelligence, she could never persuade him of anything if he thought she hadn't the proper grounds for it. For all he knew, her certainty of God's nonexistence was a subconscious punishment aimed at her overly strict parents and the God she supposedly did not believe in. But whatever reasons she gave to support her unbelief, they never struck him as altogether reasonable. He therefore argued the point and said that certainly there was a God.

Despite his cynicism regarding religion, Moishe felt a need to identify with and belong to the Jewish community. Yet he didn't quite know what his religious obligations were. This ambiguity probably was due to the semi-religious upbringing after early childhood, the largely secular nature of Denver's Jewish community, and the wide range of what people considered "proper Judaism."

Moishe and Ceil agreed that they would have a Jewish household when they married, but it would be an American Jewish household, free of the outdated rules and regulations their families had brought from the Old Country.

Of course when they began talking of marriage at the age of sixteen, no one thought the romance would last that long. And when they were eighteen and decided the time had come to carry out their intentions, their parents were concerned that they were still too young. But whatever people said and whatever they thought, the marriage was apparently meant to be.

Moishe's cousin Dorothy recollected the romance between her cousin and friend and wrote this to me:

> Your mother was a very sexy young woman. I always thought she looked like a cat. She moved like one, and with the dark hair and [hazel] almost yellow-gold eyes, she looked like one. Her movements were very natural—she wasn't even aware she was moving like that, but guys sure were. Once she started going with your father, she didn't know any other male existed. . . .
>
> We worked in the same office building one summer. She would come to pick me up for lunch. You could hear her coming down the hall in her high-heeled shoes. The young lawyers would stand at their doorways to watch her walk down the hall. This also she did not see. A couple of them asked her out. She said, "No. I'm engaged." Then your father came down to the office to see her and she introduced him. Later the guys said, "But Celia, he's just a kid!" She said, "No he isn't, he's my fiancé." He was a tall gangly kid and sometimes he *acted* like a kid, but none of that mattered—they were in love!!!

SEVEN

When we shoot the gun of anger we can be killed by the recoil.
—MOISHE ROSEN

The first sergeant leered at Moishe as he delivered one of his most disgusting insults: "Tell me, Rosen, are all Jewish women whores or just your mother?" Clearly the sergeant was trying to provoke a fight. Moishe clenched his teeth and looked around to see the other guys' reaction. They only looked away. Maybe they didn't want to risk the sergeant's anger by sticking up for Moishe, but what would it have cost for a couple of them to find him later and say, "Hey, Rosen, he's just a jerk. We don't feel that way"? But they never did. In fact Moishe knew that some *did* feel "that way."

Being hated simply for being Jewish was nothing new; still the seamier realities of military life were a somewhat rude awakening for Moishe. Throughout high school ROTC, and as an underaged member of the National Guard, he had attended weekly drills, collected his three dollars per session, and truth be told, enjoyed the activities and the classes. He had been eager for this time of military service. He could hardly believe that he would receive five and a half dollars for each day. (He'd been raised to that prodigious amount for achieving an officer's rank through correspondence courses.) Not only that, but he'd never been away to any kind of camp before. So with anticipation and a great sense of adventure sixteen-year-old Moishe packed up and left for his fourteen-day drill.

There were two significant facts of which he was unaware. First, a crisis was brewing with the Soviet Union in Berlin and Moishe's Guard unit was about to be nationalized. And second, he would be practically the only Jew in his battery.

The only other Jewish soldier Moishe encountered proved to be small comfort. Some of the guys had a habit of singing out, "Sheeny, sheeny," whenever they passed him, and he'd just grin as though enjoying a friendly joke. And once, when a group of guys demanded, "Show us your circumcision," he had dutifully complied while they snickered.

That incident so incensed Moishe that when the others left their hapless victim, Moishe was anything but compassionate. He stormed over and kicked the soldier's tail. "You want to make a fool out of yourself, then make a fool out of yourself," he barked. "But don't make a fool out of our people. When they insult you for being a Jew, stand up to them!"

Moishe had grown to his full height of six feet one inch and had won enough fistfights over being Jewish that few people wanted to pick that particular quarrel with him. But the first sergeant was not "most people." Stocky and well muscled, he was four to six inches shorter than Moishe. He used his mouth to compensate for his height as he continually antagonized Moishe with obscene and racist remarks. He used his rank as well, refusing to give Moishe his mail on time, forcing him to ask for what was regularly delivered to others.

As the insults and injustices built up, so did the pressure of Moishe's barely repressed anger. One day he was alone in the barracks when the first sergeant came in and made one of his usual obnoxious remarks. Then he inspected the lockers as though he had just made a passing comment about the weather. Whatever had been holding back Moishe's anger burst, releasing a sudden flood of rage-induced energy.

Moishe picked up a carbine and swung the butt end upside the sergeant's head. It felt so good to hurt him that Moishe was actually frightened by his anger. But even that fear could not hold back his fury as he stood over the sergeant. All the hostility he'd ever felt toward "them"—the world of Jew-hating Christians—culminated as he stood staring into the hate- and fear-filled eyes of the one man who seemed to represent them all. *He doesn't just hate me; he hates my mother, my father, my girlfriend. He was probably cheering for Hitler . . . he'd love to see us all wiped off the face of the earth.*

The sergeant rolled onto his stomach, but before he could push himself up, Moishe raised one leg and brought his combat boot down full force on the sergeant's back, hoping the blow would connect with his kidneys. When the sergeant got up, Moishe began goading him into fighting back. When he did, Moishe had the excuse he wanted to hit harder until he finally backed off, his adrenaline spent. The sergeant was disheveled and dazed, but he wasn't bleeding.

Moishe stared at him for a moment, then swallowed hard and said, "You tell anybody what I did, and I'll tell them why. I'll tell them what you've been saying, how you've been keeping my mail from me. Maybe some of the guys will back me up."

Whether it was fear of exposure or a decision to chalk up the beating as retribution for weeks of harassment, the sergeant didn't report Moishe, nor did he bother him again. His only revenge was to assign the teenager to guard the motor pool for thirty-six straight hours the next day. Halfway through that triple shift, Moishe fainted and ended up in the hospital with exhaustion, but he knew the entire incident could have ended in a far worse scenario. Before long, he found the memory of his violent outburst sickening, and it engendered an abhorrence for fighting that remained with him for the rest of his life.

———

Moishe hadn't bothered to tell his parents when he signed up for the National Guard. They were accustomed to seeing him in uniform—he'd been participating with the ROTC since he was fourteen. They could hardly be blamed if they didn't notice the difference between Moishe's activities with ROTC and the National Guard. The uniforms were identical except for the color of the piping on the service caps. All Ben and Rose knew—from what Moishe told them and what they could observe—was that his extracurricular activities with the military were teaching him discipline and building his confidence.

From the start, Moishe enjoyed his training. His high school, like many others at the time, offered students a choice between gym class and ROTC. Since Moishe did not go in for competitive sports, the choice was obvious. And whereas he considered himself a failure as an athlete, he did quite well on the rifle range. With a little practice, he earned sharpshooter medals, achieving the highest qualification ROTC gave for small arms.

ROTC provided many opportunities, including a series ten correspondence course to become an officer. He did well in these classes, went on to the series twenty, and was designated as first lieutenant. (He later stated, "I don't know what in the world that meant because I never bought an officer's uniform.")

Having grown up in the shadow of WW2, Moishe was keenly interested in military science and tactics. He was glad that Germany lost WW2 because Hitler would have killed all the Jews if he could. Other than that, Moishe described his attitude in the following terms: "I've always been interested in the military, but when it came to war, I wasn't mad at anybody. Not even the North Koreans. If the North Koreans were angry at the South Koreans, that was their problem. If the Koreans had invaded America, well, that would have been different. I would go and fight. But I learned something in high school that I never forgot: George Washington warned us against getting involved in foreign wars."

Moishe's interest in the military was based on strategy and the satisfaction he felt as he learned various skills. He also liked the gear. He wasn't interested in using weapons against people, but he enjoyed learning to operate them much as he'd enjoyed learning to operate a camera or other piece of fine equipment. His experiences with the military—like his experience as salesman—proved him more than competent and gave him confidence: a precious commodity for a teen.

Some of the guys Moishe knew began joining the National Guard, and it wasn't long before he, too, was approached during ROTC by his sergeant and a recruiter. He learned that in the National Guard, he would be expected to go to a weekly drill wherein he would march for two hours, listen to a lecture, and collect three dollars for his time. Then he would go for a full two weeks in the summer and get paid for that, too. Better yet, if he signed anyone else up, he would get five dollars for each person who joined.

And so Moishe lied about his age and signed on the dotted line. He later recalled,

> My reason for joining the military was purely mercenary. And I figured if it was anything like ROTC, it would be interesting and maybe fun. I signed up quite a few people who probably joined for similar reasons.
>
> Some of the drills were on Sunday, and they took us out to Camp George West, which was near Golden, Colorado. They introduced us to our primary weapon, a 105 mm howitzer. We used dummy shells and learned to operate as a squad.

As far as Moishe knew, the two-week summer drill would be mostly more of the same, only it would be every day—and of course he'd be away from home. But when the unit was federalized—taken into the regular army because of the Berlin crisis—the summer drill became much more. They were to help with the Berlin Airlift. However, the attorney general of Colorado didn't want to release the National Guard to the U.S. Army, so he obtained a stay and Moishe's unit remained in Colorado at Camp Carson.

Moishe considered it a happy coincidence that all this occurred just as school had let out. His girlfriend, Ceil, had been sent back East for the summer.

(Her parents, concerned about how serious the relationship had become, thought it wise to separate the couple for a while.) Other than working part time as a stock boy, he would have spent most of his time with her. Instead, he'd work full time for better pay, and he wouldn't miss Ceil any more than if he'd stayed at home. It didn't occur to Moishe that now that he was actually in the army, it might not be so easy getting out.

Everyone was restricted to the base, except for one weekend when they were allowed to go to nearby Colorado Springs. For the first time in his life, Moishe received "real mail" and greatly enjoyed the letters people sent him. Notes from his mother, from Ceil, and from another friend allayed feelings of homesickness. Ceil's letters were the most frequent and the most highly anticipated.

Moishe was in headquarters battery of the 168th Field Artillery, which was part of the 157th Regimental Combat Team. Because the numbers at the camp had diminished so greatly following World War II, Moishe was in what they called a *cadre*, that is, units that were not full. His unit had sergeants, lieutenants, captains, and so on, but no privates. So, the officers had to do everything. Moishe's official job was head of the communications section, which meant that he would lay down telephone wire. "We also reported on the artillery," said Moishe.

In addition to the official work of communications for the Field Artillery, like everyone else, Moishe was required to fill in the gaps where they didn't have enough personnel to cover other tasks. For example, there were no real cooks in the field kitchen. When asked if he had any cooking experience, Moishe truthfully answered that his experience was limited to frying hamburgers and making soup. He said, "Little did I know, this was going to get me stuck in the kitchen one day a week. But we had to eat." He also learned how to give injections because his cadre had no medics.

Moishe's military career lasted less than six months. When the school year began and Ben Rosen realized that his son wasn't coming home, he wanted to know what the army was doing with a sixteen-year-old boy. He went to the attorney general of Colorado and let him know Moishe's true age. After that, Moishe said that he was "unceremoniously dumped." There was some embarrassment because he had been designated as a reserve lieutenant. Before long, Moishe was thankful that his father had gotten him discharged; if he hadn't, by the time Moishe was eighteen, he'd have been sent to Korea with the 157th

Regimental Combat Team, which suffered one-third casualties, most of which were serious wounds that took the soldiers out of action.

Following his discharge, Moishe finally saw a doctor about an ongoing medical issue. His father used to joke, "Martin is not afraid of work. He can lie down right beside it and go to sleep." And it was true that once Moishe reached adolescence, he was continually dozing off. He really did work hard and never fell asleep in the midst of vigorous physical activity. However, if he were simply sitting or even standing, waves of sleepiness would overtake him so that he had frequent inadvertent naps. Oddly, he awoke feeling very refreshed, though the episodes sometimes lasted only a few seconds and never more than a few minutes. Moishe usually had about thirty seconds of warning before nodding off. Often, it was in the middle of a conversation, and he would sometimes excuse himself in what must have seemed a very peculiar manner.

The doctor made the diagnosis of narcolepsy. The doctor also informed Moishe that he probably had a low-grade depression, which he thought might be connected with the narcolepsy.

A prescription of Benzedrine seemed to address the narcolepsy adequately, and Moishe no longer experienced sudden drowsiness and irresistible urges to sleep. Nor did he respond to the drug as anyone without his condition would have. The Benzedrine did not make him "high," keep him awake at night, or give him extra energy: it simply ended the narcoleptic episodes.

This would have made life at school a whole lot easier, but Moishe did not return to North High School. His father felt that at sixteen, he'd had enough education and should be ready to work full time. He would have preferred that Moishe work for him, but if not, he felt it was time for his son to make a living. Ben had not needed to finish high school to become a successful businessman. He therefore did not place a great deal of value on schooling, at least not at that time. However, his brother, Dave, a partner in the business, did.

One day, Moishe's uncle Dave told him, "Benny [referring to his brother], he's a smart man, but you're like me, and if you don't go back to school, I'm going to beat the —— out of you." He went on to tell Moishe, "Your dad's wrong, and I'm right. I don't want you to grow up to be a bum like me."

Moishe was surprised to hear his uncle refer to himself as a bum. He was a veteran who'd been drafted early, and before that, he had run a "house of ill repute" in Cheyenne. He had also been a construction worker in San Diego. In fact, David Street in San Diego was named after him. Following Dave's discharge from the army, he went into business with Ben. Eventually, though, Dave quit the junk business and bought a bar. He never had children, and perhaps that made him especially fond of his nephews and nieces.

Moishe took his uncle's advice/threat about school seriously. He enrolled in night school, and between those classes and some of the extra courses he'd taken before he dropped out, he managed to finish high school at the same time as the rest of his class. He did not, however, care to pay the rental fees for the cap and gown to walk across the stage with everyone else. High school had been, in many ways, incidental to his education.

EIGHT

Power is ability. Ability is organized energy.
—MOISHE ROSEN

Moishe liked the sights and smells of the sporting goods store. The place was crammed with merchandise, much of it in boxes stacked against the wall, reaching nearly to the top of the 16-foot ceiling. Rolling ladders rumbled quietly, like a ride just starting up at an amusement park, allowing stock boys to retrieve items that were up high. Rows of glass counters encased more expensive merchandise—fishing reels, guns, binoculars, and cameras.

Moishe enjoyed being a salesman. He liked most of the people who came into the store.* He asked questions to learn about their interests, and regarded them as friends. If one of "his" customers came in while he was serving someone else, Moishe would flash a big smile and say, "Be with you in about five minutes." Usually the customer would wait patiently even if another sales person was available.**

There was one type of customer Moishe did not like—the kind who made a game of getting the lowest price possible, just for the sake of what Moishe considered, "one-upsmanship." He and the rest of the staff at Gart Brothers shared an unspoken understanding that any customer who was greedy or arrogant was fair game. They wouldn't cheat the person, but they'd make sure he didn't get a good deal. But all a person had to do was ask Moishe's advice about a piece of merchandise and the young salesman felt honor bound to point out

---

* An anecdote regarding one of the few customers to whom Moishe was not cordial: One day, "Sergeant H." of the previous chapter walked into the sporting goods store, looked at Moishe as though nothing extraordinary had passed between them and cheerfully suggested, "Bygones?" Moishe replied, "I don't know about bygones. I don't welcome you here and I don't want to do business with you." As he turned to walk away, Sergeant H. called out "We'll see about that. I'm a personal friend of Nate Gart's" (the owner).

What Sergeant H. did not know was that Moishe had told Gart all about him and the incident with the carbine. When Sergeant H. complained to Gart, and Moishe was called into account, all Moishe had to do was explain who the sergeant was. Nate Gart calmly told Sergeant H, "I'm glad that you came to talk to me. Now that I know who you are, I don't believe I care to have your business."

** When Moishe visited the store three years after moving away from Denver, former coworkers told him that some customers were still asking for him by name.

which pieces of equipment were the best value for the money . . . even if it meant taking a lower commission.

At the moment, there were no customers, and Moishe found himself puzzling over a series of strange events that had occurred over the last few weeks. He had been encountering an unusually high number of dishonest customers, and he could not figure out why.

It began when a man brought a fishing rod up to the register, and suggested to Moishe in a low voice, "How about if you and me become business partners? This rod is $15, but you could ring it up for $5, I'll give you $10 and you can keep the difference. I save $5 and you make $5."

Moishe, not wanting to offend the customer had suggested, "If you want, I can talk to my boss about a discount." Oddly, the man simply bought the fishing rod for $15.

Over the weeks, several others suggested similar schemes. Moishe had turned all these suggestions into proper sales, but many of the items were later returned for refunds.

In fact, that very day Moishe had commented to one of the partners that he could not understand why so many items had been returned. For just a moment, Moishe thought the partner had looked a bit uncomfortable, but then he shrugged and walked away. Moments later, he returned.

"Boss wants to see you," he said, jerking his head in the direction where Nate Gart was standing.

Moishe looked at his boss inquisitively.

Gart glanced at his well-polished shoes for just a moment, then locked eyes with Moishe. "You know your friend Mike (not real name) next door?"

"Sure, what about him?" Mike had been let go from his job and had asked Moishe to talk to Nate about hiring him. Knowing the guy had a wife to support, on Moishe's recommendation Nate had employed him at his pawnshop next door.

"You know how I've been asking you if you're sure the guy's a straight shooter?"

Moishe nodded. "And I vouched for him, didn't I?"

"Yeah, you did. And I'm sorry to tell you, Mike's been stealing from me. I got proof. But the fact that you recommended him, insisted he's honest . . . well I had to check you out. You cost me a lot of money."

Moishe looked at Nate in astonishment. "You hired people to check up on me?"

"What else could I do, Martin? Put yourself in my position. When things look suspicious, you gotta check 'em out. You gotta be sure, no matter how much you like the person."

Moishe nodded. He understood: bosses can't let personal feelings cloud their judgment.

———

Moishe felt his life was really on track. He was in love with a beautiful girl who'd agreed to marry him. He had a good part-time job where he felt he could reasonably expect to advance. Once he was confident that he knew something, Moishe could act quickly and decisively. He knew he was a good salesman, and he was getting better all the time. He learned very well when the topic interested him, *and* he remembered what he learned and was quick to apply it.

It hadn't been easy, changing the direction of the life he knew his father wanted for him. He couldn't blame his dad for hoping he would go into the family business. What does a man build a business for, if not to provide for his family and pass it down to his children? Moishe was only fourteen and a half when he decided to look for other employment, but he was tall for his age and often passed for an older boy. He was also more knowledgeable than might have been expected because he'd begun taking college-level courses from the Emily Griffith Opportunity School. The first course included a section on how to find employment. This gave him the information and confidence to take his father at his word when he'd said that Moishe could work elsewhere.

It was an autumn day when Moishe put on his sport coat and went to a nearby Denver manufacturing plant to apply for part-time work as a clerk. It would be a good change from the junkyard and might lead to other things.

The personnel director at the plant seemed to like Moishe, but refused him, saying, "You're qualified enough, and I'd like to give you a shot at the job, but there's one problem. Our company has never employed anyone of your race before, and I don't think it would be wise for you to be the first."

Disappointed, Moishe figured he had better stick to a Jewish-owned business and, hoping to cheer himself up, thought, *What would be a fun place to work?* It occurred to him that a sporting goods store would have all kinds of interesting merchandise—things that he might like to own—things that would be fun to sell to others. Federal Sporting Goods was owned by Joe Alpert, who was Jewish. Hadn't there been a Help Wanted sign in the window the last time he walked past? Moishe went to the store, asked for a job, and was hired as a stock boy at forty cents per hour.

If Ben was surprised that Moishe had gotten a job, he didn't show it. He simply said, "Well, you're going to have to give three dollars a week now to help with household expenses." That didn't bother Moishe, who later recalled,

> It was a good deal for me because I could go after school and work from five to nine, and then I could work all day on Saturday. That's really when I stopped going to synagogue. And at forty cents an hour, I had money left over. When my father found out how much I was making, he raised what he asked of me to six dollars a week. But I still had some left over. And I got raises.

Mr. Alpert expected all the employees, even stock boys, to wear a jacket and tie. Consequently, customers often mistook Moishe for one of the sales staff. He frequently helped customers, then took them to the store's only cash register to have their purchases rung up by a "real" salesperson. But if there was no one at the register, the customer had to wait. Moishe pointed out that this did not seem good for business, and finally, Mr. Alpert told Moishe that if no one was at the cash register, he could ring up the sale.

After his stint in the National Guard, Moishe found that his position at Federal Sporting Goods had been filled. Ben hoped Moishe would come back to work at the junkyard, but Moishe knew by then that he would never again work for his father. Meanwhile, his younger brother, Don, stepped up to the plate and was, as Moishe later described him, "the good son." Moishe watched his brother grow in their father's favor, receiving attention and approval in connection with his steadily increasing commitment to "the yard."

Ben taught Don, not Moishe, how to drive, because Don needed to drive the truck for the business and Moishe didn't. Moishe described Don as "smart—a really quick learner—very good natured, with a good sense of humor." Don was happy enough to teach his older brother how to drive, and Moishe didn't mind learning from him. However, he couldn't help noticing his father's favoritism toward Don and later reflected, "I knew my father loved me but I always felt he would have loved me more if I had loved the junk business more."

But Moishe had enjoyed his work at Federal Sporting Goods and wanted to find similar work. That is how he came to Gart Brothers Sporting Goods, which became a pivotal point in his life. At Gart Brothers, Moishe had more than a job; he had a boss who taught him life lessons.

Nate Gart, the son of a house painter who had emigrated from Russia, worked at various jobs until he had saved enough money to buy a store in downtown Denver. Then with a mere thirty-three dollars in fishing equipment for inventory, he opened a family sporting goods store specializing in hunting, fishing, and camping supplies. Like Ben Rosen, Nate was smart and worked hard; he built the business from the ground up. The store grew, and Nate's three brothers eventually joined the business. The four of them incorporated the business as Gart Brothers Sporting Goods Company.

Like Ben, Nate became one of the most successful businessmen in his field, a self-made man. He was like Moishe's father in many ways, so intelligent and observant that he didn't really need formal schooling to succeed. But he was different from Ben in that he could see the value of school for Moishe. And his relationship with Moishe was unhindered by the unique expectations and disappointments that sometimes divide fathers and sons. Ironically, Nate was able to provide a degree of the paternal encouragement Moishe needed without even realizing it.

As Moishe continued taking business classes at Emily Griffith, he soaked up knowledge with an interest and enthusiasm that surely would have surprised his grade school teachers. He recalled, "The amazing thing was, I had to do very little studying for those business classes. I was already working in a retail store, so I knew about invoices and accounts receivable. I traveled on a streetcar, and I usually took along a book to read. I picked a couple of classes in accounting, and everything I learned in business school came in very handy, either at Gart Brothers, or later, when it came time for me to operate a very different type of organization. Certain principles of financial operations remain the same, whatever kind of company you've got."

Nate was always interested to hear what Moishe was learning, and the boss was quick to appreciate any practical contributions Moishe offered. Nate was delighted when Moishe pointed out that many retailers kept small items near the cash register where customers were likely to add them to their purchase on impulse. He also took some of Moishe's suggestions about displays and how to make the most of the store's space. He gave Moishe opportunities that were unusual for someone his age, including writing some of the store advertising. In addition to giving Moishe opportunities to apply the things he was learning,

Nate was always passing on his own commonsense lessons, teaching Moishe through stories and casual conversation. Moishe described Nate Gart as shrewd and a keen observer: "He taught me to watch other people and to pick up on cues." As Moishe recalled, Nate did not have a desk. He had a chair, and he occasionally sat in it. But he preferred to be on the sales floor, and this made quite an impression on Moishe. At times Nate would stand alone by the front door and watch people walking down the street. If business was slow, Moishe would join him. Sometimes they would stand together quietly, and sometimes Nate would impart bits of street wisdom.

Though Moishe was not a partner, he felt a sense of ownership in the store and wanted to do his part to make it as successful as possible. He made it his business to know the merchandise and could show customers something they might otherwise miss on just about any item. Moishe had a strong sense of duty to the customers as well as to the store. Many of the skills, insights, and principles Moishe employed in his later work can be traced back to his work at Gart Brothers and to various lessons learned there. Moishe recalled,

> Once Nate was criticized in a newspaper article for an annual contest the store sponsored. They gave prizes for the largest deer antlers, elk antlers, the biggest trout caught for the season, etc. The article pointed out that people were shooting animals, and if their antlers were small, they would just leave them lying there until they found a bigger animal that might win a prize. It was cruel as well as wasteful.
>
> Nate Gart called the paper and told them that they were right, their criticism was justified, and he was going to change the rules of the contest, which he did. I was impressed by his apology and told him that I admired him for admitting his mistake publicly. He smiled and said, "When you're wrong, you're wrong—and in this case, I got bigger and better publicity for being wrong. Plus, in fixing the problem, I redesigned the contest so that it will cost us a lot less, and we'll get ten times as much good as we did from doing it the old way."

The necessity of admitting a mistake, the importance of publicity, and the benefit of retooling something that is flawed were not lost on the young salesman.

NINE

People are hollow because they won't open up enough to let anything in.

—MOISHE ROSEN

Another Yom Kippur had passed; the light of the crisp autumn day had given way to the chill of a dark, clear night. Elsewhere families had broken their fast together, but Moishe had gone straight from synagogue services to the sporting goods store. The boss had not required him to work that night, but he was still a part-time high school student and welcomed the opportunity for an extra three hours of wages.

Now, waiting for the streetcar at the end of a very long day, Moishe paused to tuck the velvet bag containing his tallis* under his arm, freeing his hand to light a cigarette. Inhaling slowly, he briefly mused over the synagogue service. The congregation had confessed a litany of sins, corporate and individual, intentional and unintentional. Then, light-headed, dry-mouthed, stomachs growling from hunger, they'd headed for home where they would share a long-awaited meal. But had any spiritual transaction actually occurred?

Seventeen-year-old Moishe's awareness of God had grown vague, but his awareness of himself was sharp enough. He knew that if someone were to draw his spiritual portrait, sin would certainly be part of the picture. Nevertheless, he hadn't gone to synagogue to have his sins forgiven; he had gone because he was Jewish, and it would be a shame for any Jew to be absent from synagogue on Yom Kippur, the Day of Atonement. This was one of the high holy days. Which was why he was wearing his best clothes.

Glancing around, Moishe noticed that the only other person at the stop was also dressed in a suit. He appeared to be about twenty years old, had red hair, and was gazing in Moishe's direction.

"You're all dressed up," the stranger observed. "Are you coming home from work or a party?" His voice was rich and full, making him sound older than he looked.

"Work," Moishe replied. "But before that, synagogue." He usually was not so open with strangers, but it had slipped out before he realized it. He paused,

_____
* prayer shawl

50

wondering how this stranger would react to hearing that he was Jewish. He looked like a friendly kind of guy. To Moishe's astonishment, he was more than friendly; he was downright enthusiastic as he eagerly extended his hand and announced, "I'm pleased to meet you! You know, every Jew I meet increases my faith in God and the Bible."

"Huh?" Moishe wondered if he had heard right.

"Well, sure. Every living Jew is evidence that the God of the Bible exists and that he keeps his word.* You know, Genesis 12:1–3." The man proceeded to quote, by heart, God's promise to Abraham.

Moishe was speechless. His new "friend" was not.

"Do you go to synagogue regularly?"

"No, not so much anymore," Moishe admitted. "Today was Yom Kippur. It's a pretty important holiday for us." His stomach rumbled. "Wow, I'm really hungry."

"Me, too," the man said and nodded. "I was working late and didn't have supper."

"I haven't really eaten since last night. I've been fasting. That's what we do for Yom Kippur. Besides going to synagogue."

The redheaded man seemed genuinely interested and asked, "So what does it all mean?"

Moishe shrugged. "It means that my sins are supposed to be forgiven."

"Do you feel your sins are forgiven?"

"Who knows?" Moishe shrugged again, and something in his tone touched the stranger.

Seeing the streetcar coming, Moishe crushed the cigarette with his foot. He thought this guy must be a little nutty, yet what he'd said about Jews increasing his faith in God and the Bible was intriguing. Not quite ready for the conversation to end, he smiled and said, "I'm Martin Rosen."

"Orville Freestone." The other man smiled back, and they both climbed onto the streetcar.

The two sat near enough to continue their discussion. "I believe there is a way to know that your sins are forgiven," Orville began, and Moishe could tell he was winding up for the pitch. Sure enough, Orville continued, "I believe that Christ died for my sins and made it possible for me to know God and find eternal life."

---

* This statement so impressed Moishe that in later years, he came back to it time and time again, including it in many of his sermons and lectures.

Moishe was not surprised. Since Orville wasn't Jewish, Moishe had figured he must be Christian. The strangest thing was that as he explained the Christian religion, it sounded as though the whole thing was a Jewish idea. The part about Jesus dying to take the punishment for people's sins, Orville said, was pictured in the original observances of Yom Kippur in Bible times when the Jewish high priest placed his hands on the scapegoat and recited the sins of the people. That goat was then led out into the wilderness, far from the camp of the Israelites. Another goat was sacrificed and its blood sprinkled on the altar as an atonement (covering) for sin. It all sounded weird and spooky to Moishe, but he couldn't dismiss it as Christian mumbo-jumbo because clearly Orville was describing things from the Torah.

Nevertheless, Moishe changed the subject. Orville listened and interacted with the new topic, but now and then he mentioned something from the Bible.

They both got off at Colfax and Federal Boulevard. "Well, Orville," Moishe said, "it's been nice talking to you. But I have to say, you've got some one-track mind. No matter what I say, you bring it back to religion. Look, I don't even know whether all those things in the Torah happened or not. But even if they did, it's ancient history. And I'm interested in what goes on today."

With that, Moishe figured, he'd head north to his home on Fifteenth and Federal, and Orville, who lived at Fourteenth and Federal, would go south.

"Wait a second," Orville said. "You think the Bible doesn't have anything to do with today? What would you say if I told you that the Bible predicted something that happened just a little over a year ago?"

That stopped Moishe in his tracks. "What do you mean?"

"I'm talking about the state of Israel. It's all in the Bible, about how the Jewish people would return to the land that God promised to Abraham, Isaac, and Jacob."

Suddenly Moishe found his feet were heading toward Orville's house instead of his own. Before he knew it, they had reached Orville's front porch. Instead of going home as he had planned, Moishe stayed with Orville and continued their conversation. Orville went inside briefly and came out with a small New Testament; he gave it to Moishe and said he hoped he'd read it.

It was well past midnight when Moishe got home. He found himself thinking of what Orville had told him about the Torah, why God set up the system of sacrifices, and how Jesus came to do what those sacrifices could only point to. It reminded him of something from the prayer book that had caught his eye on Yom Kippur some six years earlier.

He was eleven years old, sitting in the synagogue, finding it difficult to listen to the rabbi's sermon. To alleviate boredom, he flipped through the *machzor* (high holiday prayer book), looking for something that might stir his imagination. Sure enough, he found a section called "For the Day of Atonement." It had fascinating instructions: a man was supposed to take a rooster and swing it over his head three times while making the statement, "This is my change, this is my redemption. This rooster is going to be killed, and I shall be admitted and allowed to live a long, happy and peaceful life." And a woman was supposed to take a hen and swing it over her head and make a similar statement.

Moishe was sitting with his father on one side and his little brother, Donny, on the other. He first pointed out the section to his dad, who said in a low voice, "We don't do that anymore." Moishe glanced at his brother, who was smart and could read well. Moishe tapped him on the shoulder and pointed to the page that talked about swinging the chicken. Donny quickly read it, then looking up at his older brother, he smiled gleefully, as though he thought swinging a live chicken over his head would be a lot of fun.

When they got home, Moishe asked Ben to tell them more about the chicken. His father explained that after the ceremony, you couldn't eat the chicken because it was a sacrifice, and you had to give it to somebody in need. Donny seemed enamored by the whole idea. "Can we do it, Dad? Can we do it?" At that point, their father had ended the conversation by saying, "We've got better uses for chickens around here."

Moishe had never forgotten what he'd seen in the prayer book that day. Now it made him wonder: *If Jewish people could recite something about how a chicken's death could somehow bring life and peace to a human being, why was the story of Jesus dying for people's sins considered so very un-Jewish?*

Walking home that night from Orville's, Moishe thought *What Orville says makes sense to me, and that means I must be one dumb Jew because Jesus couldn't possibly be the Messiah.* As for the New Testament Orville had given him, Moishe shook his head, thinking, *If I read it, I might be dumb enough to believe it, and that would make me one of them [a Christian or Gentile]. If the rabbis ever get together and decide that Jesus is the Messiah, maybe I'll go along with them. Until then, I'm not having anything to do with this book.*

The tire store next door to his house had a large trashcan out front, and Moishe tossed the New Testament in before climbing the steps to his front door. Inside, he quickly undressed and flopped into bed, utterly exhausted.

Ceil had lain awake for hours, worried because Moishe had not stopped by to see her after work. It was rare for him to let an evening go by without at least a brief visit. The next day Moishe came by and apologized, explaining his encounter with Orville and how they had talked until the wee hours of the morning. Ceil didn't ask, and Moishe never mentioned what he and Orville had discussed.

In subsequent weeks Ceil met Orville and his wife, Juanita, and the four became friends. Orville later recalled how Moishe "loved a friendly argument and could take either position with equal ease." Moishe especially liked talking about philosophy and politics and, according to Orville, was "very radical"* and "always an individualist" but at the same time was "considerate and soft-spoken. The only time he ever raised his voice," Freestone added, "was when he was laughing raucously. He had quite a sense of humor!"

Juanita described Moishe as "a nice-looking young man, very intense." She said, "He was intent on living life. He had times of fun. But to him, everything was really a big deal. Everything was really important. In conversations, he'd look right at you. He was *with* you—he heard every word you said. I mean, you wouldn't dare say anything that you weren't willing to back up right then because you knew he'd ask questions. Everything that he talked about was just really important to him. I guess maybe he was interested in living. That's the only way I know how to describe it."

The Freestones went on many walks with Moishe and Ceil, during which time Moishe and Orville, deep in conversation, usually outstripped Juanita and Ceil. The women had their own conversations. Both Orville and Juanita were committed Christians, and both, in their way, attempted to share their beliefs.

Orville used comparisons and analogies. For example, Moishe insisted that it was incomprehensible that God would become man. They were approaching a large anthill, and Orville said, "Well, let's just suppose for some crazy reason, you knew that these ants were going to be destroyed when this area got redeveloped. You knew they were going to widen the street here, and the ants would be wiped out. And for some crazy reason, you wanted to warn them. How would you do it?" Moishe replied, "I couldn't." Orville replied, "You could if you become an ant."

---

* When asked what he meant by "radical," Orville mentioned how, after the Freestones moved, Moishe wrote him letters addressed to "Comrade Orville Freestone" and signed his letters as "Comrade Martin Rosen." This actually made Orville somewhat nervous. He knew that Moishe was no Communist, but his references to socialism, even in jest, could certainly have been taken amiss in those days.

Orville was referring to the danger that Jesus warned about. According to the Bible, sin separates all people from God regardless of race or religious background.* Christians therefore believe that whoever is not reconciled to God in this life will be separated from him forever in the life to come. And they believe the only way to be saved from that eternal separation is through faith in Jesus who, the New Testament teaches, died to take the punishment for our sin and then rose from the dead. Orville and Juanita tried to convey that message to all their friends, including Moishe and Ceil. But their attempts, while motivated by genuine friendship and concern, did not seem to lead to any great revelation for either Moishe or Ceil.

Juanita recalled, "During one of our walks, I asked, 'Celia, have you ever really been saved?' She looked at me—and it was quite late in the evening—but she just stopped walking and turned to me and said, 'I don't know what you mean. Am I in danger?' Then I realized that I was speaking a different language and she had no frame of reference to understand what I meant by 'saved.'"**

Moishe decided the conversations had crossed a tenuous boundary that lay between an interesting exchange of ideas and attempts to convert him. As Orville recalled, "At one point he told me, 'I really don't want these talks about religion to get so personal anymore.'" Later Orville commented to his wife, "My friend Martin will be the last person in this world ever to be saved."

The Christian couple had said all they could say on the subject and would not try to force an unwelcome conversation. They stopped talking to Moishe and Ceil about God, but they never stopped talking to God about Moishe and Ceil, praying every day that the couple would come to know and follow Jesus. They continued on friendly terms, and the Freestones attended Moishe and Ceil's wedding. They were, to Orville's recollection, the "only goyim present."***

Ceil had graduated a year before Moishe and had a job as a secretary in a law office while Moishe was still studying and working part time at the sporting goods store. But when he finished school the following spring (1950), they decided they would marry at the end of that summer. At eighteen both of them were eager for independence.

---

* "Your iniquities have separated you from your God; / And your sins have hidden His face from you, / So that He will not hear" (Isaiah 59:2). "For the wages of sin is death, but the gift of God is eternal life in Christ Jesus our Lord" (Romans 6:23).

** The concept of being "saved" or delivered from one's sins or guilt can be found in the Jewish Bible (for example, Psalm 51), but for many Jewish people it is not a widely known or discussed concept except during Yom Kippur.

*** *Goyim* literaly means "nations." It is used both in the Bible and in contemporary Jewish culture to refer to nonJews.

They set the date: August 27. The guest list consisted of some two hundred people, mostly from Moishe's side of the family. The wedding was a simple affair. Ceil borrowed a gown and veil from a friend who'd recently married. Moishe wore dark slacks and a rented white dinner jacket.

Ceil recalled, "Moishe promised to take me as his wife according to the Law of Moses, and I didn't say anything. I was not required to say anything. I just stood there under the velvet chupah* and smiled. Of course, neither of us expected to observe the Law of Moses in our new home. That was just part of the ceremony. We had already agreed that tradition was fine if we didn't take it too seriously. We would not be entangled in Orthodox rules and regulations. We would just be modern American Jews."

They lived a short time in a basement apartment before moving to another house that had been divided into apartments. Moishe and Ceil, along with another couple and their new baby, shared one upstairs bathroom with the older man who owned the house. Moishe and Ceil were glad to have the tiny space; affordable postwar apartments were hard to find.

Ceil was quite taken with the baby next door, and with the shadow of the draft looming she and Moishe decided to start a family. If Moishe were to be drafted, which they rather expected, the baby would keep Ceil busy and help ward off loneliness. If she couldn't manage alone, she could move in with her in-laws, who were always kind and supportive. To the couple's surprise and relief, however, Ceil's pregnancy earned Moishe a draft deferment.

It was a happy time. So happy that Ceil felt a surge of gratitude welling up inside her. But gratitude to whom? She realized, with a start, that it was gratitude to God. For some time she'd been far less vocal about her atheism, less secure about what she didn't believe. Now that she had her own home and was free to examine her beliefs, she realized that denying God's existence had been, more than anything, a way to break away from her strict upbringing.

Many years had passed since she'd spoken to God in her own words, and during most of that time, she had not even used the traditional Jewish prayers to reach out to him. Now she focused her mind and heart outward as she shyly and silently told God, *I'm sorry I said that you don't exist. I know that you are real. Thank you for all the good things you have given us. Please let our baby be healthy and strong.*

It was the first of several prayers that would ultimately change everything.

---

* Wedding canopy.

TEN

ow much do I owe you?" Ceil asked.

"It was sixty-nine cents," Dorothy replied, handing Ceil a brown paper bag. She was too good a friend to raise questions about the contraband it contained.

Ceil counted out the coins. "Thanks so much," she said and smiled as she placed them in Dorothy's hand.

As soon as Dorothy left, Ceil hastily pulled the thick black book from the bag. The gilt letters said "Holy Bible." She had carefully specified, "Be sure to get a *whole* Bible. You know—both the Old and the New Testament—but don't tell anyone!" Dorothy had raised an eyebrow, but didn't voice any surprise.

Now, hands trembling, Ceil fumbled past the parts she recognized from years of Hebrew school. And then, there it was, about two-thirds of the way through the Bible: the New Testament.

Now she would find out who those Christmas carols were really about and why Jesus was described as the one in whom "the hopes and fears of all the years" resided. She began with the first verse of the first book of the New Testament: "The book of the generation of Jesus Christ, the son of David, the son of Abraham." *What's wrong with that?* she thought. *It's saying that Jesus was Jewish!*

She read voraciously until it was time to prepare dinner, then she hid the Bible beneath some papers in a desk drawer. From then on, whenever she had a few moments alone she read it. The more she read, the more impressed she was that it was a Jewish book about a Jewish person who claimed to be the Jewish Messiah.

No Christian had ever suggested anything like this to her; none had even suggested that she read this New Testament. It was, she thought, her private discovery. And she intended to keep it that way.

But it was not in Ceil's nature to keep silent about her enthusiasm—and the more she read, the more she was drawn to Jesus. She just knew that he was real, and she longed to talk to someone about the discovery. But just as she knew that Jesus was real, she also knew that parents, in-laws, friends—even her husband—would be furious if they knew what she was about.

She finished the first four books—the Gospels according to Matthew, Mark, Luke, and John—each one a different perspective on Jesus' life, death, and resurrection. She started the next book, Acts, but when she saw that after the first chapter, Jesus had departed from the center stage, she stopped. She went back and reread the first four books.

Paradoxically, reading about Jesus seemed to satisfy and yet intensify an inner hunger that Ceil never knew she had. And her growing belief in him presented another paradox: it seemed to complete the near perfect life she now enjoyed, while at the same time threatening to destroy it.

Marriage and motherhood had begun a wonderful new era in Ceil's life. Born Rita Shirley Elfbaum on April 8, 1932, Ceil had nearly died at birth. She and her twin brother, Jason (Jay), had been premature. Though they survived, their mother died before they were a year old. Their grief-stricken father, Harry Elfbaum, was responsible for the sole support of his aging parents. He was also plagued with epilepsy. Lacking the emotional, physical, or financial resources to care for his children, he sought temporary foster care.

Jay went to one family, and Rita went to an Eastern European Jewish couple his wife had met. David and Mamie Starr were eager to care for the baby girl; however, Mamie would not take the child home until Harry signed certain documents. Harry was frightened that Rita, who was not well, would die if she did not receive the immediate care he could not provide. Under duress, he signed the documents—which to his dismay later turned out to be adoption papers. Rita's name was legally changed to Celia, after her dead mother, and she was no longer an Elfbaum, but a Starr.

Harry slowly rebuilt his life. He married Shirley, a wonderful, tender-hearted woman. He took his son out of foster care, but as far as the Starrs were concerned, Celia was legally theirs. A deeply religious man and highly sensitive, Harry felt it would not be in his child's best interest to disrupt her life by fighting for custody. He believed that eventually they would be reunited—and faithfully prayed for that day.

The Starrs were also very religious, though in a different way from Harry Elfbaum, whose abiding love and trust for the Almighty touched each of his relationships. Nevertheless, the Starrs loved Ceil after their fashion, just as they worked out their Jewishness in their own way. They lived a *frum* (very observant) lifestyle and saw to it that Ceil had a strict Jewish upbringing and education.

As a little girl, Ceil believed in God and used to pray to him in her own words. In synagogue whenever she looked at the ark where the Torah scrolls resided, she felt a mystical awe. When the men in their striped prayer shawls drew aside the velvet curtain to bring out the Torah, Ceil squeezed her eyes shut. She thought that God was behind the curtain and sensing that he was too holy, was afraid to look.

At age five, Ceil was taught to repeat the Hebrew prayers each day, which she obediently did, though she did not know what they meant. Prayer became a duty rather than a way for her to connect with God. At the age of six, she began Hebrew school, and before long, she knew what the prayers meant. But they had already been instilled in her as mere sounds she was supposed to make, regardless of their meaning.

As she grew older, Ceil realized that as strict and observant as her family was in its Jewish lifestyle, others kept even more rules and regulations. At the same time, most of her friends' families were far less Orthodox. Those discrepancies confused Ceil. Why did her family observe some regulations but not all? Why did other Jews get away with doing less? Were all those rules really from God? Before long, her confusion turned to apathy. By the time she graduated from Hebrew school (age twelve), she figured that if God existed at all, he was a rather unpleasant authority figure who exacted a heavy toll from Jews for the privilege of being his chosen people.

She knew that she had been "chosen" by her adoptive parents as well, and as far as she could see, their choice had not been the best thing that ever happened to her. When Mamie told Ceil that her natural father had not wanted her, she suspected that it might not be true. But when her mother told her two conflicting accounts blaming different people for her childlessness, Ceil began seeing a pattern of discrepencies. Sadly, her adoptive mother proved to be an unhappy, emotionally damaged woman who believed her own fabrications and blamed others for her misfortunes and discontent. Ceil's adoptive father, Dave, was kind, but he seemed to lack the fortitude to defend himself or his daughter from his wife's manipulative ways.

Ceil's experience of Orthodox Judaism often reminded her of her mother: arbitrary, heavy-handed, all-consuming, and never satisfied no matter how hard one tried to comply. Eventually, Ceil wanted no part of it. And because her only knowledge of God came from Orthodox Judaism, she thought she wanted no part of him, either.

By the time Ceil was married, she'd had it with being chosen and was ready to do some choosing of her own. She still identified as a Jew but was thankful to keep her own household where there was no need to follow the many rules and regulations. She was very content with her husband and new baby, and she was very thankful for her in-laws, who treated her like she truly was their daughter.

All these positive circumstances melted Ceil's rebellion and left her feeling so grateful that she could no longer deny the God she had trusted as a very little girl. She wanted to know him, and she wanted her child to know him. But when she reached out with that first prayer, she never imagined that there would be more prayers or that the answers to them would lead her to Jesus. Now with that forbidden black book challenging her, what was she to do?

———

On October 18, 1951, Moishe Rosen became a father. Linda Kaye (who later preferred to be called Lyn) was born safely, speedily, and only one day later than anticipated. In those days, fathers were not allowed in the birthing area but were often seen pacing the floor while their wives were normally rendered unconscious with drugs. Moishe didn't have much time to pace. Having gone out for a cup of coffee, he was hastily summoned as Linda was quickly arriving, only four hours or so after their break-of-dawn ride to the hospital. Ceil described Moishe as "kind of awed by this screaming, squirming little wet thing—but happy to be a father and glad to take on the responsibility." The new parents were only nineteen and a half years old.

Lyn was the first grandchild for the Rosens as well as the Starrs, and both sets of grandparents doted on her. When the senior Rosens vacated Moishe's childhood home on Federal to move to a slightly nicer neighborhood eight blocks away, Moishe, Ceil, and the baby moved right in.

It was a happy time for the young couple. Moishe was doing well at work and often looked for opportunities to surprise Ceil with a gift. Music was one of her chief joys, and not long after Lyn was born, he brought home a record player and a collection of 45 rpm recordings. The collection contained some songs by Mario Lanza, a popular tenor. Among his vocals was a selection of Christmas carols, which Moishe knew that Ceil particularly loved.

He had no idea that a Christmas carol had once caused Ceil to consider what no Jewish person was supposed to consider. Ceil had taken high school chorus for class credit, and the group had a major role in the school's Christmas program. She would either have to sing in the concert or fail the class. She really wanted to sing, so the fact that she had to in order to pass provided the perfect excuse to do so despite her parents' wishes. (They had never allowed her to attend, much less sing in, a Christmas program.) She concocted a half-truth about having to be at school that night, smuggled her costume out of the house, and went to the performance.

Ceil later recalled, "We moved across the stage in a kind of slow dance, singing, 'O come, O come, Emmanuel, and ransom captive Israel.' Though we had rehearsed the song many times, I suddenly found myself pondering its meaning. The song seemed to be saying that Jesus was somehow for Israel, for us Jews. For a moment, I was deeply impressed by this possibility. But then I quickly shrugged it off. What did it really matter? I didn't even believe in my own Jewish God, so why should I believe in Jesus, the gentile God?"

Three years later Ceil, at home with a newborn, put on the Christmas collection. Suddenly the words of "O Little Town of Bethlehem" struck her as they never had before. She wondered what was meant by "the hopes and fears of all the years are met in thee tonight." Did the hopes refer to the Messiah? But who would fear the coming of our Messiah, and why?

Ceil knew the Gentiles believed that Jesus was the Messiah. Were her own people afraid to think about Jesus because it might be true? She listened to another song, "We Three Kings," and thought about the miraculous star that supposedly led the wise men to the baby Jesus. Might it have actually happened? Song after song seemed to challenge her to consider whether its message might be true until she felt driven to ask God.

And so, Ceil prayed once again, but this prayer was far more radical than the last: "God, I'm ready to do what you want now, even if it means going back to all those rules. I'll keep kosher, observe the Sabbath laws, and be an Orthodox Jew again if that's what you want. But please show me. Do you want that? Or is there truth to what the Christians are saying about Jesus? What should I believe? What do you want me to do?"

When summer came and she still couldn't stop thinking about Jesus, she asked her friend Dorothy, who was also Moishe's cousin, to get her a Bible at the dime store. Almost from the moment Ceil began reading, she was captivated.

She could barely hide her growing excitement. Occasionally she would blurt out some tidbit she'd learned to Moishe or Dorothy: "I just found out that the Lord's Prayer my grade school class used to recite every day came from the New Testament," or "Guess what? I never knew that the term 'salt of the earth' came from something that Jesus said, did you?" Moishe and Dorothy were the only two people on earth to whom she would admit that she had read, much less believed, part of the New Testament. But her "revelations" provoked little more than a quizzical look or an uncaring shrug from them.

By the end of summer, Ceil was fairly bursting to discuss Jesus. She remembered Orville and Juanita (once the baby came, they had not done much to keep up the acquaintance.) and casually asked Moishe if he'd heard anything from Orville lately. She was crestfallen to learn that Orville and his family had recently moved to Gallup, New Mexico. She silently offered up a third prayer: *Oh, God, please help me find someone to talk to about Jesus.*

She soon forgot about that prayer, so was somewhat surprised when, one blustery February afternoon, a middle-aged woman trudged up the snow-covered steps to her flat and rang the doorbell. Hannah Wago was a missionary who had taught a Bible study at the church led by Orville's father. The Freestones had continued praying daily for Moishe and Ceil, and during one of these prayers, they had felt impressed to contact Mrs. Wago and ask her to visit their friends.

Mrs. Wago had braved ice and snow to travel across town. She had brought a reference Bible, as well as numerous pamphlets written for Jewish inquirers. When Ceil realized that Mrs. Wago had come to talk to her about Jesus, she suddenly remembered her prayer. Overcome by the reality that God had heard and answered, she retreated to the pantry to wipe away tears that she was embarrassed for a total stranger to see.

Ceil recalled, "Mrs. Wago brought a chart that helped me understand the problem of sin and how the Jewish Bible says it separates us from God. The chart also showed how Moses and the Hebrew prophets had talked about the Messiah. . . . I couldn't believe my eyes when she showed me the fifty-third chapter of Isaiah. It was such a perfect description of how and why Jesus died, though it was written hundreds of years before he was crucified. I wondered, why, during all my years of attending Hebrew school, had no one told me about those passages?" When she showed the passages to Moishe and told him she believed they were predicting Jesus, he wasn't as angry as she had feared he would be. He said, "It's fine if you want to believe all that. Just . . . don't . . . tell . . . *anyone.*"

Mrs. Wago visited Ceil regularly, delighted to find that her young pupil absorbed Bible lessons like a sponge. She explained to Ceil that she was supposed to profess her faith in Jesus publicly. This could be done in a church, where, after the sermon, an invitation would be given for any new believers in Jesus to formally announce their faith. Moishe was not at all happy about what was happening but he agreed that Ceil could go to church as long as it was a one-time event and she went as inconspicuously as possible. Mrs. Wago accordingly arranged a ride for her on Easter Day.

Ceil recalled, "In those days, women wore hats to church, so if anyone in our Jewish neighborhood saw me wearing a hat on Sunday morning, especially Easter, they could easily guess where I was going. When my ride came, I ran to the car with my hat in a paper bag; I did not put it on until we were far from my neighborhood."

When the invitation came, Ceil walked down the center aisle of Trinity Baptist Church. After the service, many people welcomed her and promised to pray for her and for Moishe, that he, too, would come to know Jesus.

After that, Ceil respected Moishe's wishes not to tell people about her new beliefs, with one exception: she kept trying to tell *him* about Jesus, trying to get *him* to read the tracts. Irritated, Moishe said that he would rather Mrs. Wago not come to their home anymore. Ceil did not protest. Why not continue their lessons over the telephone?

Moishe became increasingly upset. She obviously wasn't getting over it as he'd hoped she would if he didn't make a fuss. The longer it went on, the more he feared that sooner or later, the secret would leak out. One day he tried calling home from work repeatedly, and the phone was continually busy. She must be talking to Mrs. Wago. Moishe came home and ripped the telephone from the wall. The next day the repairman came, and Ceil continued to study with Mrs. Wago over the phone—but they kept the lessons brief.

Moishe began applying other pressures. He pointed out what she already knew: if their families found out, they would be disowned and disinherited. They would be shunned by the Jewish community. He might even lose his job. How could she continue down this road?

Ceil never considered herself especially courageous, but though her heart was pounding, she replied calmly, "I asked God to show me what was true, and he did. I can't deny what he showed me. If I had to choose between you and God, I'd have to choose God. Don't make me choose!"

Moishe backed down; Ceil clearly meant what she said, and he did not want to lose her. On the other hand, maybe he already had lost her. He knew that it was wrong for Jews to believe in Jesus. What was he supposed to do? He downed a couple of shots of whiskey for courage—something he never did—and went to see his father.

"Dad," Moishe began, "I have a real problem." He hesitated before blurting out, "Ceil says she believes in Jesus. She reads the New Testament. She prays. I can't convince her to give it up. Do you think we should get a divorce?"

"Shame on you," his father said, "You've been drinking."

"You know I don't usually drink. It's just that I'm really worried."

"You can't be serious about divorcing your wife," his father said. "She's a nice Jewish girl. She's the mother of your child and my granddaughter. And she's a *good* mother. You're not going to do any better than the wife you've got. You shouldn't drink if it gives you such silly ideas."

Despite his father's chastening, Moishe went home relieved. He didn't want a divorce. He just wanted to do whatever a good Jew was supposed to do under these circumstances. Then it occurred to him that he had an untapped resource—the rabbi.

Moishe just *knew* that there had to be a good case for why Jesus could not be the Messiah. All Moishe had to do was educate himself, hear the rabbi's case so that he could explain it to Ceil. That would give him the ammunition to blow all this "Jesus stuff" out of the water.

Moishe visited the rabbi who had performed their wedding ceremony and explained his dilemma. "Ceil is an intelligent person," he said. "I just need you to give me the intellectual reasons that will convince her she made a mistake."

Rabbi Bryks began to explain how Christians had gotten the Hebrew Scriptures all wrong. "For example," the rabbi said, "the Christians say our prophets predicted that a virgin would conceive—become pregnant—and that Jesus fulfilled that prophecy. But the verse that they think predicts Jesus is only talking about an *almah,* or young woman, giving birth. The Hebrew word for 'virgin' is *betulah.*"

This sounded promising, but Moishe wanted to be certain: "Is *almah* ever used to mean 'virgin'?" To his dismay, the rabbi replied, "Yes. Sometimes."*

---

* The Septuagint—the Hebrew Scriptures translated into Greek by Jews in the Diaspora, long before Christ—uses a Greek word in this passage, *parthenos,* that implies virginity. That is significant since those who chose the word to relay the meaning of the prophet clearly were not reading Christian theology into the text. Moishe later discovered there is a Hebrew Scripture verse (Joel 1:8) in which the word *betulah* is used to describe a woman mourning the husband of her youth. A widow was presumably not a virgin.

Each time the rabbi explained that the Christians misunderstood or mistranslated the Hebrew prophecies, it was the same. There was more than one possible meaning.

Finally Moishe shook his head and said, "Rabbi Bryks, these arguments will not convince Ceil, and frankly, they don't even convince me. There must be better reasons why we don't believe."

The rabbi smiled mischievously. Then he said, "Well, think on this. It takes two to tango."

Moishe wasn't sure what dancing had to do with it. The rabbi explained that when it came to the virgin birth, it simply was not possible.

Moishe later recalled, "What Rabbi Bryks didn't know was that in that one statement, he completely undermined the case—not only for Christianity—but for Judaism and any other kind of theism." For Moishe, the rabbi's reasoning created more problems than it solved. If God could not manage this one miracle, how did he manage to create the world, part the Red Sea, or do any other miracles? And if God couldn't perform miracles, then the Bible must be wrong, in which case being Jewish meant no more or less than being Italian or Greek or African or Mexican—so why should it matter whether or not Jews believed in Jesus? Moishe felt he had been cut adrift.

For weeks, Ceil prayed for her husband. She had given up discussing her new beliefs with him since she had already done her best to explain them and did not want to provoke him any further. She didn't realize that there was a new softness, a new sweetness in her demeanor that continued to speak to him of Jesus, even when her words did not.

As for the tracts that Ceil often left around the house, Moishe recalled, "Some were serious and talked about messianic prophecy from the Jewish Bible. I could not ridicule our own Scriptures, so I ignored those pamphlets or threw them away. But if I found a pamphlet that I could ridicule, I would read it out loud in a sarcastic tone of voice so that Ceil would know that I was making fun of it."

Ceil continued to pray, and she stopped leaving so many pamphlets around the house. But one day she deliberately left a little booklet about heaven lying on a table.

It was a Saturday night when Moishe picked up that booklet. It wasn't one of the "serious" pamphlets, but for some reason, he did not read it out loud. Seeing the hyperliteralist interpretation of heaven—where people would enter through pearly gates and walk on streets of literal gold—he almost laughed out loud. He thought, *Heaven's not like this at all—uh-oh!* The "uh-oh" was the shock of realizing for the first time that he actually believed heaven was real.

Moishe began to unpack his thinking and was surprised to find faith. He not only believed in heaven, he believed in the Bible. He believed exactly what he'd fought so hard to disbelieve! There was no big sign or miracle. There was no closing argument. It was just that Moishe suddenly knew that he no longer had a choice. Deep inside his heart of hearts he saw that Jesus was the Messiah, and he knew just as certainly that if he didn't admit it, he'd be a liar. And he reminded himself of his mother's maxim: *the man who lies to himself is the biggest liar in the world.* He had chosen to look away from Jesus for as long as he could. But once he caught a glimpse, he could not deny what he saw.

Ceil recalled, "That night, Moishe turned to me in bed and said, 'I believe all this stuff that you believe about Jesus. What do I do now?'" Though she and so many others had been praying for that moment, she could hardly believe it. She managed to say, "You're supposed to tell God that you know you have sinned and need the forgiveness Jesus made possible by dying on the cross. Then you're supposed to go admit that publicly. I did it by going to the front of the church when the minister asked who wanted to declare their faith in Jesus for the first time. That's when you formally tell people that you want to start a new life by following Jesus. And then . . . ," she hesitated because she hadn't yet done what she was about to tell him, "you're supposed to get baptized." She added, "Getting baptized doesn't mean you become a gentile. It's not like the Inquisition where Jews were forced to be baptized and turn their backs on our people."

Once Moishe knew what he was supposed to do, he didn't want to lose any time. He said, "Well, tomorrow is Sunday. Let's go to that church you went to a couple of months ago."

The next morning Ceil returned to Trinity Baptist Church, this time with her husband. It "just happened" to be Pentecost Sunday. Christians celebrate Pentecost as a special day in the history of Jesus' followers, even though it is actually a Jewish holiday, Shavuot,* which falls seven weeks after Passover.

---

* The Torah records how God gave this as one of Israel's harvest festivals, and in particular, it was a time when the Israelites were to offer the firstfruits of the spring harvest. Giving God the first and best part of the harvest showed gratitude to him as the giver of all good things and also trust that he would provide the rest of the harvest to take care of the Israelites' needs.

According to Jewish tradition, Shavuot also marked the anniversary of Moses' receiving the Law on Mount Sinai. Christians believe that on the Shavuot after Jesus was resurrected, God fulfilled his promise to write his law on people's hearts (Jeremiah 31:31–33). You can read more about this in *Christ in the Feast of Pentecost,* by David Brickner and Rich Robinson, published by Moody Publishers.

The church service was certainly unlike anything Moishe had ever experienced in synagogue. There is no denying that he felt some culture shock, and that culture shock would continue in the days to come. Nevertheless, at the end of the service, Moishe walked down the same aisle that Ceil had walked. United in their new faith, they began to attend church regularly. In July, 1953, both were baptized.

ELEVEN

All colors look bright when you have enough light.
—MOISHE ROSEN

It's no wonder the Bible describes this as being born again, Moishe thought. *There's so much to learn!* He was somewhat overwhelmed, not only by the seemingly endless information, but also by all the cultural differences he had to navigate simply to avoid making a spectacle of himself at a Sunday morning church service.

There were also physical differences between the church and the synagogue. At church, there was no holy ark for the Torah at the front of the sanctuary, and no *ner tamid* (eternal light) hanging by a chain from the ceiling. The racks on the backs of the church pews held big hymnbooks and some Bibles, but no prayer books. Many people brought their own Bibles from home; Moishe and Ceil had brought theirs as Mrs. Wago had instructed. But these details could barely begin to account for how strange Trinity Baptist Church seemed in comparison to the Orthodox synagogues Moishe had known.

Saturday morning synagogue services had lasted—from the very beginning to the very end—about four and a half hours. However, it was understood and accepted that people could arrive after the services began and/or go home before they ended. People greeted one another as they entered and left the services, and sometimes they even engaged in brief conversations. As for the actual service, there were no musical instruments, except the *shofar* (ram's horn) for the high holy days. Much of the worship was read aloud, at times responsively, from the *siddur* (the prayer book). Everyone started and finished at roughly the same time, but they all read at their own pace.

Moishe was surprised to find that Sunday morning church services were only an hour and a half. They started and ended punctually. Latecomers appeared to be very embarrassed and apologetic as they found their seats, and no one left before the close of the service. Worshippers entered the sanctuary quietly and sat, face forward, without saying much to one another until it was time to leave. When the congregation read a Scripture passage responsively from the back of the hymnal, everyone seemed to know just where to pause so that they were exactly in sync.

He hadn't been prepared for any of this the first time he'd come to church. He expected it to be a one-time experience. Probably, he thought, they would return for holidays and special occasions. He soon realized that he was expected to attend church every week: Sunday morning, Sunday evening worship, and Wednesday night prayer meeting.

As he and Ceil climbed up the front steps of the old red brick building, Moishe felt a sense of bewilderment. Ceil was carrying the baby, wondering a little anxiously how she would behave during the service. They were relieved when a man met them at the door to extend a welcome. Smiling at Lyn, the usher explained that the church had a nursery, and Ceil followed as he led the way.

That left Moishe standing alone in the lobby. The usher returned soon enough with Ceil and said, "Let's get a good seat for you." Moishe thanked the man, silently noting that unlike the Orthodox synagogue, he could sit with his wife. Yet he wondered why or how a good seat had been reserved for them. In the Orthodox environment of Moishe's youth, the synagogue president held a discreet understanding of what each family could afford, and annual dues to support the synagogue were set accordingly. In return for these dues, the men of each family were assigned numbered seats. Higher dues meant seats closer to the front. The elders sat up front against the eastern wall in seats of honor. Less affluent men sat in the back of the sanctuary.

The usher led the couple out of the economy section and into what Moishe recognized as the first-class section of the church. Finally the usher motioned for the couple to be seated in the second row, handing each of them what Moishe assumed was a program. Moishe felt honored that the church would assign him and Ceil such special seats. "Now if there is anything I can do to help, let me know," the usher concluded. Moishe thought how wonderful it was that the church could afford to hire ushers.

The program, which he later learned was called the bulletin, had several words that he didn't know: *invocation, prelude, doxology,* and *benediction.* Sometimes a few words were followed by a mysterious number: "A Mighty Fortress Is Our God—347" or "Just as I Am—583." Presumably, their meaning would become clear during the service. But when Moishe got toward the end of the bulletin, the words *Prepare for Communion next week* caught his attention.

Communion? Moishe did not want to be unprepared. The organist had begun to play, and Moishe had no idea that this was to signal a time of quiet reflection. He looked back at the usher who had said to let him know if there was anything he could do to help—and made a beckoning gesture. The usher made his way down the aisle. Moishe pointed to the bulletin and asked, "This word, what does it mean?"

The usher whispered, "I'll tell you later," and turned to leave.

Moishe grabbed his arm. "If I wanted to know later, I would have asked later." *The insolence of this usher!* he thought. *Why do they pay a man to insult the worshippers?* Little did he realize that church ushers were volunteers, and that this usher taught part-time as a seminary professor.

The usher, somewhat taken aback by this response, nevertheless remained composed. He replied, "You know what Passover is, don't you?" Moishe nodded. The usher continued, "Well, Communion is for Christians what Passover is for Jews."

Finally, Moishe thought, *something I know about*—because he certainly knew all about Passover.* It was a family reunion where people got dressed up in their best clothes. There would be a big meal prepared especially for the holiday and (in his home) a little bit of a ceremony. There would be unleavened bread, *matzo*. And some fun songs and games. Communion sounded like it was going to be pretty good, but there was still the matter of preparing for it.

The usher had managed to slip away, but Moishe sought him out after the service. "This Communion, how much does it cost?"

The usher replied, "We don't charge for Communion. You can put something into the offering if you want."

Moishe continued, "Well, should we bring anything?"

"No."

Moishe couldn't think of anything else to ask about preparing for Communion. Probably it meant to bring a good appetite, or maybe it was a reminder to allow extra time for the event.

The following Sunday, Moishe arrived at the church with a healthy appetite and a sense of anticipation. Ceil headed straight for the nursery like an old pro. When she returned, Moishe led them to their seat, bypassing the usher. He'd noted the location carefully the previous week and assumed they would be expected to return to it whenever they attended.

---

* Decades later Moishe and Ceil wrote an in-depth book on the subject titled *Christ in the Passover* published by Moody Press (now Moody Publishing).

He'd expected to be greeted with the savory aromas that signaled a Jewish holiday meal. But as he and Ceil approached their seats a shocking sight awaited him.

Down at the front was what he recognized to be a funeral bier. When a Jewish person from Moishe's synagogue died, the *chevra kedushim* (holy brethren) washed the body and left it covered with two shrouds. The dead were to be buried within twenty-four hours. Yet what Moishe saw at the church appeared to be something or someone prepared for burial. Under the white cloths, there was a lump where the head should be and a lump where the feet should be.

He thought, *This is terrible taste, to have a funeral and a meal in the same place.* But then, he didn't see any meal or any indication that there was to be a meal. As he kept thinking about the body at the front of the church, the idea of the meal grew less and less appealing.

The service seemed to go according to the previous week's routine. The congregation sang a few hymns (he now knew that the words and numbers in the bulletin were the hymns and pages on which they could be found), and the choir performed an anthem. Then the pastor, Donald MacDonald, spoke. His message was longer than most rabbis' homilies—about forty minutes—but Moishe didn't mind. MacDonald was an excellent teacher and preacher. Moishe appreciated the way he explained the background of the time and place pertinent to whatever Scripture passages he used in his sermons. He even took notes, soaking up information with characteristic interest and intensity.

Following the sermon, eight men dressed in black walked down the center aisle. Moishe later learned that they were the board of deacons, but they seemed to him more like the Trinity Baptist Drill Team; all their movements seemed coordinated. They arrived at the table where two deacons were deployed at each end, the others stood on the sides of the table, and the pastor was in the middle. With perfect precision, they grasped the ends of the shrouds.

Moishe's stomach lurched as he realized they were going to uncover the body. This was a sin and he felt he should not look—but curiosity overcame him. What he saw was a puzzlement: aluminum pots and pans. The pots had covers, each with a cross in the center. The pans were shallow, like plates. The pastor called on somebody to say a prayer over the bread, and one deacon prayed, thanking God for the bread that represented "the body of Jesus that was broken for us."

They began passing the pans throughout the pews, and being so close to the front, Moishe was one of the first recipients. As a pan reached him, he saw that it contained matzo that had been broken into very small pieces. Finally, something that actually related to Passover! Moishe picked out a piece and ate it. Then he noticed that everyone else was holding his or hers, so he pretended to hold his matzo too.

The deacons returned to the front, and the pastor said, in a very solemn voice, "Take and eat." Everybody ate a piece of matzo, and Moishe pretended to eat what he had already eaten.

Next the pastor asked someone to say a prayer over "the cup," and another deacon prayed, thanking God for "the blood of Jesus that was shed for us." Then they passed the big uncovered pots. Moishe knew that there wasn't going to be real blood; at Passover, the wine symbolized the blood of the lamb, just like the matzo symbolized its body. And sure enough they passed around cups of wine, except they were more like glass thimbles than cups. Moishe took one and this time, he held onto it. When everyone had been served, the pastor said, "Drink ye all of it," and Moishe drank all two swallows of grape juice!

Then they sang a hymn about the tie that binds as the offering plates were passed. After that, people started filing out. Somewhat bewildered, Moishe went to his favorite usher. "Excuse me," he said. "When will we be having Communion?"

The usher, equally bewildered, replied, "You've just had it."

Moishe could feel his stomach rumbling as he nodded a polite acknowledgment. He thought, *They invite you to a Passover feast, they give you a crumb of matzo and a thimble full of grape juice, and then they have the nerve to make jokes about Jews being stingy.*[*]

————

Despite the culture shock, Moishe dove into his new life of faith with zeal. This was not so much a sign of great spirituality. In large part he was so dazed and amazed by God's reality in his life that he couldn't stop thinking about it. Moishe later described being a new believer in Jesus as "a very heady experience."

He had no family or friends who knew how to "do" Christianity, so for

---

* The "Communion story" became a standby in later years when Moishe spoke to students at Bible colleges and seminaries. He'd greatly embellish it with perfect timing, exaggerated gestures, and facial expressions that delighted students. At the same time the story helped hearers understand the serious reality of how cultural rituals that they took for granted could be very confusing to others. Because the story became such a fixture in his testimony, this third person narrative does include some of the embellishments Moishe added through the years. For example, while most Jewish people find ourselves objects of racial stereotyping at some point, the reader is not to suppose that anyone at Trinity Baptist Church joked about Jews being stingy.

the first few years, Moishe was highly influenced by people and institutions who'd had a part in introducing him to Jesus. He learned by imitation as well as by instruction. He began each prayer, "Our dear gracious heavenly Father we come unto thee in prayer . . ." because that was how he heard other, more mature Christians pray. He also noticed that no one at church smoked cigarettes before or after the service. On inquiring about this, he was told, "The Scriptures say that one's body is the temple of God." This was not a particularly compelling argument to Moishe at the time, but he decided he better quit anyway. It wasn't easy, because he had smoked heavily since he was sixteen, but he did quit—and put on forty pounds. Smoking had somewhat curbed Moishe's appetite, and without cigarettes he was hungry a great deal of the time. Moreover, as with most people, his interest in food went beyond satisfying hunger; he found pleasure in particularly good food. Ceil recalled, "He had been so skinny, he actually needed most of that weight."

It wasn't that Moishe was enamored of Christian culture or eager to meet the expectations of his new mentors. Truthfully, Moishe often found Mrs. Wago irritatingly pushy with her Bible studies and her insistence that he and Ceil not only read but also memorize certain Scriptures. Still, he respected her and faithfully studied the Bible under her tutelage.

But there was more to this new life than acquiring information. Moishe recalled, "You have this impulse that you just want to tell people; you want to sing about what God has done. You don't always think through the order or the consequences of how you tell people."

If there was one thing for which Moishe later felt remorse, it was that he'd told a great many people about his new beliefs before telling his immediate family. It was easy enough to blurt out to his cousins Donald and Dorothy, "Can you believe it? All this time, we've been wrong about Jesus. He really is the Messiah!" As far as his parents and brother, Moishe had every intention of telling them, but, as he recalled, "I was waiting for a good time to tell them about my faith, and I regret that they first found out about it from others." By the time they did find out, about four months had passed, and Moishe and Ceil had already been baptized.*

The family usually got together twice weekly, on Friday nights and Sunday afternoons. When Moishe's brother telephoned one day to say that their father

---

* Trinity Baptist Church occupied a building that had no facility for baptizing by immersion (which is more in keeping with the Jewish cleansing ritual known as the *mikvah*, where the entire body must be submerged). Pastor MacDonald conducted baptisms on occasional Sunday evenings at the First Baptist Church of Lakewood, Colorado. Moishe and Ceil were baptized there on July 28, 1953.

had requested that Moishe come over at a specified nonroutine time (Wednesday night), Moishe knew that something was up. He later explained that it was rare for his father to ask to see him and even rarer to be invited to talk in the living room. The living room was for insurance salesmen and other people who wanted to sell something. Moishe said,

> I sat down, a bit tense, so my father broke the ice: "What's this I hear, that you've been telling people you believe in Jesus?" I couldn't have asked for a better icebreaker, so I stood up and took the family Bible off the shelf. It needed a good dusting. I sat down, but my father remained standing.
>
> I began flipping through the pages, talking much too fast yet somehow unable to slow down: "Well, you see, Dad, over here it says that when the Messiah would come, he would be born in Bethlehem." And then I was off, flipping to another passage, telling how it had been in our Bible all along and we'd missed it. Finally, looking somewhat bewildered, my father sat down.

Then his mother and brother joined them.

Moishe recalled,

> My father was very patient. He didn't say anything as I rushed from one text to the next, sometimes fumbling to find the reference I wanted. Finally, I stopped, like a wind-up toy that had run down. At that point, my father reached over and closed the open Bible. He said, "This book has come between me and you, and until you can give it up, you can't be my son."

That was it. Whether or not the Hebrew Scriptures seemed to point to Jesus as the Messiah was completely beside the point. Ben was committed to the Jewish community's position, which meant that believing in Jesus as Messiah was not an option. To veer from that position was considered the worst kind of disloyalty. His father's reaction came as a shock; it was painful and hard to believe it had actually happened.

Moishe later reflected,

> Some people might think that what he said was unreasonable. But I knew he was doing what he thought was right, though it was difficult for him. All I could say was, "Well, Dad, I want you to know that I love you more than ever,

and I really do respect you." To me, those were the key issues. And my father answered, "Well, if you respect me; if you see me walking down the street cross over to the other side so that I don't have to."

In recounting this story Moishe emphasized that his parents never treated him or Ceil as though they were villains. They never acted as though either of them had deliberately wronged the family. As for his brother, Moishe had the impression that he simply wanted to keep the family together.

Moishe's uncle Dave, however, was infuriated when he heard the news.* Moishe recalled, "With the colorful life he'd lived, Uncle Dave wasn't at a loss for a swearing vocabulary. I'll never forget how he turned red in the face as he shook his finger at me and finally said, 'You . . . you . . . you . . . *Christ lover,* you!' It was astonishing to realize that the most shameful thing he could think to call me was actually a compliment. After what Jesus had done for me, I wanted to be a 'Christ lover.'"

The sad truth was, being a Christ lover meant something very different to Moishe's family than it did to him. For centuries, Jews had been persecuted in the name of Jesus. Belief in him was anathema to Jewish people, and Jews who embraced him were seen as traitors who had crossed a line. They were no longer considered part of the community. What Christ did has never been so much of an issue to most Jewish people as what has been done in his name.

Moishe continued to tell everybody and anybody he could about Jesus, including people at the sporting goods store. Nate Gart slowed him down by reminding him, "It's your job to sell sporting goods, not Jesus." He then showed Moishe that he more than understood the gospel, describing to his young protégé Christian beliefs at least as well as Moishe could have described them. Nate calmly explained that he would not forbid Moishe from talking about Jesus at the store, but that if he wanted to keep his job, he would have to keep his sales up. He commented that he wasn't surprised that Moishe had become "a Christer" as he put it—that it was usually people like him who became fanatically involved.

By then, Moishe was the buyer in the camera department and assistant to the corporate manager. It was a lot of responsibility for someone his age, but Nate

---

* Despite Uncle Dave's explosive reaction, Moishe said, "He was also the first one in the family who showed me any respect. After I finished Bible college and I came to Denver to be ordained, he said, 'I don't want to encourage you to follow this religion, but I'm glad that you followed my advice and got an education.'"

Gart had invested a lot in him and appreciated his work. In fact, he withstood significant pressure from Ben Rosen, who wanted him to fire Moishe.

Ben really wanted his son back and somehow believed that if things weren't going so well for him, he'd be forced to give up this Jesus *mishegas*.* Moishe was a young man with a wife and baby to provide for, and his job was clearly a vulnerable spot.

What did Moishe think about his father trying to get him fired? "My father was not the type of person who would fire anyone because of his religion," Moishe said. "I am sure if someone asked him to do what he wanted Nate Gart to do, he would have seen immediately that it was unfair. Plus he was not in the habit of threatening people. He must have found it distasteful, but I guess he hoped it might pressure me into doing what he thought was right."

Moishe had heard stories about other Jewish people who struggled over whether to accept the gospel, knowing that they would be rejected by parents or friends. His experience was very different. Unlike Ceil, he hadn't been seeking the truth when he found it or, as the case may be, when *it* found *him*. He had never wanted to know if the gospel was true, was not open-minded about it, and never pretended to be. But once he saw the gospel as true, he never considered acceptance as a choice. He said,

> To me, it was simple: if something was true, it was true. If people disliked you for believing it, there was not much you could do about it. Things were not true or false because you wanted them to be. . . . I don't know if I missed a great implication, or if God somehow just salved my heart and mind with some kind of anesthetic to help with the potential pain. I like to think that I simply knew God would take care of us.
>
> When my family disowned me, I felt a terrible loss and I missed them— but I couldn't ignore the truth or apologize for what I believed. I had enough sense that I would not try to argue that I was right and they were wrong. I knew the rift was very painful for them—as much as for me. I never doubted their affection for me; they were simply doing what [they thought] was required of them.

Sadly, Ceil could not say the same thing for the Starrs. She and Moishe had acquiesced when the Starrs asked them to see a rabbi—it was to be one visit

---

* Yiddish word for nonsense or craziness.

out of respect for Ceil's parents. When she had first pointed out the messianic prophecy in Isaiah 53 to her adoptive parents, it had shaken her father, who had never seen the passage. He was eager for the rabbi to prove that Jesus was not the suffering servant described in the Hebrew Scriptures. Upon meeting the rabbi, Mr. Starr became impatient and asked the rabbi in Yiddish, "What about Isaiah 53? What about Isaiah 53?"

After much hemming and hawing, Rabbi Bennett explained that having just moved, he did not have his commentaries unpacked. He would be glad to speak with them about the passage when he could refer them to those writings.

The interview had not gone as the older couple wished, and they had wrongly assumed that the young couple would be willing to return. Mamie Starr threatened that unless her daughter and son-in-law were willing to continue sessions with the rabbi, she and her husband would have nothing more to do with them. When this threat did not produce the desired effect, a furious Mamie ended the relationship. Ceil was grieved, particularly at having lost her adoptive father.

Moishe reflected, "The Bible says that when your father and mother forsake you, then I [the Lord] will take you up (Ps. 27:10). We found that to be true. We had a new family in the church. Not a substitute family because no one can replace your family—but a different kind of family."

The cynicism Moishe once felt about God was gone. He was delighted in being able to believe in miracles, being able to believe in prayer. Mrs. Wago had stressed the importance of prayer and reading the Bible, and Moishe used his break times at work to read the Bible and pray. He noticed that the Pillar of Fire Church, about seven blocks from the store, had a sign out front that said, "Open all day for prayer." At that church Moishe found a place of quiet solitude to read and pray.

One day during his break, Moishe was reading chapter 20 in the book of Acts. He came to verse 21, which described the apostle Paul as he was "testifying to Jews, and also to Greeks, repentance toward God and faith toward our Lord Jesus Christ." Moishe thought how great it would be if someone like Paul would bring the gospel to Jews in modern times, and he prayed that God would send someone.

What happened in that moment was difficult to describe. As he reflected on the verse, Moishe knew that he was reading about someone else. He knew that these events were from a different time and had nothing to do with him.

Yet the verse seemed to be illuminated in his heart and mind so that he knew that God was speaking to him through it. He didn't hear a voice or see a vision, but the message was clear: *Why not you? Why not spend* your *life telling people about Jesus?*

Moishe did not know what form this would take. He only knew that something very significant had happened; God had communicated to him through that verse in a way that went beyond his usual understanding of the Bible.

Herein lies a pretty piece of symmetry. As it turned out, the very street preacher that Moishe and Ceil used to pass every Sunday on their way to the movies—the one that prompted Moishe to wish out loud that he could believe something with so much devotion that he'd be willing to face ridicule as that man was doing—was one of the clergy from the Pillar of Fire Church. That was where God called Moishe to preach the gospel.

TWELVE

It's not so bad to be out on a limb if Christ is the branch.

—MOISHE ROSEN

Ceil had taken the streetcardowntown to meet Moishe at the sporting goods store. Out of the corner of his eye, he saw her near the door. He rang up a sale, counted back the customer's change, and started toward her. As he reached the door, one of the Gart brothers shouted after him, "Hey, Rosen, where you going?"

"It's my lunch hour," Moishe explained, still on his way out.

"No, it's not, We're too busy; we need you to cover." He punctuated his demand with some rather colorful language. Moishe liked and respected three of the four Gart brothers; unfortunately, this happened to be the fourth.

Moishe felt caught between his duty to the store and to his wife. Normally, he would not have hesitated to get back to work. But Ceil arranged her day so they could have lunch together.

Moishe swallowed hard, forcing himself to remain calm. He said, "But my wife made a special trip. She wouldn't be here if you'd told me earlier you wanted me to work through lunch today."

The man shrugged."Well, that's too bad," he said, adorning the terse phrase with a colorful adjective.

None of the other brothers used language like that in the store, much less in front of a lady. Finding this lack of respect for Ceil intolerable, Moishe announced once again that he was going to lunch.

"If you do," the man growled, "don't bother coming back. You're fired."

Moishe put a protective arm around Ceil and left without another word. They walked to their favorite lunch stop: Joe "Awful" Coffee's—where the coffee wasn't awful. (The owner's last name was Coffee, and the restaurant was named for a locally famous boxer, Joe "Awful.") Moishe, acutely conscious of being newly unemployed, considered getting hot dogs at the dime store instead, but didn't want to spoil the day.

"You don't have to worry, you know," he told Ceil reassuringly. "I'll start looking for another job right away."

"I'm not worried." She tried to match his optimistic tone.

"I think it could be a pretty good adventure, looking for a different kind of work," he said while they ate. "I've been doing the same thing for six years now. Probably it's time for a change."

Ceil nodded. "I'm sure we'll be fine."

Moishe already had an idea of the kind of work he wanted to do. As a teenager, he'd been influenced by a writer/philosopher named Eric Hoffer (later known as the longshoreman philosopher) and his book titled *The True Believer*. Moishe had heard a radio interview with Hoffer, in which the man explained that most philosophers were too "heady" to understand everyday life or care about working-class people. He insisted that until a person had worked with his hands, he was not worthy to be considered a philosopher.

Moishe had a philosophical bent and found Hoffer's ideas challenging. He'd even wondered occasionally if his skill as a salesman was taking the easy way when he ought to be shoulder to shoulder with those who lived by the sweat of their brow. True, he'd sweated plenty while swinging a sledgehammer in the family business, but then he'd had no choice.

After lunch, he went home and began poring over the classified section of the newspaper. He avoided sales opportunities in favor of manual labor. Before long, he found an opening for a carpenter's helper. With his good work history and positive attitude, Moishe got the position without much trouble. Soon he was shoveling concrete, sanding wood, hammering nails—and discovering that he was absolutely no good at it. Six weeks into the job his boss shook his head sadly and said, "Rosen, I never seen anybody work so hard and fail so badly. I hate to do this, but I won't be able to use you after this week."

Next he tried driving a truck. That job ended on the very first day when the boss asked to see his Social Security card and driver's license. Moishe could drive a truck, and he'd gotten driving experience in the army, but he'd never gotten a license because he had no car.

A month before Easter he found work in a wholesale florist shop. After Easter, sales dropped and Moishe was laid off. From there he got a job as a shipping clerk in a department store, but he was fired for being too slow.

One after another, Moishe attempted a series of jobs for which he was ill suited. The worst of it was that earlier, when he'd returned to the sporting goods store to pick up his last paycheck, he'd discovered the entire "firing" incident had been bogus. Nate, the senior partner, had never authorized the brother in question to fire anyone.

"Why'd you take my brother so seriously?" Nate asked. "If you'd have come to me, I would have worked the whole thing out." But Moishe hadn't realized that was an option.

After a string of failed attempts to work with his hands, Moishe decided that respect for manual labor was all very well, but doing work he was actually good at was even better. He thought about returning to Gart Brothers, but even if Nate wanted him back, Moishe would still have to humble himself to get his old job—and he wasn't yet ready for that.

When a friend mentioned that the Fairmount Cemetery had an opening for a sales manager, Moishe made an appointment. He asked Ceil to pray for him as he left for the important interview. Moishe arrived at the cemetery's office, confidently answered the interviewer's questions, and felt relieved as the interviewer nodded his satisfaction. Moishe then asked a few questions of his own and learned that his would be the only full-time salaried sales position. Four part-time salesmen, older men, worked during the evenings, and three women looked for customers from 3:00 to 5:00 p.m. They all worked on commission. "You can run the operation however you see fit, as long as sales remain up," the interviewer explained. "You seem very well qualified; the job is yours if you want it."

Moishe wanted it.

He sized up his staff within the first week. The four salesmen were buddies. In addition to selling cemetery plots they were in the real estate business, and some sold merchandise on the side. The women were likewise working other jobs.

The group had developed a strategy, and one of the salesmen had explained it rather crudely. "Get 'em while they're weeping," he advised his new sales manager. "Someone comes in to buy a plot for mom, that's the time to ask him or her about a personal resting place. I tell them, 'We can get you a place next to the dearly departed, but it's a desirable location and I can't promise it will still be available if you wait.'" The other employees nodded approvingly.

Moishe recoiled inwardly but did not say much. He didn't want to quarrel with them over their ethics. He asked a few questions, ascertained that each one did, indeed, have other sales jobs and sources of income. He knew that there'd be trouble if he let some go, but not others. He wanted to start fresh with a new set of employees.

The following week he called a meeting of the staff. "I know it's short notice, but I'm going to have to let you all go. I think you knew there might be some restructuring when the company hired me. I appreciate all your work, but I'll be bringing in a team of dedicated salesmen who will be working solely for the cemetery."

Moishe's membership at Trinity Baptist Church had brought him into contact with several luminaries from Denver Seminary (then called Conservative Baptist Seminary in Denver), including Dr. Vernon Grounds, who at that time was the dean.* Dr. Grounds had shown himself a friend to Moishe, and through him, Moishe learned that many seminary students needed part-time work. Moishe felt that ministers-in-training would be sensitive in caring for bereaved customers. He visited the seminary and recruited his entire sales team from the student body.

It was the kind of move he would later refer to as "convergence" because it brought together multiple purposes. It provided more compassionate care for his customers, and it helped the theological students cover their school and personal expenses. Finally, it provided a dedicated staff whose commissions depended solely on the cemetery, which was advantageous for the company.

Selling burial plots wasn't nearly as much fun as selling cameras, but Moishe did well at it, and the sales job at Fairmount Cemetery turned out to be an important, if brief, chapter in his life. First, it helped him develop a spiritual discipline. This began as he walked through the cemetery grounds, initially to acquaint himself with the property he would be selling. As he passed through the rows of headstones, he found himself reminded of various people he cared about, and he began to pray for them. When he found, quite by accident, that he could walk and even observe his surroundings while praying, it revolutionized his prayer life and became one of his better habits for decades to come.

In addition to prayer, working at the cemetery provided a context for Moishe to do what he loved best: tell others about the hope he had found in Jesus. Many customers left, not only having bought a burial plot, but also having received something even greater at no cost: the joy of reconciliation with God and the promise of eternal life through Jesus.

---

* Dr. Grounds later became the president of the seminary.

Finally, one of the men Moishe hired from the seminary helped him take the next step in his call to ministry, a step that would help prepare him to change the face of Jewish missions.

———

Moishe grew up in an era when it was the norm to be cause-oriented. It was understood that people were meant to dedicate their lives to something beyond their personal satisfaction. To him, "witnessing" (telling people how and what God had done for him) came naturally. He recalled, "From the start, I witnessed to everyone that I could. And maybe even to some that I should not have, because I was at work on my boss's time."

He recalled, "Many people prayed with me, but I noticed that only a few stuck. That's when I realized that it wasn't too hard to get somebody to pray with you to receive the Lord, but that didn't mean they were eager to start a new life. So, I realized even before I became a missionary that one shouldn't push." As a result, Moishe was never tremendously excited over the news of someone's initial decision to follow Jesus. He always figured it was best to wait and watch for evidence that the person had truly had a life-changing encounter with God.

Much of what Moishe learned in his earliest days of faith was from Trinity Baptist Church. He formed his first opinion of what a good sermon should be from his pastor, Donald MacDonald, whom he described as

a very analytical preacher. . . . MacDonald's genius was that he could give the backgrounding in such a way as to illuminate the Scripture in its original meaning. He'd paint a scene, draw you in. You didn't feel inadequate or focused on the fact that the preacher knew all these details that you didn't know; you were too busy listening and envisioning the details he described.*

Many people at the church were scholars—several were professors from the seminary—and were much better formally educated than our pastor. But none of them claimed any greater knowledge; he was a phenomenon. And on top of that, he was a superb musician. He played the trombone and on Sunday evenings, he had this brass quartet. His music as well as his preaching brought a great deal of excellence and dignity to the ministry of our church—and that meant a lot to me.

---

* Decades later, Moishe patterned some of his signature sermons, including "The Centurion," on MacDonald's style of preaching.

Harold Deinstadt was one of the seminary students Moishe had hired to work with him at the cemetery; it was he who helped clarify Moishe's call to ministry, and thus he played a pivotal part in Moishe's life. Harold really could not pinpoint a time or place related to their conversations that led to Moishe's ministry:

Martin felt God had called him to be a witness to the Jewish people, and I encouraged him to get the training to do so, and before you know it they left for Bible school in New Jersey. We saw each other daily, and I tried to be a help to him as a new Christian. He later told me I'd had a real influence in his life, and that has been a real point of satisfaction and joy for me as I have followed his career. But once Martin left Denver, that was the last of any regular contact I had with him. After I graduated from seminary, we took a church in Maine, and since we were back East we made a point to go to his house and stay overnight there in New Jersey."

Moishe had a much more crystallized memory of the role that Harold Deinstadt played in his life:

He was one of the Christians who taught me a great deal, by his example and through our daily conversations. At one point he asked me if God had called me to witness for him, and I said "yes." Then he wanted to know what I intended to do about it. I knew that God had called me that day at the Pillar of Fire Church, but I hadn't realized that I was supposed to do anything about it, other than what I was already doing—which was to tell everyone I could about Jesus. Harold pointed out that God had called him to be a pastor, and as a result he had trained for the ministry and would go on to be the pastor of a church. If God had called me to be a witness to the Jewish people, what was I going to do about it? Harold got me in motion.

That was how Moishe realized that when God spoke to him about being a witness to his people, he did not mean it as a hobby or a part-time job. After all, there were missionaries, like Hannah Wago, whose full-time occupation was to witness to Jewish people. Moishe spoke to Mrs. Wago about this, and before long, the American Board of Missions to the Jews (ABMJ) had offered to sponsor his education and training. He applied and was accepted to Northeastern

Bible Institute (which later became Northeastern Bible College) in Essex Fells, New Jersey.

Naturally word reached Ben that his son was planning to become a missionary. One day, to Moishe's great relief, he received an answer to a fervent prayer. His brother, Don, called and said, "Dad wants to see you." The meeting was arranged, and a reconciliation of sorts took place.

Since the heart-wrenching session a year earlier with the elder Rosens, Moishe and Ceil had honored Ben's edict that they have no direct contact with them. They had, however, made it possible for Don to take Lyn to her grandparents' house for weekly visits. Ben now made it known that he did not want to be estranged from his son and daughter-in-law any longer. They would be welcome in his home as long as they did not attempt to discuss religion.

Ben also made it known that he was genuinely concerned about his son's mental health. He could not fathom how a sane Jew would choose such a life. He'd seen that his son was willing to be rejected, even disinherited—and for what? Had Martin considered that it might be a delusion? Would he make just one appointment to see Dr. Cohen, who was a psychiatrist? Ben was willing to pay for the visit.

Moishe could see that his father was not being sarcastic or mean-spirited, and he agreed to see a doctor, strictly for his father's peace of mind. It began with a phone call. "Before I make an appointment there are a couple of things I need to know," Moishe told the doctor. "Is it possible, do you think, that a sane Jew could believe that Jesus is the Messiah?" If the doctor felt that was grounds for declaring him insane, Moishe would not have seen any point in going. However, the doctor did not dismiss the possibility as insane. Moishe continued, "Then, if you examine me and find me of sound mind, will you give me a written statement to that effect?" When the doctor agreed, Moishe made the appointment for the very next day.

At the psychiatrist's office, Moishe explained that he was there because his father wanted assurance that Moishe was not insane.

"Can you tell me why you think he doubts your sanity?" asked the psychiatrist.

Moishe began, "I have become a believer in Jesus, and lately I have felt the hand of God guiding me . . ."

The doctor leaned forward and asked, perhaps a little too eagerly, "Tell me, Martin, just where on your body do you feel the hand of God?"

"No, no!" Moishe quickly explained. "That's idiomatic. I didn't feel the hand of God physically. I just meant I had an inner conviction, a strong sense that God had a certain direction for my life." The psychiatrist's initial assumption was not lost on Moishe. He realized that in just a year he had picked up a great deal of church jargon. He determined that he would never talk to anyone who wasn't a Christian in a way that he himself would not have understood before he became acclimated to Christian culture.

Moishe continued to explain his plans to go to Bible school and become a missionary. The doctor asked routine questions and concluded that Moishe probably had a condition that he described as a low-grade depression, which he did not regard as serious, nor did he suggest any treatment. He wrote a brief letter certifying that in his professional opinion, Martin Meyer Rosen was of a sound mind, with no indication of insanity. Moishe often joked that no matter how often people accused him of being a *meshuggener* (crazy person), he had written proof of his sanity.

Meanwhile the job at the cemetery continued to go well. Moishe not only kept his sales relatively high, but he had many opportunities to tell people about Jesus. Yet none of them were Jewish. Jews didn't buy in Fairmount Cemetery because Denver had a Jewish cemetery, and members of the community would not have considered it proper to be buried elsewhere.

More and more, Moishe found himself thinking about Gart Brothers Sporting Goods Store. Nearly all the employees were Jewish, and Moishe cared about many of them. Not that he begrudged gentiles or strangers the opportunity to hear the gospel, but he longed to tell his own people about the Messiah. He recalled, "There were only a few months left before I would be leaving Denver. I couldn't stand the thought of leaving without doing my best to be a witness to the people at Gart Brothers. So I decided I better humble myself." He got his job back, but he knew he had to keep his sales up to stay on the job. He did, and he had that job until the family moved to New Jersey.

Moishe never stopped thinking of himself as a Jew, not only by birth and upbringing, but also by culture and heritage that no one could take from him. But he was a Christian by faith and specifically a Baptist. He learned that it was common among Baptists to get a preaching license when one went away to study for the ministry. Accordingly, Moishe asked to speak to the pastor and the deacons at his church. He gave his testimony, explained his calling, and asked if they would license him. To Moishe's surprise and disappointment, the board concluded that since they didn't know if he could preach or not, it would not be proper to license him at that time. "But," Pastor MacDonald told him, "should you choose, after your education to come back, we would be happy to hear you preach. If your education and preaching are satisfactory, we will do better than issue you a license. We will ordain you."

Though disappointed, Moishe recognized that it was a fair decision and offer. The pastor promised to correspond with Moishe while he was in Bible college, and he kept that promise.

At the end of August 1954, Moishe and Ceil stored a few pieces of furniture with a friend and loaded up the family's 1949 Hudson with the rest of their worldly goods. Then they set out on the two-thousand-mile trek to New Jersey. It was exciting, yet that adventure might easily have come to an abrupt and tragic end. Moishe explained,

> I had been informed that our Hudson automobile was in excellent working order. We got to Columbus, Ohio, and checked into one of those old-fashioned motels. They rented out one-room cottages and on either side of each cottage there was a carport.
>
> I have always been a somewhat cautious person. That night I inspected the car, checking all the fluids under the hood and noting the air pressure in the tires. The temperature had been hovering near a hundred degrees each day of the trip. Who knew from air-conditioning? The heat did not seem to bother us much. But that night I had difficulty sleeping. It was like my own voice was speaking to me and saying. "Tires, look at the tires." Well, I was in my pajamas, but I got dressed and went out with the flashlight to check all around the tires. I did not find anything wrong, so I went back to bed. Just as I was dropping off to sleep, I heard it again: "Tires, tires, tires, tires."
>
> Once again I went outside, and this time instead of looking at the outside of the tires, I got under the car with a flashlight and shined it on the inside of the tires. . . . There it was: a big bulge on the sidewall of my right front tire. The following day we would have entered the Pennsylvania Turnpike, which had no speed limit at that time. I couldn't help but think that in the hundred-degree heat that front right tire would have blown at the worst possible time. "Thank you, Jesus," I said. I knew that it had not been my voice but God's.

The next morning I went to get a new tire and the man who looked at the old one marveled that I made it from the motel to the tire shop. Tragedy averted, and that is what I can say about many of the "God-incidences" in my life. I can't say that things like that happened on a regular basis and I have always been reluctant to use the words "God told me, or God showed me." But he certainly showed himself able and willing to watch over our family that evening.

PART TWO

Prelude to
Jews for Jesus

THIRTEEN

Patience is the virtue we want most . . . for those around us.

—MOISHE ROSEN

Pink mashed potatoes?" Moishe pronounced the word "puhtaydas." His upper lip curled back of its own accord as he bent down to sniff his dinner.

He looked at Ceil expectantly, as though she might be able to identify the foreign substance. She dipped her fork tentatively into the mixture, and delicately took a bite, if something that required no teeth could be called a bite.

She lifted an eyebrow and swallowed. "I have no idea," she shrugged. "It doesn't taste like anything."

"It's hash," a second-year student across the table informed them briefly.

"It's what?!" Moishe looked at him in disbelief.

"It's hash," the other repeated. "Corned beef hash."

Moishe took a forkful. "Feh!" he exclaimed. "They call this hash?"*

"Yes, we call it hash. Some people like it." And having finished his portion, the young man rose, picked up his plate and walked away.

Moishe shook his head. "Who could like this?"

As if on cue, three-year-old Lyn leaned over in her high chair, waving her spoon in Ceil's direction.

"Mommy?"

Ceil quickly loaded up a spoon with the pinkish mixture and directed it toward the tot's face.

"Mmmmmmm, nummies!" Lyn opened her little mouth and was soon smiling appreciatively through a face full of "hash."

Moishe grinned. "It must remind her of the baby food you used to feed her."

As the two laughed, Moishe's loud and rather unusual guffaw seemed to echo throughout the small dining room. Though not understanding the joke, Lyn shrieked with laughter, wanting to join the fun.

---

* The once-a-week "hash" was made with canned government surplus corned beef, but the ratio of potatoes to meat was very high as the school was on a tight budget.

Suddenly the small family found themselves the object of stares, mostly curious, but one or two disapproving. Ceil's smile faded.

"Our Eastern classmates may have a different sense of propriety than we do," she said.

"Easterners?" Moishe asked, bemused. "You think that's the difference?"

Ceil pursed her lips. There was no sense saying what they both knew. The entire first week had proven that they, the Jewish family from Denver, did not exactly fit seamlessly into the very reserved, conservative Christian culture of Northeastern Bible Institute. She sighed, but then brightened as a short, energetic woman came bustling over to their table.

"Hello, Martin, Celia." The woman smiled, patted Lyn on the head and said, "Hello, you young whippersnapper." Then she offered, "Can I take your plates? Or are you still working on the hash?"

Moishe knew Catherine from the alphabetical seating in several of his classes. First came Martin Rosen, then Sylvia Royce, then Catherine Siewell.

Moishe shook his head. "Catherine, I don't see how anyone can eat this stuff."

"Oh, I know what you mean," Catherine nodded vigorously. In fact, everything about her was vigorous. "It's ghastly." Her arm shot out as she grabbed a bowlful of a brown, sticky substance from the table. "That's why they have this stuff out all the time, ya know. Here, let me make you some peanut butter and jelly sandwiches."

Catherine was some ten years older than the Denver couple, which set her apart from the other students. She was a strong, no frills, no nonsense, extremely bright, outspoken, and somewhat eccentric young woman. Her presence cheered the couple considerably, though Moishe didn't have the heart to tell her that he wasn't especially fond of peanut butter and jelly sandwiches.

"You know, Ceil," he said thoughtfully. "It doesn't do much good to kvetch about the food. Let's see what we can do to make it better."

"Ka vetch?" Catherine repeated with alacrity. 'What's that? Some Jewish word?"

"Yes," Ceil replied. "It means to complain." Then turning to her husband she asked, "What have you got in mind?"

"Well, I'll just stop by the grocery store in Caldwell before it closes and I'll pick up a bottle of garlic powder and some Tabasco sauce."

"It couldn't hurt," Ceil agreed.

"Garlic powder and Tabasco sauce, well I'll be. You're a hoot, Martin. You'll shake things up around here if ever anyone could." And laughing robustly, Catherine bustled off, leaving the couple to shake their heads in amusement.

———

The trip from Denver to Essex Fells had been a wonderful time for the three Rosens. They started out at the break of dawn each morning to beat the summer heat, enjoying the quiet countryside as the sun came up. They usually packed in an hour or two of drive time before stopping for breakfast. Finally, they arrived at the school, ready to begin a new life.

Essex Fells proved to be hot, humid, and lush with greenery. Moishe drove the family car across the tracks of a tiny railroad station straight onto the campus of Northeastern Bible Institue. They admired the main building with its pretty white steeple, and Lyn was especially delighted with the pond on campus and the lovely trees.

The married dorm was just across the street from the main campus. The Rosens settled their belongings in their attic apartment before going on to the Greater Boston area to see Ceil's birth family in Dorchester. That visit was a landmark experience for the young Rosens after the irreversible rupture in their relationship with Ceil's adoptive parents. Whatever connection they'd had with one another had been crushed by the weight of disapproval over Moishe and Ceil's faith in Jesus.

Once Moishe realized that they would be moving back East, he strongly encouraged his wife to attempt a reunion with her birth father. She had occasionally corresponded with her twin brother, Jay—mainly small talk—during his years of military service overseas. Now Moishe and Ceil wrote to Jay, telling him they were moving back east with their little daughter. They also explained that they believed in Jesus as Messiah and Lord and that they would understand if the family wanted nothing to do with them because of their faith.

The response came swiftly; the family would be overjoyed to see Ceil and meet her husband and daughter. With a sense of nervous anticipation, the Rosens drove some two hundred miles to Dorchester, a predominantly Jewish district of Boston.

Moishe and Ceil had outfitted Lyn in a red cape for the occasion. When they arrived at the apartment door, Ceil bent to adjust the little red hood over the girl's blonde curls and prompted, "Okay, ring the bell and say what we practiced."

Moishe lifted his daughter so that her pudgy little finger could reach the bell. She pushed hard and waited expectantly. Soon the door was opened by a smiling lady, and Linda Kaye Rosen delivered her first of many play lines. With a dimpled, gap-toothed smile just like her daddy's, she announced, "Hello, I'm Little Red Riding Hood, and I've come to visit Grandma!"

In an instant, any doubt of how the young believers in Jesus might be received by Ceil's side of the family was gone. Shirley, face beaming with happiness, ushered the little family into the Elfbaum home and into a new and sweet relationship. With tears, Harry explained how all his life he had prayed constantly that one day the Almighty would give him back his daughter. Now at last that day had come. His two eldest, the twins, were together once again, and they were joined by their half brothers, Gerry, Stanley, and Larry, the sons of Harry and Shirley.

None of them seemed to care a bit that Moishe was training to be a missionary. Harry was thrilled that his little girl had met a Jewish man who was a good husband and father. Lyn quickly stole everyone's heart as the first grandchild of Harry and Shirley and the first niece of all the sons. It was difficult to say good-bye after the initial reunion, but now that they had been reunited, the relationships would last a lifetime.

The Rosens returned to New Jersey and settled in with help from Emil Gruen, the ABMJ missionary who had recruited Moishe. He lived in nearby Livingston with his family, and they were very kind to the Rosens. They loaned them some items that their own children had long since outgrown, including a crib.

The first day of Northeastern was an orientation. For Moishe, this proved to be an introduction not only to the school, but also to the culture. He had already experienced and recovered from some amount of culture shock through regular attendance at Trinity Baptist—but the new school culture was to pervade each and every day, including his home life. Moishe recalled,

That first day we received mimeographed sheets and spent a lot of time in prayer; many of the prayers had been printed out for us. Some were very moving and I still remember one of them: "Lord, if this is the time when you want to call me and prepare me for your service, please make my heart and mind and will ready to receive it from you." Another prayer that I remember, but didn't really understand at the time was: "Help me to put aside the foolishness of this world and seek the substantial things of heaven." I wondered what the word *substantial* meant and how we were supposed to seek the things of heaven.

I also remember thinking that some of what they required was silly. One of the printed handouts was titled "Ministerial Decorum." Part of the "decorum" was a dress code. Men were supposed to wear coats and neckties on campus, preferably dark suits. That made me uneasy, so I asked about it. I was told that I had to find a new level of dignity that represented my profession.

In later years, Moishe freely admitted that he had an "attitude." Anything stated in absolutes rubbed him the wrong way, and he often challenged his teachers. "I do not know what was in me that was so contrary," he said, "but I enjoyed doing that. It was not that I thought I knew more than the teachers, but I wanted to prove that certain ones did not know as much as they thought. I got along much better with those who were not so quick to make sweeping, absolute statements."

By their second summer at school, the little family discovered public beaches and occasionally drove down to the Jersey shore, sometimes bringing along their friend and fellow nonconformist, Catherine Siewell (later Damato).

Catherine quickly became fast friends with the Rosens. She recalled,

> It was either the first or second day at Northeastern that I saw Moishe—then Martin—and Celia come walking through the main hall toward the dining room. I thought they looked very exotic. They appeared solidly American, but different. I wasn't much aware of Jewish people at that time. Somehow or other we spoke, and I took to both of them immediately. Moishe had a terrific sense of humor; he and I pretty much laughed at the same jokes. Eccentric is his middle name. I think that's why we hit it off so well.

The Rosens found Catherine fun and easy to be around, as well as a truly godly person who had an exemplary commitment to help others. Occasionally she even babysat.

Applying himself academically was challenging for Moishe, who had not been to college full time before. He'd just taken courses at Colorado University. At the time, he hadn't cared much about his grades. Now that his education was being sponsored by the ABMJ, Moishe felt obligated to do reasonably well, not only in gratitude for their support but in order to prepare properly for ministry. Ceil helped with his studies, typing his papers, helping him memorize the Greek alphabet as well as poetry for his literature class.

Even more challenging than the academic discipline was trying to understand how to relate in this new context. Moishe was not only learning facts, he was learning, or at least trying to learn, the value of being polite outside of the workplace. He was also learning the discipline of taking some classes not because they interested him, but because they were required.

He accepted that he was at this particular school because he had put himself in the hands of the mission agency that was sponsoring him. His experience with the army and the National Guard had taught him to think in certain terms. As he put it, "If you're in the army, and they send you to the Aleutian Islands, you don't wonder if you might be happier in a warmer climate. It's the Aleutian Islands for you."

Initially Moishe had asked his sponsors if he might enroll at Moody Bible Institute in Chicago, which was founded by a great evangelist for the express purpose of equipping people to bring the gospel to unbelievers. Emil Gruen agreed that Moody was a fine school but patiently explained why Northeastern was a better choice. It would enable Moishe to be close to New York City, which was the largest Jewish community in the world. He would have the greatest mission field practically in his backyard, and he would be with a well-established organization where he could see how to do things right. Moishe accepted this, and his outreach experience in New York City did prove to be invaluable, as were some of the connections that he made there.

However, Moishe later critiqued some of his choices:

I made the mistake that most people make when they go to Bible college or seminary; I let the school start organizing my time and my witness and my ministry. I was seeking out and witnessing to people before I went away to Bible college. But once I got to school, there were structured opportunities and scheduled activities to minister to people in jail and at rescue missions.

In a sense, I began to rely on the school and the mission to put me in contact with people. I went from being a very active witness—trying to talk to everyone I met about Jesus—to being passive, waiting until it was time to go here or go there for the purpose of telling others about Jesus. I lost some of my natural enthusiasm, and the zeal that had made me a good witness was blunted. The school and mission seemed to be satisfied with too little.

At one point, the pendulum swung the other way as the school scheduled a conference known as Deeper Life Week. Ordinary classes were suspended so that students could listen to the four speakers. Each speaker had a day in which to speak three or four times, emphasizing a particular aspect of spiritual life.

All the speakers set parameters for the minimum amount of time and effort that students should give for that particular aspect of spiritual life. One speaker explained that each student should have devotional time of at least an hour of personal prayer time. Another said that students should spend at least half an hour in daily Bible reading. Yet another told of some godly person who didn't allow himself to go to bed at night until he had led at least one person to the Lord.

Moishe took each admonition seriously and felt weighed down by his inadequacy. As for the third admonition about leading one person to Jesus each day, he recalled,

> I knew I couldn't do that, but I made a promise that every day I would try to explain the gospel to at least one person who didn't know Jesus. This promise was not easy to keep because everyone connected to the school was a professing Christian.
>
> Each day of that conference put more pressure on me. I felt terribly guilty that I did not measure up to the standards set forth. Finally, the week came to an end, and I realized that I had not explained the gospel to *anybody*. . . . I decided to go down to the bus station, where I knew the driver stopped at midnight and left at 12:15 a.m. I reasoned that at least I could talk to the driver about Jesus. . . . The bus driver saw me coming. He jumped in the bus, slammed the door, and began the route early.

This ludicrous scenario helped Moishe realize that he had taken the deeper life speakers too literally and that spiritual growth would be a matter of reasonable efforts on his part and plenty of grace on God's part.

Moishe's passivity and attempt to conform were temporary and did not mean that he had become docile. Chapel proved a good example. Certain speakers came with an obvious agenda to recruit missionaries, and they spent their allotted time promoting their own organizations. Moishe grew very annoyed with this type of speaker. Equally annoying were others who repeated the same message over and over: "When you get out in the real world. . . " and they would go on to say what a different life students could expect from the sheltered upbringing they'd had. Moishe wasn't sure who they were addressing, but he felt he'd come from "the real world" to be at the school.

Although he attended chapel on most days, Moishe and Catherine occasionally used the time to get coffee and donuts if they suspected a speaker would not be worth hearing. When they were confronted about this breach of a school rule, Moishe stood up to the president of the school and said, "If you and the rest of the faculty would sit through chapel and see how awful some of these speakers are, you'd understand why I skip some of them. It doesn't help my spiritual life when speakers act like we have to show we are dedicated Christians by going to this field or that field. I already know the mission I'll be serving with. I feel like I'm taking a browbeating every time I listen to one of these organizations that make you feel guilty if you won't consider serving with them or donating to their cause. And the ones who talk as though we have no idea what the real world is like treat us like we are children." He paused, wondering if he was about to get thrown out of school.

The president simply said, "All right, you two are a little older than the other students, and you may use your discretion to be excused now and then. But don't make an issue of it or flaunt your absence."

Moishe enjoyed hearing some of his favorite faculty members at chapel, and he also made a point to be in chapel when anyone from the ABMJ was speaking. Charles Kalisky did not promote the ABMJ; instead he talked about Israel. Henry Heydt, also from the ABMJ, did not promote the mission either. Moishe said, "I appreciated the way the speakers from the ABMJ tried to give something meaningful to benefit the students without making a big deal about the mission. And I noticed they never expected an offering or used guilt to solicit students' support. Both of these things made me proud to be associated with them." This stark comparison led Moishe to a conscious and lasting decision: if ever he got a chance to speak at any school's chapel, he would be sure to give something meaningful to the students rather than try to get them to give to him or his mission.

Moishe also attended chapel whenever Charles Anderson, the school president, spoke—even though Anderson had excused Moishe from going. He said, "Dr. Anderson had this very practical and straightforward approach that I liked."

Charles W. Anderson was not only the president of NBI; he was the founder. The school had started as Brookdale Bible School on the campus of Brookdale Baptist Church, where Anderson was pastor. The church and school remained affiliated, and students were generally encouraged to attend Brookdale Baptist Church. This was fine with Moishe and Ceil, whose only church experience had been at a Baptist church similar to Brookdale.

The teacher who most influenced Moishe was William Lincoln, of whom he often said: "If William Lincoln taught a sewing class I would have taken it. I would have taken any class from him because I knew that I would learn more about God and about life, no matter what subject he taught." Lincoln taught church history, and he was not an easy grader. Moishe recalled:

William Lincoln was so enthusiastic for God—a person of deep feeling. He would talk about the Saint Bartholomew's Day massacre that happened centuries ago and his eyes would fill with tears. He must have taught the material countless times, but you could see he felt just awful about the lives that were lost so many years ago. He was also the first person I heard say that Jesus had a wonderful sense of humor.

Lincoln's only graduate degree was a THB from Princeton. But he was a very well-educated man who had concluded that all education is self-education. He showed me that going to school gives one the opportunity to learn—but no one can teach you anything; you teach yourself.

Lincoln was not as strait-laced as some of our teachers. He knew the value of strategically used sarcasm. For example, somewhere I picked up the idea that if people didn't hear the gospel, God would not hold them responsible for their sins—that if they lived mostly righteous lives, they would go to heaven without receiving Jesus. I brought this up in class, and he stood there and nodded his head. Then he said, "If that's true, maybe we should stop preaching the gospel and keep Jesus a secret. Think of all the people we're sending to hell by preaching the gospel." Then he went on to explain what the Bible teaches, but his ironic or sarcastic approach was just what I needed to get my attention. Later in life I often used that same approach.

Wesley Olsen was another highly influential teacher, and he, too, had a way of using irony or sarcasm to get Moishe to take a second look at what he was thinking and where it would lead. Olsen taught biblical theology and systematic theology. He encouraged the students to think through carefully the things they thought they knew. When he'd ask a question, any student who tried to give a predigested answer would find that this professor would go along with it just so far, and then, as Moishe described it: "Bang! He would cut you off so dramatically, so logically, so incisively that you had to give up your whole preconceived idea, and then he'd start to teach you. He used the Socratic method. He was very interactive." When it was his turn to teach, Moishe well remembered Olsen's style and adopted it to train missionaries.

Moishe recalled negative lessons as well. The school had a canteen where students were allowed to dish up their own sundaes, malts, or milkshakes and pay on the honor system. To Moishe's horror, when the school year ended, the "honor system" had landed the school a good fifteen hundred dollars in the red. "It was not just people forgetting to leave money, but to lose that much money, somebody had to be stealing from the money that we did leave. That proved to be the case, and the thief was discovered. But the fact that one of us was stealing—and at a school that charged only a hundred dollars a year in tuition—was upsetting because it showed a frightening level of corruption in our midst. I thought that even among the most dedicated Christians there are wolves among the sheep," he said.

At the end of Moishe's first year at Northeastern, Dean Bleecker approached him. "His general attitude was serious," Moishe explained,

and he said, "We've been discussing your adjustment to school." Well, of course it was quite an adjustment so I was interested to hear his conclusion. He said something like: "You've been doing very well, and we know that academics are a struggle for you. And we can see you working, and we appreciate what you've done for your practical Christian work." I had been going to Patterson Jail, as well as working with the ABMJ in New York City.

Then the dean said, "I think it might help with your adjustment if you could have a little more of your own family life." And then to my great surprise—and I felt so privileged—the dean told me that they wanted to excuse me from the rule that said we had to live in the married dorm. He even suggested a nearby neighborhood where I could find affordable outside housing. This solved so many problems for us, because the nearby neighborhood was Montclair, New Jersey, where many Italian families lived. Not only were people's temperaments in that neighborhood far more similar to our own, but what could be better than having an Italian landlady who was proud of her cooking—and who loved the smell of garlic as much as we did? It never occurred to us that the cultural differences we experienced at Northeastern were two-sided . . . and that others were very happy for us to find a home more to our liking off campus.

Among all the adjustments and lessons of that first year of Bible school, Moishe was also still learning what it meant to have a personal relationship with God. Toward the middle of his first semester, Moishe had a paper due that was crucial for his grade, and it had to be typewritten. Unfortunately, Moishe's typewriter needed repair. He only needed $3.50 to get it fixed, but he said, "It might as well have been $3,500 because I didn't have it.

"I was desperate. It was then and there that I learned to petition and pray, and God encouraged me with a swift answer." When Moishe went to his student mailbox, he found a check for five dollars from the Public Service Company of Colorado. It was the refund from a service deposit. He cashed the check and took his typewriter to be repaired. "I got my typewriter, the paper was finished on time, I was still in school, and I knew that God had answered prayer," said Moishe. "*So, maybe it's all right to ask for things*, I thought. It wasn't long before I needed to ask again."

In the move from Denver, his overcoat and other winter clothes had gotten lost. That meant when he went from New Jersey into New York City to do volunteer work at the ABMJ, he had only a suit coat over a sweater to keep him warm. Moishe explained,

As I went to my assigned place and began my work, Hilda Koser, the missionary from Brooklyn, came to me and said, "Mr. Rosen, I hope you don't mind my asking you, but a man from Kalamazoo died, and his wife sent me all of his clothes. He didn't die of anything contagious. He was evidently a rather tall man like you, and all of the people to whom we minister in Brooklyn are much shorter. I wouldn't insult you by offering you secondhand clothes, but I know that the man's wife would be so pleased if she knew who the clothes went to."

Hilda Koser couldn't have known how much I had been praying for an overcoat! I said I would take a look at them after I finished my work. . . . The man must have been rather well off. There were several Hart, Shaffner, and

Marx suits and, best of all, two overcoats! All of the clothes—the shirts, the suits, even the barely worn size thirteen shoes—were exactly my size, and the styles were what I would have chosen. This was too good to be true!

I had barely finished praying before God had greatly answered. That kind of thing went on for several weeks. I would have a need, I would pray, and my prayer would be quickly and decisively answered in a unique way. Then, after perhaps six remarkable answers, I prayed yet again, and what I asked did not happen. It was as though God were telling me, "I've shown you that I can answer prayer and that I will answer prayer, but not every time that you ask it."

I don't expect God to give me everything I ask of him, but I know that he answers, and I continue to ask, even for little things like parking places, and they often come to pass in remarkable ways.

FOURTEEN

The right enemies help more than the wrong friends.

—MOISHE ROSEN

Moishe was honored, awed, and perhaps just a little frightened that Harold Pretlove had asked to see him. Pretlove was the acting missionary secretary, which meant he was the chief executive officer of the American Board of Missions to the Jews. He was a mysterious figure to Moishe. A slender man whose suits matched his gray hair, Pretlove regarded the new missionary with a friendly, if somewhat detached, air. He said, "We've been thinking about what to assign you for your volunteer work."

Moishe nodded. In addition to sponsoring his education at Northeastern, for which the tuition at the time was one hundred dollars per annum, the ABMJ had generously provided a stipend of two hundred dollars per month for living expenses.

Moishe felt it was right that he be expected to do some work in return. He and Ceil had been coming on Tuesday and Thursday nights to attend training classes that the ABMJ provided for staff and laypeople who were interested in Jewish evangelism. They also took part in the mission's weekly worship service on Sunday afternoons. But Moishe expected an additional assignment and had been somewhat surprised by the lack of direction he'd received in the first few weeks. Nevertheless, he was totally unprepared for what came next.

"I think that it would be good for you to take charge of our outdoor meetings." Pretlove smiled beneficently.

Swallowing hard, Moishe hoped he could respond to Pretlove's assignment without stammering: "I'd be glad to participate, Mr. Pretlove, but I don't think I can be in charge of something I don't know anything about."

The boss had a solution: "Well, the Lord himself will teach you, just as he taught Moses how to lead."

Moishe tried to imagine that it might possibly happen that way. His Yiddish name, after all, was a derivative of the Hebrew name Moshe (in English, Moses). *If only I could have a rod to throw down, and it would become a snake to impress people,* he thought. But he feared he would have to make do without any signs or wonders.

Pretlove continued with optimism: "You'll have a couple of weeks to get volunteers, and if you stand up at next Sunday's service and ask for people to join you, I'm sure that you'll find many, many who will want to help."

With a combination of dread and hope, Moishe stood before the congregation of some eighty people the following Sunday and said, "We're going to have an outdoor meeting next week before the service, and we're wondering if there are any volunteers to help us. If you'd like to volunteer, will you raise your hands?" All hands remained motionless. Perhaps if no one volunteered, he would be let off the hook. "Well," he added, "think about it, and if you'd like to help, let me know after the service."

After the service, up came up Madiline Osbourne, a Bible college graduate who she said she didn't know anything about outdoor meetings, but would help if Mr. Rosen would tell her what to do. "And," she added, "Maybe I can get my dad to come, too."

"Can he preach?" Moishe asked hopefully.

"Well, no, and he can't hear either; he's deaf."

Then came Anna Frank, a dear lady who was bent over with age and with scoliosis. She smiled warmly as she cocked her head to look up at the rookie missionary. "I know about outdoor meetings, Brother Rosen; I've been to many. I can't speak because I'm too old, and if I open my mouth wide, my teeth fall down. But I'll go and I'll pray for you, and I'll help."

With three volunteers and the possibility of a fourth, the outdoor meeting was now inescapable. Moishe felt he'd best not wait for "God himself" to teach him how to lead such a meeting. After the service, he went to Joseph Serafin, an older missionary, and Serafin told him to come back Tuesday and he would show him "the ropes."

On Tuesday, Serafin provided Moishe with a real soapbox to use as a portable platform, a portable organ, and the American flag. Serafin explained that Moishe would need to find someone to play the organ and that he had to display the flag: "New York law requires that we display it. Shows we're not Communists and all that. You sing a hymn or two, have each of your volunteers get up and give a little testimony, and then you give your message."

"Mr. Serafin, will you come with me?" This was the most instruction Moishe had received, and it would be a big relief to have someone with Serafin's experience come along. Unfortunately, the older man would be at his own church at that time.

Over the next few days Moishe prepared a message based on Hebrew Scriptures that predicted the Messiah, and Ceil typed it, some eight pages, single-spaced. The appointed day came. The Rosens went to their own church in New Jersey and had a quick lunch before Moishe headed into the city. He was at the mission center by 2:30.

The small group prayed, then prayed some more. Then Mrs. Frank, also known as Momma Frank spoke up, but not to the Almighty. "Brother Rosen, don't you think it's time we go now?" Moishe smiled wanly and agreed. He wrote a note to Mr. Osbourne, who must have been about 80 years old, and the note said, "We're going to ask you to give a five-minute testimony."

Mr. Osbourne had not been born deaf and could talk well enough. When he saw the note he asked rather loudly, "What's a testimony?"

"Just tell how you came to believe in Jesus," Moishe wrote, and Mr. Osbourne nodded.

They prepared to go. The "portable" organ required two people to carry it. With all of the other things they had to take, they decided to leave it behind. Moishe folded his notes into his Bible and grabbed the soapbox. Someone else took the flag, others took hymnals, and out the door they went.

Moishe had picked a location a couple of blocks from the mission, which stood at Seventy-second Street and Broadway on the upper west side of Manhattan. The group set up shop and began to sing "'Tis So Sweet to Trust in Jesus." But Moishe was tone deaf, and the others found it difficult to hold the melody—all except for Mr. Osbourne. He had a strong voice, and once he got going, the rest of the group followed him. He had absolutely no idea that he was leading the singing.

Mr. Osbourne also had the distinction of being the first to speak. The others stood there as he proclaimed to no one in particular, "I didn't know anything about religion, and I really didn't care and, Madiline, that's my daughter over there, she got saved and went away to Bible college and when she came home, she told me that I needed to accept Jesus, so I did." Then he stepped down.

Daughter Madiline was a graduate of a reputable Bible school and knew a great deal more than Moishe, a first-year Bible student. She began to tell why she believed in Jesus, and she had worked her story into a four-point sermon. Unlike her father, she was not content to deliver her message to the empty sidewalk. She lifted her voice in an attempt to send it soaring across the street to some passerby. She sounded a bit shrill, but her speech was well organized. *Why didn't they ask her to lead this?* Moishe wondered. *She seems to know what she's doing.* Then it was Anna Frank's turn, and she told her story. It was very moving—at least Moishe thought so. He was the last one left.

For the first of what would be a hundred times or more, he mounted that soapbox. He held his Bible open in one hand and clutched his notes in the other. He began reading from the sheets, attempting to refer to the Bible when appropriate. *Please, God, don't let there be a gust of wind,* he pleaded silently.

From time to time he looked up from his reading and was thankful that nobody was there to return his gaze. He was trembling so hard that he could hear the box beneath him, clattering against the pavement. He wondered if anyone else could hear it and tried raising his voice to drown out the sound. He finished, and once again the little group sang "'Tis So Sweet to Trust in Jesus" before trekking back to the mission.

Before the 3:30 worship service began, Anna Frank got hold of Moishe and, with a sweet smile, said, "Brother Rosen, you worked so hard to bring such a nice message. I know you're young, but you're going to be a good preacher. But you know what I think?"

"No, what, Mrs. Frank?"

"I think next week, it would be nice if we went where people could hear us." There was nothing for him to do but smile back and agree.

———

Moishe realized that the act of facing his fears and getting through his first outdoor meeting was a personal victory. He also knew that the meeting had been an abject failure, and he was determined to learn how to succeed in his assignment.

Over the course of a month, Moishe observed several outdoor meetings. The first few proved to be of little help since they could not seem to hold a crowd. Then Moishe heard about an outdoor meeting on a Sunday night on Fifty-seventh Street, just south of Columbus Circle. It turned out to be a one-man event from the Catholic Evidence Guild. The speaker had his American flag, and he had defined his space with long tubing and a platform in the middle. He began talking, and it wasn't long before he drew a very large crowd.

Moishe recalled, "As I watched the man work, I realized that for the first time I was seeing someone who understood how to interact with people on the streets. The man was personable and confident as he began by calling out to passersby." The speaker posed the question: "How can Jesus be God and man at the same time?" and asked his listeners if they had ever wondered about that. Apparently some had because they stopped to listen. "He gathered a crowd and got his point across, all in about six minutes," Moishe said. Then he asked if anyone in the crowd had a question. Some people shuffled off after the first question, but others stopped to listen for a while. The speaker fielded questions for an hour or so. When he finished, a few people from within the crowd handed out invitations to a nearby church.

Moishe introduced himself to the street preacher and explained that he, too, was an outdoor preacher. The other seemed neither impressed nor interested in conversing. But Moishe needed a teacher, so he continued asking questions until he learned that the man had taken a seminar on street preaching held by the Paulist Fathers.

Moishe told no one at the mission, but began attending a two-hour Thursday night class at the Paulist Fathers' headquarters in New York City. The organization offered beginner, intermediate, and advanced classes. Each lasted four weeks; over a year, Moishe took all three classes. He learned how to interest passersby, and he learned about hecklers and how to handle hostility. He also learned how to position himself facing the buildings, so he could bounce his voice off them to amplify his volume.

Moishe's intrepid volunteers stayed with him, and a couple more from Bible colleges joined him here and there. Ceil practiced a few hymns and played the organ as needed, though a volunteer named Richard was a more experienced organist and helped at times.

Until he left New York in 1957, Moishe was out street preaching at least once a week during the school year and four times a week during the summer. The basic value of outdoor preaching, to him, was to raise an image, letting people know that some Jewish people had come to believe in Jesus.

Meanwhile, his boss, Harold Pretlove, continued to be a mysterious figure. Moishe initially interpreted Pretlove's strange ways of speaking as an otherworldly kind of godliness. As they interacted more regularly, Moishe began to wonder how the man had achieved his position in this mission to the Jews—it wasn't merely that he was not Jewish, but he seemed to understand so little about Jewish people on a personal level.

A painful instance proved itself upon the student missionary when his boss asked him to procure three record albums. The mission had a decent sound system, and Pretlove wanted recordings of Jewish music for the staff to enjoy during their lunch hour. Moishe found this an agreeable task until the boss handed him ten dollars and instructed him to bring back three albums. "But, Mr. Pretlove," he said, "record albums usually cost $4.95. This is enough to buy two albums; I don't think I can bring back three."

"I know they usually cost five dollars each," Pretlove agreed, "but you're a Jew. You'll be able to get the price down."

Embarrassment for the older man and respect for his position suppressed the younger's ire. He took the money and felt extremely fortunate to find albums that were $3.95. Still, he had been instructed to bring back three, and he had a distaste for haggling. With a sigh, he reached into his pocket to supply the remaining two dollars required for the purchase. In the 1950s, two dollars were not small change for a student with a wife and a child.

Pretlove smiled expansively when Moishe handed him the three LPs. "I just knew you could do it," he beamed.

Moishe did not want to contradict him, but he made a mental note: *If I'm ever in charge of anything, I'll make sure I know what things cost, and I'll never ask anyone to purchase something with insufficient funds.* He long remembered the humiliation of that experience as being greater than his first awkward attempt at street preaching.

Over time, Moishe came to enjoy street preaching. Though he never got over the initial nervousness, once he got going, he found pleasure in hitting his stride. He discovered that the financial district was a good venue, especially during the lunch hour. Other street preachers came there regularly, and they shared a degree of camaraderie.

Eventually Moishe commissioned a carpenter to make him a folding pulpit with a handle, and he carried it on the subway along with books and tracts. Nobody in Manhattan used electronic amplification, and neither did he. But he'd learned how to project his voice and he enjoyed interacting with the crowds.

He learned to appreciate the hecklers; they often drew the interest of the crowd and could really make the meeting a success. Most hecklers were not vicious; they liked the attention and interchange, and they liked to try to stump their "competition." Moishe recognized it as a kind of urban sport and grew to enjoy the game as well. Occasionally he got to know his opponents and was able to speak to them privately about spiritual matters.

Once, when Moishe was talking about the Son of God, an older man shouted out, "God doesn't have a Son!"

"Did you say God doesn't have a Son?" Moishe asked.

"That's right."

"Then how come I believe it?"

"Because you're stupid."

"It seems to me it says so some place in the Bible."

"In your Bible, maybe, but not in mine. I'm a Jew. If you can find a place in the Bible where it says God has a Son—I mean in the real Bible, not the New Testament—then I'll convert and preach your religion myself.

"Do you have a Jewish Bible with you?"

"Do I look stupid, that I should carry a Bible around like you?"

"I've got a Jewish Bible. Can you read?"

"Of course I can read."

"Well, you sound like a Hebrew scholar, but I wasn't so sure if you could read English."

"Well, I can read fine."

Moishe turned to Proverbs 30:4. "Okay, read it out loud."

"'Who hath ascended up into heaven and descended?'" the heckler read.

"Now that's God, right?"

"Right," the heckler agreed. "Next it says, 'Who hath gathered the wind in his fists?' That's God, not the Son of God."

"Keep going," Moishe prompted.

"'Who hath bound the waters in his garment?'"

"Now that's poetry, it just means. . . ."

"Okay, okay, that's God," the heckler interrupted, then proceeded, 'Who hath established all the ends of the earth?' That's God! God! God!"

"Keep reading," Moishe said.

"'What is his name?' Not Jesus! It's Adonai!"

"Yes, now read it louder, read the next line."

"'And what is his son's name, if thou knowest . . . .'" As the man's voice trailed off, Moishe began preaching.

Another time, on Wall Street, a heckler stood right in front of Moishe, gazing straight up as though he was watching something of marvelous interest on top of a building. Before long, everybody's neck was craned, trying to see whatever this man was seeing. Moishe lost the crowd until, in one of those moments that he believed was from God, a quotation from the New Testament book of Acts popped into his head. He called out, "Men of Galilee, why stand ye gazing up into heaven? This same Jesus, which is taken up from you into heaven, shall so come in like manner." By then, he had leather lungs and a voice like a trumpet, and his pronouncement rang out all over that busy street corner. He launched into a talk on how Jesus was going to return to earth, and he was able to regain the crowd's attention.

Afterward, the man who'd started it all approached Moishe. "You really trumped me on that one, didn't you?" he observed good-naturedly. Moishe smiled and asked his name. Leon was Jewish, but not religious. Years later their paths crossed again, and once again it was a friendly encounter.*

Moishe had come a long way from that first meeting. He had recognized and approached his inadequacy as a problem to be solved, and he succeeded in solving it. Occasionally the crowds he drew were large enough that the police had to clear a path on the sidewalk. Eventually they asked to be notified when he planned to hold a street meeting, so that there'd be an officer nearby if crowd control was needed.

The large crowds also attracted the attention of the Anti-Shmad League, a group that opposed the mission and its representatives. One Sunday afternoon while a volunteer was giving her testimony, a man pushed his way to the front and began yelling into Moishe's face. Someone grabbed his left arm and someone else tried to grab his right arm, but he thrust it straight up into the air so they couldn't reach it or the Bible that he held aloft.

The man who was shouting began punching Moishe in the stomach. To the young missionary's relief, he soon heard police sirens wailing, and an officer quickly made his way to the front of the crowd. To his dismay, however, Moishe was accused of punching the fellow who was shouting, and the man produced a pair of broken glasses as evidence of the supposed assault.

Suddenly, several people in the crowd nodded their heads in agreement with the story, and the officer ordered Moishe to come down to the station. Moishe told his volunteers to return to the mission and not to worry. He spoke to them with a confidence he did not entirely feel. He was weeks away from

---

* Years later, Moishe was in Southern California, preaching in MacArthur Park to a fairly good crowd. Suddenly they all began looking up. Then he saw Leon, who apparently had not recognized him. Moishe smiled and called out, "Leon, don't worry. Jesus really is coming; you don't have to keep looking up."

graduating from Bible school, and Northeastern had strict rules. One student who was arrested for failing to pay parking tickets had been suspended, and Moishe did not remember him returning to school, much less graduating.

Moishe, the policeman, and thirteen "witnesses" walked to the station, where the desk sergeant began filling out a report. After all of the "witnesses" had made their statements and signed the report, another man came forward.

He was the retired captain of a nearby precinct. Within moments, the situation was entirely reversed. The man announced that he saw the whole thing and stated that he was Jewish and didn't believe a word of what Moishe was saying, but he was ashamed of his own people for what they had done: "This guy didn't do anything," he said, indicating Moishe with a jerk of his head. "He was just standing there, and they grabbed him and started hitting him." He then pointed out who had done the grabbing and who had done the hitting. "And," he added, "nobody was wearing glasses."

As some of Moishe's accusers began moving toward the door, the desk sergeant stopped them and said, "You have all committed a felony by turning in a false police report. You can't leave, but even if you do it won't matter. I've got your names and addresses right here." Turning to Moishe, he said, "It's up to Mr. Rosen if he wants to file a complaint."

Moishe, overwhelmed by the situation, said to no one in particular, "I need to pray about whether to make a complaint." He sat down on a bench and silently prayed. He soon returned to the desk sergeant and said, "I'm willing to forgo the charges on one condition. I want these guys to come to our outdoor meetings every Sunday to keep the peace."

The desk sergeant replied, "That is your prerogative, Mr. Rosen, but I'll make a notation on my report that if you decide to file charges, you've got the next ninety days to do so."

Moishe nodded. He had only two months left until his graduation, and then he would leave for his next post. He didn't know of anyone else who planned to continue the outdoor meetings after he left.

The sergeant asked the accusers if they agreed to the terms. After gathering the group into a huddle, the leader said yes.

Moishe recalled, "This was a glorious turn of events, because after that, each Sunday when I arrived to begin the outdoor meeting, a small, ready-made, albeit less than enthusiastic crowd was waiting for me."

In the years that followed, Moishe often retold this incident as he trained other missionaries. He described it as the perfect illustration of the value of a hostile witness. One person with integrity and absolutely no particular fondness for the accused can give a far more credible defense than any number of friends. This was one of many reasons why Moishe always appreciated good, honest opposition.

FIFTEEN

The truth is never cheap, but the righteous can always afford it.
—MOISHE ROSEN

Moishe passed his destination—Caldwell's National Newark and Essex Bank—and pulled into the parking lot of a church. He had no idea how he would pay the doctor and hospital bills for the baby girl who was born six days earlier. He was fond of telling people that "Ruth came into the world with a full head of black hair," a fact that made far more of a first impression on him than had the initially yellowish complexion. Now, rosy pink and healthy, his new daughter was ready to come home.

Although they had planned this pregnancy, the thrifty young couple hadn't exactly planned how to pay for it—and that was highly unusual for them. The Rosens had all of one hundred dollars in the bank, and Moishe knew that would not be nearly enough to pay for the medical costs. He hoped that he could negotiate the rest and pay over time.

When Moishe entered the bank, only one teller stood behind a window, but fortunately there were no other customers. Moishe was eager to get back to the hospital in Newark, arrange payment, and take his wife and new daughter home.

To Moishe's chagrin, the teller was engrossed in a sociable conversation with another employee. She did not even turn to acknowledge him as he stepped up to her window. *Why don't you stop your yammering and try doing your job already?* he silently excoriated the teller. When at last she acknowledged him, he pushed his bank book toward her and said tersely, "I want to withdraw the balance from my account and close it." The teller resumed her conversation with her coworker as she checked the records. He had $103 in the account.

Well, it is three dollars more than I expected, he thought as he signed the withdrawal slip. He watched distractedly as she counted out three single bills into one pile and ten other bills into a second pile, once again talking to the other employee. He didn't bother to examine the bills; he shoved them into his pocket and strode out the door.

He was halfway down the block before he pulled the money out of his pocket to straighten the crumpled bills and realized the teller had given him three single bills and ten twenties! Her lack of attention had resulted in a one-hundred-dollar error in his favor. For a moment he was elated. *Praise God for how he's provided!* he thought. But within seconds he sighed because he knew that God didn't provide that way, and he knew that he had to go back to the bank.

This time, adding insult to injury, he had to wait in line for the teller. When it came his turn he informed her, "You made a mistake when you counted my money." She eyed him somewhat disdainfully and said, "I'm sorry sir, once you leave the window, the transaction is final."

Making every effort to remain calm Moishe replied, "Well, you better hope that's not true because you gave me two hundred dollars instead of one hundred. I don't know what you believe, but you can be thankful that I believe in Jesus because he's the only reason I came back." Then he counted back five of the ten twenty dollar bills and returned them to her with a grumpy glare. It was not the most gracious expression of faith, just proof of the genuine difference beliefs can make. The teller did not thank him for possibly saving her job, nor did he expect her to.

Moishe then drove back to Presbyterian Hospital and went straight to accounting. To his great surprise, he learned that he owed nothing. They were still covered by a Blue Cross policy they had signed up for in Denver, and the hospital accepted insurance payments as full remuneration from ministers or ministerial students and their families. Scarcely able to believe it, he sought out Ceil's obstetrician, who explained that, like the hospital, he never charged ministers or seminarians. Just as Moishe had known that God had not been at work through the teller's poor work ethic and subsequent mistake, he felt with a very grateful heart that the kindness of this doctor was certainly God's provision—and his way of reminding Moishe that honesty was the best policy.

He told Ceil the good news about the medical expenses, and they left the hospital with light hearts and their precious new baby. They were eager to introduce her to "big sister" Lyn at last.

———

Becoming a big sister had not been the happiest day of Lyn's life, not because of sibling rivalry but because of a nasty cut she'd received while playing in the backyard with the neighbors. The day Moishe's second daughter was born, he returned home to find his older daughter with a cold washcloth pressed against her bleeding forehead. The landlady who had been watching her explained what had happened and assured Moishe that it was not as bad as it looked. He took Lyn to the emergency room, where she got stitches.

Lyn was not the only one to experienced drama that day. Moishe was sound asleep at home after a very eventful day, when, at midnight, a doctor woke Ceil in her hospital bed. He said, "Mrs. Rosen, I'm sorry to wake you, but there's a problem with the baby and we need your permission for an emergency procedure."

A terrified Ceil responded, "What? What's wrong with my baby?!" After the birth, she'd had only a fleeting glance of the newborn before the nurses had swept her away for various tests. Earlier in the pregnancy, the doctor had cautioned Moishe and Ceil that there might be an incompatibility between the RH factor between the mother's blood and the baby's. The couple had optimistically dismissed the prenatal warning as a possibility, not a probability.

Now the baby needed a total blood exchange, and the doctor needed Ceil's signature to authorize the procedure. After the doctor rushed away with the signed permission, the nurse looked at her sympathetically and asked, "Mrs. Rosen, would you like me to call your husband?"

The couple had no phone, and Ceil did not want to awaken the landlady. "No," she said. "I'll wait till morning. Unless . . . something happens before then."

"Now, nothing's going to happen. The pediatrician on call will take excellent care of your baby. I know she is very sick, but you just wait and see. She'll be so much better in the morning."

Ceil spent a dreadful night with little sleep. She was desperate to talk to her husband, and the night seemed endless. At last morning broke and she could make the call.

Moishe was scheduled to speak that morning, an engagement that she had forgotten. She was shocked when the landlady, Mrs. Ciancetta, explained that Moishe was not home, but she was caring for Lyn. For the first time in their married life, Ceil was upset that Moishe was not with her when she felt she really needed him.

When he arrived that afternoon, totally unaware of the crisis, the worst was over, just as the nurse had predicted. Ceil was so relieved that she did not communicate much of what she had felt about Moishe's absence. Meanwhile, the doctor who had performed the blood transfusion came to introduce himself and to explain what had happened. As he extended his hand the young father grasped it firmly, trying not to show his surprise. The doctor who had saved his daughter's life was black.

Moishe had not met many African Americans in Denver. In general, he was not given to thinking in stereotypes. But recently he'd harbored a growing prejudice without realizing it. The Italian section of Montclair where they lived abutted a predominantly black neighborhood. Ceil had grown increasingly uncomfortable about walking to the store because she had to pass some day laborers who ogled women as they walked by. Ceil would have been uncomfortable no matter the color or ethnicity of the men, but it happened that they were African Americans. Knowing this, Moishe had been nursing a growing dislike toward a group of people with whom he had had very little personal experience.

He hadn't even realized his prejudice until he gripped the hand that had so skillfully cared for his baby girl in the middle of the night. In that moment, he knew that he would never make an assumption about any man or woman based on skin color. This doctor also waived the fee for the lifesaving procedure he had performed. All in all, Moishe had lived and learned quite a bit during the first week of his younger daughter's life.

———

Life in Montclair was far more agreeable to Moishe and Ceil than their first year of campus residence. Initially they shared a house owned by the Cassies, a warm, caring Italian family. Moishe's fond memories of life in Montclair included tantalizing aromas of genuine Italian cooking from Mrs. Cassie's kitchen and the occasional samples she would bring upstairs.

Four-year-old Lyn was a very sociable child, so in the summer, Moishe and Ceil looked for a daily vacation Bible school (DVBS) where she could meet others her age. Grace Presbyterian Church, which was within walking distance of their apartment, had such a program.

Their only experience up to this point had been with Baptist churches. As Moishe recalled,

> These churches did not stress being Baptist, but they did emphasize the importance of believing the Bible—and a couple of people had explained to me that

"we" [meaning that particular church] were Baptist because we took the Bible seriously. Based on that, I concluded that if somebody wasn't a Baptist, they didn't take the Bible seriously. I didn't know what Presbyterians, Methodists, Lutherans, etc. believed, but it seemed to me that if they really believed the Scriptures, they would be Baptists too. So much for deductive logic. I added two and two and got three.

Despite Moishe's early doubts about non-Baptist denominations, he and Ceil enrolled Lyn at the DVBS at Grace Presbyterian Church. Through Grace, Moishe discovered that genuine Christians belong to churches of various denominations. He later said of the Presbyterian pastor, "Frank Hunger was more of a Christian than I was. He was a thoroughgoing evangelical who believed in missions. At one time, he had served as president of Biblical Seminary. And as our family began to attend the church regularly, he personally undertook to encourage me. The people of Grace Presbyterian were very kind to Ceil and to me. . . . They didn't seem to expect a whole lot from me, but they honored me by having me teach an adult Sunday school class."

As the time drew near for their second child to be born, the family had moved to a slightly larger place in Montclair. Moishe got a part-time job at Sears Roebuck in anticipation of the higher rent.

Though Lyn was quite young, she retained several memories of the family's Bible school days and of her father's dealings with her, including the following:

I didn't know that others would have considered us poor while he was in Bible college; and I don't remember a sense of going without with the exception of one event. Dad had taken Mother to the doctor for a prenatal visit and while he waited, he took me to a bakery to buy cream puffs. They were so big that I needed both hands to hold mine. When it came time to cross the big street, I clutched my cream puff in one hand while my other hand was safely in the grasp of Dad's huge strong fingers.

As we reached the other side I dropped my cream puff—before I had even tasted the filling. I was very disappointed and began to cry. I could see that Dad felt terrible as he explained we couldn't afford to go back for another one, but that if I didn't mind the bite marks, I could have his. More than fifty years later I can honestly say no cream puff ever tasted so sweet.

Lyn trusted her father implicitly. When it was time to remove the stitches she'd gotten on my birthday, he took her to the doctor, who also happened to be the coroner of the county of Newark. Moishe recalled that he "had a bedside manner that would work better with dead people."

The doctor snipped the three or four sutures in Lyn's head. It didn't hurt, but it frightened her. When she began to cry and pulled away, the doctor was so unnerved that he couldn't finish. Moishe offered to help, and the doctor handed him the tweezers. Lyn immediately calmed down as her daddy pulled out the stitches.

With her dad in charge Lyn quickly returned to her good-natured self, and the doctor relaxed. Apparently he was trying to build a regular practice, so he asked Moishe, "Do you have a family doctor?"

Moishe did not, and agreed to have a physical. The doctor was very thorough, and after the exam, he announced, "You've got narcolepsy."

Moishe shrugged. "When I was sixteen, I dozed off all the time, but I think that it went away after I was married."

The doctor replied, "Well, it's back." He went on to describe several symptoms of narcolepsy, and Moishe had all of them.

Moishe's doctor prescribed amphetamines, which again became part of his daily regimen, this time for the rest of his life. He explained, "What amphetamines do to most people, they don't do to me. I don't feel nervous or jumpy. In fact, if I don't take them, it's harder for me to sit in one place; it's harder for me to focus."

He certainly needed all the help he could get to focus. Life in New Jersey would have been full enough had it consisted only of school and family life—not to mention the part-time work at Sears during the last year or so. But Moishe's purpose in being there was to prepare for ministry, so the ABMJ was a very prominent aspect of his life during those three years and not only during the summer when school was out.

At the mission center Moishe was surprised that people addressed one another as "Miss," "Mister," or "Mrs." whenever anyone else was present. Even those in the higher echelons addressed the staff and volunteers that way. In describing those days, Moishe explained,

> We were all treated very respectfully—not like young kids who were just learn-
> ing the ropes. The missionaries called each other by first name in private and

as long as we were by ourselves, the missionaries encouraged us to call them by their first names too. There was what they call esprit d' corps, a special camaraderie that we all felt because we were insiders. It was a professional, yet pleasant atmosphere.

The mission quickly became my family, and they had a cradle-to-the-grave program for their constituents, including cemetery plots where Jewish people could be buried. They were very good at helping Jewish people in need.

During the school year, Moishe went to the mission center only on Tuesdays, Thursdays, and Sundays. Like the other missionaries, he had a desk on the sixth floor. However, Moishe did not spend much time at his desk. Early on, he'd developed a rapport with Joe Serafin, the man who told him the basics of conducting a street meeting. Serafin, a Hungarian, was not part of the missionary staff. He was a utility person hired to run the elevator and perform various errands. Yet he often stood outside the door, telling passersby about Jesus. Moishe liked to stand there with Joe and listen as the older man shared his faith. Serafin told Moishe, "Don't let yourself become a desk jockey. People spend too much time sitting at their desks. You can't witness on your seat; you gotta use your feet." This made perfect sense to Moishe, and he never forgot the admonition. Later, when it was his turn to supervise field missionaries, it was one of his guiding principles.

Moishe was one of several students whom the mission was sponsoring through Bible school, but they did not all attend Northeastern. Somehow, it fell to Moishe to supervise the group, an assignment he did not particularly want. He agreed conditionally: "If I have to be in charge, I need the authority that goes with the responsibility." The mission met those terms, and Moishe had his first job supervising other missionaries.

Part of being in charge was looking out for the interests of those he supervised. Sometimes he had to speak to Harold Pretlove on their behalf, but the man was no Joseph Hoffman Cohn, who had been the consummate leader of the ABMJ. Moishe was sorry that he never had the chance to meet him. (Cohn died shortly after Moishe and Ceil became believers in Jesus.) Yet his influence at the ABMJ remained pervasive. According to Moishe,

People were always telling stories about Dr. Cohn. Nobody ever called him *Joe* Cohn; it was always *Dr.* Cohn. He was a very strong chief who didn't appreciate challenges to his leadership from the staff. And what they told me about him greatly influenced me. I got the impression that he knew how to do things the right way.

Everybody talked about how tough Dr. Cohn was, and they recollected his style of supervision. Once a week, he'd come in and call a meeting of the staff. He'd bring an inspirational word. Then they would discuss the work, and after the discussion, Dr. Cohn would go to his office on the second floor. The missionaries would come in one by one and account for their week's work. . . .

I remember hearing about Dr. Cohn and what a good memory he had and how much he delighted in catching a cheater. There was no judicial hearing. There was no process. If he felt someone was not honest in reporting their work, that was it. Anyone who lied or cheated to misrepresent the amount of work they were doing was gone. And though I never met him, I admired his ability and his resolve to weed out any sort of dishonesty.

Following the death of Dr. Cohn, the leadership of the mission was divided three ways. Harold Pretlove was officially in charge, but Daniel Fuchs and Emil Gruen each had their own areas of authority and, Moishe believed, did the actual work of running the mission.

Gruen had recruited Moishe and was a great encourager. Moishe particularly appreciated the way in which he corrected people. Moishe recalled, "After hearing me preach he gave me some good suggestions: He told me, 'You started with your voice very loud and you trailed off. It's much better if you build as you go. Save most of your breath for the end of a sentence.' Then he demonstrated how to do it. He also told me: "When I'm on my way to speak to any group, I always pray that God will give me a love for the people who come to listen."

Moishe thought of Emil Gruen as a very loving person with "a very strong sense of propriety. He set a very balanced example, and that helped me to see what was expected of me.* I learned from Emil that you never became pals with those you ministered to. You were there to minister, and that was the attitude. People you ministered to could expect certain things of you, and not others, and that was good. I appreciated the professionalism."

---

* After Moishe left the ABMJ, Emil Gruen was one of many coworkers who encouraged him as he began the ministry of Jews for Jesus.

Other people who influenced Moishe were Henry and Margaret Heydt, Sydney Parker, and especially Daniel Fuchs. Dr. Heydt had been the president and founder of Lancaster School of the Bible and was a theologian. He was more or less the resident "answer man" at the ABMJ. Sydney Parker was a missionary. As for Daniel Fuchs, Moishe said, "He was really my mentor. We had common interests, including photography.'"

Parker's influence was somewhat complex, as Moishe recalled:

My friend Sydney Parker in a sense influenced me in a negative-positive-negative way. His theology was what would then be called neoorthodoxy. Now they would simply refer to it as liberalism. He challenged me at a good time in my life because I was at a very formative stage.

He taught one of the training courses I took; it was on Jewish thought and theology. But instead of teaching what I would call Jewish theology, he explained certain theories of how the Bible was written, and he espoused ideas that don't fit within the evangelical framework.

Sydney took courses at Union Theological Seminary, and he liked to take me to sit in with him. I soon realized that Sydney didn't believe exactly the same way I did. He did believe that Jesus died for his sins, and he said he believed in the resurrection. I didn't quite know in what way he believed because he didn't seem to take things too literally, but he did have faith. And he was trying to enlighten me. Eventually, when it became known what he was teaching, he had to leave the mission.

The interesting thing is, when I went and I listened to these great liberals of the day, they didn't influence me. Their attitude toward the Bible was to take it apart and dissect it, and what they were saying didn't speak to me. Most of my biblical education was establishing the trustworthiness of Scripture, and that's always been my conviction. But it was good for me to hear the other side.

Moishe was learning from everyone he could, including Isaac Finestone, leader of another Jewish mission known as Messengers of the New Covenant in Newark, New Jersey. Finestone invited Moishe to a Bible study that he taught in an informal way.

When Moishe got there, he found forty or fifty people sitting around a big dining room table, some at the table, others in a second row around the table, and still others in chairs here and there. Finestone was slow to speak and encouraged others to participate. Like Fred Kendall (his half brother, who was also in ministry), he occasionally broke out into a song, and the people sang with him. Moishe felt it was a very Jewish way of studying—everyone's Bibles out on the table—and it gave a certain equality to have the leader teaching from a sitting position. Moishe used that method for years to come.

The New Jersey years were packed with all kinds of lessons for the new missionary. But there were some things that he seemed to know intuitively—things that sometimes surprised those who were more experienced than he. Some fifty years later, Moishe received an e-mail from a man he'd known during those student days with the ABMJ: "I remember how you helped an elderly Jewish man who was very sick and smelly go to the bathroom at the mission. I avoided him but you did not. I saw a part of you that impressed me, which not everyone has had the privilege of seeing: a sensitive and caring heart. Daniel asked me to train you when you were a student, but I soon saw someone who could have trained me."

The incident that this man was referring to was something that Moishe would have shrugged off as simply doing his duty. He recalled helping that man, but he didn't see that it set him apart from others. He never regarded himself as particularly pious or holy, but he did use the phrase "practical piety," referring to doing one's spiritual duty without any spiritual glow or holy feelings about it. Practical piety pushed Moishe to do what was difficult, and it also helped him to overcome the more obvious types of temptations. It was the kind of piety that reminded him that God was always with him and there were no secret sins.

Not all temptations involved grappling with sin, however. One of the most dangerous temptations Moishe encountered taught him an important lesson and demonstrated God's protection in a bizarre way. He recalled,

There is a kind of twilight zone when going to sleep or waking up. And that time of semiconsciousness is when I've often heard the voice of temptation. One such incident occurred during a ferry trip. . . . I remember coming home on the ferry boat in July on one of the hottest days of the year. I went to the upper deck to get fresh air. . . . Soon I was looking down at the foam where the prow of the boat was cutting the wake. I was so hot and tired, and as I stared down into the water, I was somewhat hypnotized by it.

Then I heard the words in my mind, *Jump off, dive in, cool off in the cool, cool, water.* And over and over again, in my mind I was hearing how cool it was down there. I wanted to jump in . . . but as much as I wanted to climb over the rail, my hands wouldn't let go of the rail. Suddenly I looked at my hands instead of the water and when I realized . . . what I was trying to do, I snapped out of the hypnotic state. In a flash, I realized that temptation had come straight from hell. It was really spooky. I never had any inclination, before or since, toward any kind of suicide. But going over that rail would have been suicide.

I concluded that hypnotism is dangerous and should be avoided. And I also learned something about temptation. The temptation wasn't to kill myself; the temptation was to cool myself. The thought of death didn't occur to me at all.

It was an important lesson: temptation lures people to pursue some sort of relief, but the result is deadly.

Moishe later recalled, "I can't say that I heard from God, but my hands sure did." It's amazing to think just how easily Moishe's life and influence could have been cut short apart from God's strong and saving grip.

SIXTEEN

There is no such thing as a hopeless situation;
it seems insoluble because people have grown weary of trying.
—MOISHE ROSEN

Zimmy is retiring . . . again." Daniel Fuchs smiled wryly at Moishe.

Moishe had never met Elias Zimmerman, who was in charge of the ABMJ's Los Angeles operation. However, he and Fuchs had developed the kind of relationship—professionally and personally—that was characterized by the older man's willingness to speak candidly.

Noting Moishe's raised eyebrow, Fuchs continued in his low, husky voice, "Oh, Zimmy's been talking about retiring for years. He says his health is declining. To me he seems pretty fit for his age, but then who am I to say? Every year he says he can't afford to stay on at the salary we pay, so we've been giving him raises to keep him on."

Moishe nodded, not entirely sure what Elias Zimmerman's situation three thousand miles away had to do with his own.

Fuchs, as though sensing this, got to the point: "Listen, Martin, I think it might not be such a bad idea if we encourage him to go through with it this time. He's of an age when he ought to be able to retire if he wants to, and frankly, I wouldn't mind having a younger man in his place. It's a great posting, Los Angeles."

Uh-oh, Moishe thought. *Now I see where this is leading.*

"I know you and Ceil have been having a hard time finding a place in New Jersey. Maybe it's b'shert,* you know? It occurs to me that you might be just the man to breathe some new life into the Los Angeles work. Are you interested?"

"The answer is no," Moishe answered without hesitation. Then he quickly continued, "I . . . uh . . . uh . . . appreciate your confidence in me." He stammered as he sometimes did when he wanted to be heard and sensed an interruption coming. "But I . . . uh . . . have been looking forward to full-time ministry here. I've developed a love for the greater New York area. There are more of our

---

* A Yiddish phrase roughly translated "meant to be."

people here than anywhere else in the country, and I want to reach them. So, if given a choice, I'd like to stay put."

Fuchs seemed disappointed, but he smiled in a fatherly fashion. "I thought you might feel that way. But think it over, Martin. It's a great opportunity. Talk to your wife about it, will you?"

The recent Bible school graduate nodded. Of course, he assured Fuchs, he would certainly mention it to Ceil. He reflected on his situation most of the way home. It had been an understatement to say that he and Ceil were having a hard time finding an apartment anywhere in New Jersey. Impossible was more like it. And it made no sense because for the first time in his life, affordability was not the issue.

It was understood that the couple probably would not be able to afford a place large enough to hold fellowship meetings and Bible studies on their own. The mission had indicated a willingness to subsidize rent if necessary. Moishe and Ceil had looked for apartments to rent in southern New Jersey, particularly East Orange, West Orange, and Montclair. For a time they even considered moving as far as Atlantic City to open a new mission branch, but nothing seemed available there, either.

Several weeks had gone by, and they were no closer to finding an apartment than when they'd begun. Moishe had prayed and prayed, and though he had seen God provide for his needs numerous times throughout his Bible college days, suddenly it was as though the Almighty had turned a deaf ear. Moishe puzzled over this briefly, then let the clickety-clack of the narrow gauge commuter train lull him into semi-sleep.

At home over dinner Moishe mentioned casually to his wife, "Daniel asked me today if I wanted to go to California and, you know, work there instead of here."

Ceil was visibly startled. "What did you tell him?"

"Well, of course, I said no."

"Why of course? Isn't it a possibility?"

Moishe looked at her curiously. "How is it a possibility? I've got people I'm visiting here in East Orange. Once we find a place, I can start a weekly Bible study, like what Finestone is doing. And we're so close to the city—probably the greatest place anywhere and the most Jewish city in the world."

Ceil shrugged. She was happy enough in New Jersey and she loved living on the East Coast, close to her family in Boston—but she wasn't as enamored of New York City as her husband was. "I understand, but you know, maybe the

Lord is trying to tell us something. Maybe we're supposed to go to California, and that's why we're not finding an apartment here."

Moishe replied, "I don't know. I hadn't really thought of it that way. I guess I just assumed that God wanted us to stay here."

"So you'll think some more about Daniel's offer?" she pressed.

"Yeah, I'll think and pray about it."

There was no bolt from the blue, but Moishe found it more and more plausible that God might have closed the door for them in New Jersey so that they could go through that open door to California. The next time he saw Daniel, he asked, "Do you still want me to take that post in California?"

"Yes, absolutely. Have you changed your mind?"

"I wouldn't exactly say *I* changed my mind, but my mind's been changed. I think it's the right choice, given the circumstances and I . . . well, I feel confident that if this is what God wants, it'll be the best thing."

"Good!" Dr. Fuchs was visibly delighted. "I'll let Zimmy know you're coming. We're giving him a trip around the world as a retirement gift, but he's promised to be available when he gets back to help the new man in the transition period."

Moishe nodded. He wasn't that thrilled to be the new man in California when he'd already begun trying to build a small work in New Jersey where no one expected him to fill anyone else's shoes. But at least he'd have help. "When does Mr. Zimmerman leave for his trip? You know I've got plans to be in Denver for a couple of weeks this summer. My parents have agreed to see us, and I've got to go before the ordination council at Trinity, my home church."

"Oh, you don't need to worry about that," Fuchs assured him. "We can fly you out from Denver to meet Zimmy. He'll introduce you to everyone you'll need to know before he goes on his trip. You spend a little time with him out there, get yourself oriented, and then come back to Denver for Ceil and the girls."

With a mixture of apprehension and anticipation Moishe returned to his pretty young wife that night and sang, albeit a bit off key, "California here we come . . ." She, laughing, sang back, "Not quite where we started from . . ."

On a hot July morning in 1957, Moishe loaded up the four-year-old white Dodge, a rather nice hand-me-down from one of the senior missionaries, and the family set out for their new home—Los Angeles, California, via Denver, Colorado. The first two-thirds of the cross-country trip passed uneventfully. Then, after fields and fields of alfalfa and corn and sunflowers, there was Denver, nestled at the foot of the Rocky Mountains.

Moishe's parents delighted in their first granddaughter—her vocabulary had grown and she could express even more of her personality than ever. They were also happy to meet their second granddaughter for the first time—though by comparison to her sister, she was cautious and shy and never wanted to be very far from her mother.

Some changes had occurred since Moishe had left Denver. His brother, Don, had married; he and his wife, Elaine, were expecting their first child. Don had become an indispensable part of Ben's business that would one day become his own.

Ceil's adoptive parents had moved away without informing anyone where they were going or how they might be contacted. Rumor had it that they had moved to Israel.

With his family comfortably ensconced in Denver, it was time for Moishe to fly to Los Angeles, meet Zimmy, and scope out his new post. Moishe liked to travel by car and train, but had never flown anywhere. The flight would be a real adventure. As Moishe kissed Ceil and the girls good-bye, he felt a growing excitement for this new phase in his life.

On the plane ride Moishe mentally rehearsed what Daniel Fuchs had told him about Elias Zimmerman. In 1938, Zimmerman began his work as a missionary in Boyle Heights, then a very Jewish area of Los Angeles. It was the end of the Great Depression, when many people rode the rails because they were homeless. Zimmy, as many called him, had a reputation as a good preacher and had begun his outreach as somewhat of a rescue mission. He'd preach to those who came and then serve them sandwiches or sometimes soup.

Now, in 1957, the days of the rescue mission were long gone, and Zimmerman was renting part of a Free Methodist church for Sunday afternoon services. These meetings were still in Boyle Heights on the East Side of Los Angeles, though more and more Jewish people were moving to the West Side. Moishe understood that he was to be Zimmerman's successor but was not expected to follow in his footsteps too closely. The work had been declining over the years, which was why Fuchs wanted a new missionary there.

From the airport, Moishe took public transportation to the downtown May Flower Inn where Zimmy (or his assistant) had booked him a room. It was a smallish, commercial hotel near the library and the Church of the Open Door. Upon checking in, Moishe asked the desk clerk if there were any messages for him, as he hoped for further instructions. No messages, no phone calls. It was midafternoon the next day when Zimmerman finally rang to let Moishe know that he would pick him up at five o'clock.

With a sigh of relief, the young missionary contemplated what to do for a couple of hours. He walked around downtown Los Angeles, which had nothing of the bustling excitement of Manhattan. He thought everything seemed too spread out for anyone to bustle.

At five o'clock Zimmerman arrived and welcomed Moishe enthusiastically, assuring the new missionary that he anticipated "great things" from him. They drove west from downtown to a small white house at 5020 West Pico Boulevard. Burl Haynie, who was employed by the ABMJ, was there to show Moishe around what was to be the Rosens' new home. Somewhat sadly, Mr. Haynie explained that he had remodeled the mission house for himself and his wife, hoping they could minister there together. Things had not worked out as he had planned, but Mr. Haynie hoped that the Rosens would find themselves very happy and very much at home there. Moishe thanked him and complimented him on the work he had done.

After Haynie gave him a tour of the house, Moishe allowed the fact to sink in that this was to be his family's home. The move became more of a reality and he began to envision the possibilities and grow excited about the future. He could not wait to tell Ceil that they would have an upstairs *and* a downstairs bathroom all their own!

Zimmerman did not introduce Moishe to many people, but he did connect him with a few helpers that evening. One was an assistant whom Moishe was apparently to inherit. He also met Ken and Betty Jacques, who were keenly interested in reaching Jewish people with the message of Jesus. Dr. Jacques was an orthopedist, and the couple had a lovely home in the Hollywood Hills, which they opened for monthly meetings attended by believers in Jesus and seekers alike.

The following day, Zimmy also introduced Moishe to a couple who would supposedly "take care of" him for the rest of the week. "Because," as the retiree explained, "my wife and I leave for our trip tomorrow."

Moishe did his best to hide his shock and disappointment that the man who was supposed to show him the ropes was departing so soon. He tried to use the short time that he had to ply Zimmerman with questions about whom he would be calling on to study the Bible and discuss spiritual matters and various other details concerning the work.

Zimmerman wasn't prepared to give details then, but once the Rosens moved out to Los Angeles, he'd see to it that they were "all set." After all, Daniel Fuchs wanted Moishe to make his own mark, so the older man did not want to encumber or restrict him with too much of his own style. With a cheery good-bye, Zimmerman bid Moishe farewell, suggested he spend the rest of the week sightseeing, and left him in the care of the "host" couple who, as it turned out, had plans to head for their vacation cabin.

With no work to do, no one to show him the ropes, and no desire to go sightseeing without his family, there was no reason to remain in Los Angeles for the rest of the time originally planned. Fortunately, the airline had plenty of open seats on an earlier return flight to Denver, and Moishe was able to change his ticket and head back early. He had an ordination to attend.

———

Moishe's initial resistance to the move west had not been unusual. He later conceded, "That has almost always been the case for me with God's will. I was always pointed someplace else, moving ahead, doing what I thought I was supposed to do. I wasn't seeking; I wasn't looking. It seems as though God has always come to me as an interruption." In fact, he often found that what he'd taken to be an unwelcome change of plans was actually an answer to his prayers for God's leading, as in this move to California.

The stop in Denver was a high point. But as happy and hospitable as Moishe's family was about the visit, there was an underlying tension. The conditions of their reconciliation caused Moishe to feel guilty; he was not allowed to discuss religion. His whole life was dedicated to telling others about the amazing relationship with God that was possible through Jesus; it seemed wrong to keep silent about that relationship when he was with the people he cared for most. Yet he felt he had no choice. He'd always hoped, and in fact had been led to believe by some well-meaning Christians, that eventually his family would see the positive changes in him and begin to ask about God. They never did. That was painful for Moishe—and it also made it awkward for him to discuss his other reason for being in Denver.

Pastor MacDonald and the elders of Trinity Baptist Church were happy to fulfill their promise concerning Moishe's ordination. The church had called an ordination council of about twenty-four church leaders and elders before whom Moishe presented himself to be questioned on his Bible knowledge, theology, and doctrine. The council found Moishe's responses satisfactory, and he was invited to give his testimony the following Sunday night, after which he was to be ordained as a Conservative Baptist minister.* It was with a sense of accomplishment and gratitude that Moishe received his ordination. He valued the connection to the Conservative Baptist Association throughout his life.

Moishe explained to his father that he had been qualified to be ordained—and though he realized it was highly unlikely that Ben would attend the service, he had invited him anyway. Moishe recalled, "My dad looked at me and said, 'I guess if I were a Christian, I'd be very proud of you. But I'm not a Christian.' That was his way of giving me what amounted to a compliment without compromising his principles."

The time in Denver went by quickly. Moishe and Ceil had stored some of their belongings at a friend's home, and it was somewhat bittersweet to ship those belongings to California. Denver was no longer home base, and when they returned, it would be as visitors.

Now the Rosen family was in the home stretch of their road trip, and Moishe was eager to get to Los Angeles.

He organized it so that they would travel through the desert at night, but even so, the summer heat of the Mojave was brutal. In those days air-conditioned cars were only for the very wealthy—most people simply rolled down their windows. Moishe and Ceil carried plenty of water in the car, and Ceil continually soaked washcloths to keep each family member cool.

At last, the four Rosens pulled up in front of their new home between two and three in the morning. After getting some sleep, the family surveyed the house. Ceil and the girls were happy with the grassy backyard, which had an avocado tree and a few other plants and a fence so that—oh, joy—the family would be able to have a dog!

The property also included a large garage, but the mission had been renting that space to a carpenter/cabinet maker, George Devries, who lived nearby. George was rather new in business and had a wife and family to support. Moishe knew that if he claimed his right to the garage, it would put his new neighbor out of business. There was no way the carpenter would find a comparable deal on rent anywhere. So they struck a bargain; Devries built, at his own expense,

---

* When Pastor MacDonald discovered that Moishe did not know any Greek (the language in which the New Testament was originally recorded), he secured Moishe's promise that if the council ordained him, he would do a year's study in Greek. Moishe kept that promise by taking a class at Biola.

a carport right next to the garage, and with the Rosen's needs thus met, he continued to rent their garage.

George and his wife, Elfrieda (Elfie), were German Jews whose families had fled Hitler. Their oldest boy, Jerry, was about Lyn's age, and soon two more little boys came along. The Devrieses were excellent neighbors, and the two families became fast friends.

It would be an understatement to say that Moishe got off to a slow start with the work in Los Angeles. Zimmerman came back from his trip, but his promised help never materialized. From him, Moishe had inherited a Tuesday night Bible study on the East Side of LA in a formerly Jewish neighborhood. The same six or seven people trudged to these meetings each week.

Moishe recalled, "After my first Tuesday night meeting, I remember thinking that the people who attended were looking at me rather expectantly. We had already served refreshments and I could not imagine what else I was supposed to provide. Then Ken Reeves, the man who had previously assisted Zimmerman, observed, 'You didn't take care of their car fare.'" The attendees were used to receiving a dollar, and as Moishe said, "The bus fare was nowhere near a dollar in those days. I concluded that he'd more or less been paying people to attend."

It wasn't long before Ken Reeves seemed inclined to move a good two hours south and do missionary work in San Diego. This move suited Moishe quite well because he'd never asked to have an assistant.

Moving the work from Boyle Heights to West LA made perfect sense, but Moishe wasn't entirely sure how to go about it, other than moving the Bible studies to the mission house on Pico. "In actuality," Moishe recalled, "God began the work there without me."

During Moishe's Bible school years, Ceil had attended missionary training classes with him at the mission center in Manhattan where she learned about children's ministry. Now that she had a school-age daughter who needed to learn the Bible, Ceil had jumped right into the LA work by starting a Bible club. It was a small group, consisting of Lyn and some of her neighborhood school friends. Before long Ceil was teaching stories from the Old Testament, with a view toward prophecy and New Testament thinking. Two of the neighborhood children, Harry and Elsa Cohen, heard about the Bible club and asked their mother if they could attend. She gave her consent.

Harry and Elsa's mother, Hilda, was a Holocaust survivor. Having lived through the camps, she firmly believed that God had spared her life for a purpose. She desperately wanted to know more about God, and now two of her children were studying the Bible with Jewish neighbors who believed in Jesus. Something was building up inside her until one day she seemed ready to explode.

Moishe described his first meeting with Hilda Cohen:

This short lady came stomping up to our front door, and we let her in out of courtesy. She talked in an excited way and I could understand that she felt very strongly about something, but it was hard to understand her. She had a heavy Dutch accent. I could see on her left arm the tattoo of the concentration camps. She only knew a few words of English, and she said that she had heard that I was a domine. At first I thought that she was saying "domino" and I was confused. But in her broken English, she told me "a man with a Bible." I said, "A minister?" She said, "That's right." And she pointed to me with a questioning look, so I nodded my head that yes, I was a minister. And we just stared at each other because we had this language barrier.

At that time, the American Board of Missions to the Jews had a missionary couple, Dr. Elias Den Arend [sometimes called Eddie] and his wife, Margaret. They were from Holland, and he was a Jewish believer in Jesus. They were in San Jose, and they were coming to visit us in a day or two. So I told Hilda Cohen that we had another domine coming to visit and he was from Holland. She wanted to know if he was Jewish, too. And I nodded my head. She asked, 'And he believes in Jesus like you?' I nodded yes, and her face broke out into a big smile and she said, very emphatically, 'Good!' She was so eager that the next morning she knocked on the door and wanted to know if the domine from Holland was there yet. I took her address and promised to come tell her when they arrived.

Moishe did as he promised. The Den Arends talked and prayed with Mrs. Cohen, and she received Jesus as her Messiah. Then the three of them went over to Hilda's house. "Before long, her husband, Isaac, had also prayed to receive the Lord," Moishe said.

The ministry slowly began to percolate. Moishe planned his week around regularly scheduled meetings. First was the weekly Bible study on Tuesday nights, which was moved from Boyle Heights to the Pico house. Moishe liked this informal style of teaching. It did not elevate him but helped him to facilitate group study and discussion. Following the study, Ceil served refreshments.

On Sundays, Moishe preached outdoors in the park. His experience with hecklers stood him in good stead. Before long, a frustrated opera singer who happened to be an Italian Jew took to singing loudly whenever Moishe tried to speak. Moishe spoke privately to the man (whose name was also Moishe) and told him, "I know you don't agree with what I say, Moishe, but for me this is a living. I'm paid for preaching. I have a wife and two children. Let me preach. Let me do my work." The opera singer appreciated the request and actually began singing to help Moishe draw a crowd. He sang traditional Jewish songs, operatic arias, and sometimes songs from a Christian hymnal until he moved from the area. Before he left, however, he told Moishe that he believed in Jesus.

There were several such incidents that, if told all together, would seem to indicate that Moishe Rosen was off to a great start in Los Angeles. But these anecdotes, while true, did not represent everyday life and ministry.* The fact was, on days when no meetings were scheduled, Moishe would wake up each morning and decide what he should do that day. If there was someone for him to visit, he'd visit. If not, he'd work on preparing his Bible study. He often spoke at churches, and frequently he met Jewish people who wanted to know more about Jesus. Sometimes he received a knock on the door from a Jewish inquirer. How did they know to knock on his door? For one thing, a small plaque on the front of the house read, "Reverend Martin Meyer Rosen."

Having just been ordained, he was rather proud of the title and took satisfaction in referring to himself as "Reverend." Besides, it was useful in establishing initial contacts. Nevertheless, in later years he came to regard the use of his honorific titles an unnecessary and unwholesome desire for status. He dropped the title altogether and discouraged his staff from using titles as well.

The Pico address was also listed in the phone directory under the American Board of Missions to the Jews. It was not surprising for someone to stop by and ask for gospel tracts to use in telling Jewish friends or neighbors about Jesus.

---

* Moishe came to insist on detailed reporting because anecdotes, while often encouraging, could not account for amounts of time spent, number of people called or visited, number of tracts handed out and doors knocked on, and so forth. His own lack of accountability in those first few months taught him the importance of planning, preparing, and reporting on one's work.

Moishe's ability to connect with people was a vital part of his ministry, but as yet he did not know how to plan for or organize such opportunities. He simply took them as they came. Despite his slow start in Los Angeles, the ten years Moishe spent there became a pivotal point in his development as a mission leader.

SEVENTEEN

Every knock is a boost.

—MOISHE ROSEN

It was early evening, and still light outside the little mission house on West Pico Blvd. The girls were off playing and Moishe was telling Ceil about his day as she cleared away the last of the dishes.

"I wanted to tell you about a man I met with today. His name is Abe Schneider, and he was a truck driver before he became a missionary. He does door-to-door canvassing and he thinks I should do it too, you know, to help get the work going. So I went with him to see how he does it."

"Uh huh." Ceil nodded to indicate that she was listening.

"He has a big smile, like this," Moishe grinned expansively, "Well, not quite like that; his smile is better than mine and his teeth are nicer. But he knocks on the door with this big smile and when someone opens the door, he says—now picture this, with that big smile on his face!— 'Could I ask you a question? If an atom bomb hit Los Angeles today, what would happen to you?'"

Ceil's eyebrows shot up as she gasped, "Really?"

"Yes. Imagine how embarrassed I felt. But the strangest thing was . . . some people really wanted to talk about what might happen to them when they died. And would you believe, one person listened to the whole gospel and decided to believe, then and there!"

"So are you going to do it?"

"Go door-to-door? I guess I can try it. But when I do it, I'll leave out the bomb part."

"What will you say?"

"Well, what about this: Hello, my name is Martin Rosen and I'm from the Beth Sar Shalom Hebrew Christian Fellowship. We have a Bible study every Tuesday night and I want to invite you.' He paused. "Then I could hand them a post card that gives the time and place of our study. And if they want to know more, I'll give them one of our tracts, like, 'What is a Christian?'"

"I guess it might work," Ceil said, somewhat doubtfully. "When are you going to try it?"

"I don't know. I'll have to get the post cards printed up first."

The doorbell rang. "Are you expecting anyone?" Ceil asked, as he went to answer the door.

"Not particularly," he said.

"Well, if it's anyone with a bomb, tell them that we don't want any," she called after him.

Moishe opened the door and found himself eye to eye with a tall, blond, handsome young man. "Are you Martin Rosen?" he asked in a soft southern drawl.

"Yes." Moishe wondered why the young man was wearing a tweed sport coat in August, when the weather was still hot.

"My name is Tom McCall, and I'm here to be your assistant. Daniel Fuchs hired me."

"He . . . he did? I hope you'll excuse me, Mr. McCall. Daniel never mentioned anything about it to me. Are you sure you're supposed to be my assistant?"

"Yes, very sure."

"Well, uh, uh, come in."

Moishe ushered in his guest and introduced him to Ceil.

"Mr. Rosen, I'm enrolled at Talbot Theological Seminary in La Mirada," Tom explained. "I'm supposed to work with you half-time. Daniel said I would learn a lot from you."

The last thing Moishe wanted was an assistant. He had "inherited" one from Zimmy but had been relieved when the former assistant had asked to go elsewhere. What was he supposed to teach Tom, when he was still learning the ropes himself?

"Well, tomorrow's Sunday. I guess for starters, you can join me in the park for outdoor evangelism."

The next day the two men went to MacArthur Park. Moishe was curious to see how Tom would acquit himself and, much to his surprise, Tom did well. Most street preachers Moishe had seen presented themselves as great beholders of the truth who were imparting what they knew to those wise enough to stop and listen. Tom was different.

He's very approachable, Moishe thought. *That humble and vulnerable manner is not just a show for outdoor preaching. It's the way we should be as missionaries.*

Moishe was happy to have someone else to preach with him on Sundays, but it seemed to Moishe that Tom was making plans and decisions without too much regard for his "boss's" input.

"I don't think it's such a good idea for Tom to look for a home in Downey," he told Ceil one night. "It puts him too far from the mission and the neighborhood where he's supposed to minister."

"Did you tell him that?"

"Yeah, I told him."

"And?"

"And he's set on living in Downey." Moishe shrugged. "What am I going to do, fire him? I didn't hire him to begin with. I like the guy a lot, but I don't feel like I have any leverage with him. I just wish I knew what Daniel was thinking."

"Can't you ask him?"

"He probably expects me to figure things out for myself."

"You have a good relationship with Daniel—"

"Yes, I know. I don't want to bother him with this."

"You're sure?"

"Sure. Hey, isn't Ed Sullivan on tonight? Let's turn on the TV."

———

Moishe never did quite get the hang of supervising Tom McCall who was very smart and very determined to do things his own way. As a seminary student, Tom had knowledge that outstripped Moishe's Bible college education, causing Moishe to stretch a little in order to fulfill Daniel's promise that Tom would learn from him. Moishe began to prepare lessons that were different from the sort of thing Tom would learn at Talbot. The twenty or so lectures on how to witness to Jewish people helped him formulate ideas that he would use with future trainees. They also formed the basis for a booklet Moishe wrote titled "How to Witness Simply and Effectively to the Jews."

As for the door-to-door work, Moishe was not looking forward to it, and it took quite a while before he got started. For the most part, people took the postcard invitation to the Bible study and said, "Thank you." Occasionally someone would ask a question; now and then someone would be hostile. Over the course of eighteen months, Moishe recalled, "I did talk at length to a few people. But from all the invitations that I handed out, only one couple that I know of ever came to the Bible study. Afterward, they told me very cordially that they had been curious enough to come, but that once had been enough. I never saw them again."

Moishe found that one of the most effective ways for him to meet people who wanted to talk about Jesus was already in place when he moved to California. It had been organized independently of the mission long before Moishe's arrival. Lawrence Duff Forbes, whom Moishe once described as "the father of messianic Judaism," began the project—a monthly Friday night fellowship meeting—and once it got going, he left it to others. Through Betty Jacques who, with her husband, hosted the gatherings in their Hollywood Hills home, Moishe learned the value of such meetings and how to conduct them.

The evening typically included a special speaker—sometimes a Christian celebrity Betty knew from her church—who told of his or her faith journey. Often a talented soloist brought a touch of class to the music. The Jacqueses were generous and the refreshments were elegant. A core group of Christians attended the meetings and invited their friends, many of whom were Jewish.

Moishe attended most of the meetings, and Ceil came when she was able to hire a babysitter. The Jacqueses always made the Rosens very much at home at the fellowship meetings, though as Ceil noted, "They were in a very different social strata than we were." Betty introduced them to some of the "Hollywood people," including Roy Rogers (who autographed a Bible for Lyn), David Nelson and his wife (of *Ozzie and Harriet* fame), and Donna Douglas, who played Ellie Mae Clampett on *The Beverly Hillbillies*. These entertainers were well known in the late 1950s and early 1960s. The Jacqueses also introduced Moishe and Ceil to personal friends who lived in Bel Air, a number of whom were Jewish or had Jewish friends with whom Moishe met to discuss the gospel.

During their early years in Southern California, Moishe and Ceil became members of the First Baptist Church of Hollywood, pastored by Dr. Harold Proppe. Dr. Proppe, an "old school Baptist," befriended Moishe and made quite an impression on him. Among other things, in warm weather he wore a linen suit, and in cooler weather he wore a morning coat. Moishe explained,

> When I say Dr. Proppe was an old-fashioned Baptist, first of all, he was an orator. His elegance of language was phenomenal. He had a sense of decorum. . . .
> I went there as much as anything because one person could make a difference in that congregation.

Dr. Proppe's interest in Moishe was typical of his desire for people in his congregation to do what they could to tell others about Jesus. He recognized potential in the young missionary and wanted to encourage and challenge Moishe. Dr. Proppe was very frank with him about potential pitfalls in ministry and Moishe took his warnings seriously.

Moishe was at a point in his life where he certainly needed to be encouraged as well as challenged. Throughout the first year or so, Moishe did not realize where he was lacking until his boss, Daniel Fuchs, came to spend ten days with him. Fuchs was one of the most important and highly regarded Jewish believers in Jesus at that time. The fact that he wanted to spend an extended period of time with Moishe—living at his home and shadowing him throughout his work days—came as a bit of a shock to the young missionary, who felt both honored and intimidated by the plan.

The mere act of figuring out how to spend his time with Dr. Fuchs showed Moishe just how little he'd been accustomed to scheduling his work and how much he had relied on people and activities to present themselves. Daniel's visit was exactly what Moishe needed to learn how to plan his time wisely and organize opportunities rather than wait for them.

He later reflected, "The conclusion I drew from my own life was that one doesn't do a novice any favors by allowing him to set his own pace and be entirely responsible for his own work schedule. Novices need to work alongside someone who can set a good example."*

Dr. Fuchs confided to Moishe that he'd come because somebody had made a complaint that Moishe's ministry wasn't developing. That was certainly true and Moishe was able to see and admit it—but since no one had spoken to him about it, he was naturally unhappy that someone had reported it to Daniel behind his back. Daniel would not name the person who made the complaint. Moishe recalled,

> The fact that Daniel wouldn't say who complained made me suspicious of people around me. Years later, he told me who the person was. It really hurt my feelings, because it was Elias Zimmerman, who had always told me what a wonderful job I was doing and what a wonderful person I was. But behind

---

* Moishe came to believe that one of the most common problems in any ministry is that people, when allowed to work at their own pace, often do not challenge themselves to stretch beyond the minimum acceptable effort. He found that underchallenged ministers either tend to become depressed over low levels of achievement or else deceive themselves into thinking that a low level is higher than it really is.

my back, he complained that I wasn't doing enough work. He might have challenged me to do better and shown me how to do better, but he didn't.

I decided that, if I ever got in that position [of being a boss], I would never heed any complaint if the person insisted on being anonymous. If somebody complained, they had to sign off on their complaint. If they didn't care enough to attach their name to it, and stand by it, I was just not going to take it seriously. A lot of my principles came as counter measures to bad experiences.*

Daniel did not realize that referencing the complaint with no name attached was likely to engender suspicion. Nevertheless, Moishe did benefit from the criticism because Daniel Fuchs cared enough to help Moishe turn the situation around.

Moishe was grateful for the time Fuchs spent with him. He was honored that his mentor and boss stayed in his home when he could have been far more comfortable in a hotel. Fuchs made it very clear that he had not come to scold Moishe, but to bring him along and build him up. Moishe said,

He was a good coach. He didn't give a lot of directives, but he knew how to make helpful suggestions. When he taught something, instead of saying, "You ought to do this." Or, "Here's what you need to do" he would start out by applying the situation to himself. He'd say, "I found a way of doing this that might work for you," or, "You might want to try it this way." He was also very commendatory of anything that I did right. He said that he'd learned a lot from me, and that meant a great deal. Daniel knew that part of giving was showing the other person that they had something to offer. The ten days he spent with me revolutionized my life.

Within five years, the LA work had grown to the point that the mission sought a larger facility to accommodate it. They secured an excellent property on the corner of Lexington and Lodi. The small mansion had once been the home of Mary Pickford, one of the most important actors and producers of silent film, and cofounder of the United Artists film studio. More recently the building had been owned by Calvary Church of Hollywood, a split-off from First

---

* Daniel probably wanted to prevent friction between two of his staff by not disclosing names, but Moishe felt that anonymtity caused more problems than it solved.

Presbyterian Church of Hollywood. Eventually, Calvary Church rejoined First Presbyterian and no longer needed the building. They offered the ABMJ a terrific deal; if the mission would buy the property for the price of the land, they would donate the building. It required only minor renovations to adapt it for the mission's use. Moishe oversaw those renovations.

The mission no longer needed the little house on Pico Boulevard, and accordingly, they sold it. As long as Moishe and Ceil resided in the building where the mission work was centered, they had lived rent-free. For the first time ever they saved up a significant sum toward a down payment for a home of their own. Daniel Fuchs encouraged the couple's desire to become homeowners and did what he could to help make it possible.

Their savings, along with a generous gift from Mary Hensley, a friend and supporter of the ministry, enabled them to purchase a three-bedroom ranch house in North Hollywood.

These moves, one to a new mission facility and the other to a new home that the family could call their own, signaled a new era in Moishe's life and ministry.

EIGHTEEN

A careful artist doesn't need a big brush.

—MOISHE ROSEN

At least we're not late," Moishe told Ceil, who had gotten up at the crack of dawn to accompany him on the two-hour drive to San Diego. He was half apologetic as he explained that the breakfast meeting to which he'd been invited was actually a luncheon and would not begin until one o'clock. Ceil loved Southern California and didn't mind having extra time to explore beautiful San Diego.

The morning passed quickly enough, and they returned to the church. Moishe had spoken at several such gatherings and was accustomed to an audience of fifteen or twenty area pastors, but this time more than sixty attended. The young missionary was delighted to find the ministers keenly interested in communicating the gospel to Jewish people. After his message, they were eager to hear more. Moishe remained, fielding questions for most of the afternoon.

The following afternoon, Moishe dropped Ceil at the airport and prepared to enjoy the long drive ahead. He was heading for El Paso, Texas, 725 miles away. By 2:00 a.m. he reached Gila Bend, Arizona, low on gasoline and even lower on energy and alertness. He found an all-night gas pump/convenience store, fueled his green Plymouth station wagon and dreamily downed three hot dogs, a glass of milk, and a cup of coffee. He was still 370 miles from El Paso. Fortunately, he did not have to speak that morning.

He was just about to get in his car when he felt a couple of sharp pokes—first in the back of his arm, then in his ribs. A gruff voice demanded, "Give me your money or your life."

Moishe turned to see a teenage boy who did not look nearly as ferocious as his threat had sounded. But he did look jumpy. Moishe took a deep breath to compose himself and said, "You can have my money; all I have is six dollars in cash. But you can't take my life. That belongs to Jesus, and whatever he wants me to do with it, I'll do, and however long he wants me to live, I'll live. If you use that knife on me, you'll only put me in a far better place than this. But one of these days you're going to die, and then where will you be?"

"Are y-y-you a B-b-baptist?" came the unexpected reply.

"Yes, I am," Moishe answered, somewhat surprised. He saw that the teenager was shaking and gently but firmly took the knife from him. It was a switchblade. He clicked it shut, and the kid actually seemed relieved.

"Mister, I've never done anything like this before," he said. "I've gone to church and Sunday school all my life. My parents and grandparents taught me what was right. But you get to be a certain age and well, you know. You get tired of being some Goody Two-shoes."

A trailer was parked at the edge of the lot, and Moishe saw a man motioning for the would-be mugger to come back. The boy was shaking his head and gesturing for the guy to stay away.

"Mister, is it okay if I get in your car? I promise I won't try anything, but I think I better get outta here."

Moishe agreed, and they drove out of the parking lot. The boy explained that he had a job in the convenience store and a "real pretty girl" had come in that night and flirted with him. When he got off work that night, she introduced him to her "boyfriend." They promised him quite an evening and the girl said she'd like to show him a "good time," but first he had to get the money to pay for the liquor. The girl said she could show him how to get the money easily enough, so he called his parents to say that he was working late. The girl then gave him a knife and assured him that he wouldn't really have to use it. It would be easy enough to scare someone into handing over cash.

Once the crisis had passed the boy could see that the prostitute and her boyfriend/manager were only using him. But of all the "victims" he might have tried to hold up at knifepoint, a Baptist minister? The implications were not lost on the young man.

Before long, the sixteen-year-old was praying, asking God's forgiveness and saying that he wanted to surrender his life to Jesus once and for all. Moishe added his amen and drove the boy home. He was so tired, he didn't even think to ask the boy his name or write down his address. He simply drove on toward El Paso.

When he could go no further, he checked into an economy class motel where he quickly fell into a sound sleep. He awoke just a few hours later. It wasn't until he'd paid for the room that he recalled that something strange had happened the previous night. He remembered the boy with the knife, but of course that couldn't have been real. It must have been some crazy dream, he thought. And so he dismissed it—until he got to the car. There, lying on the front seat was a switchblade knife.

———

The weapon from this event quickly became a symbol to Moishe—not only of how God intervenes to save people in radical ways, but also of how that salvation transforms lives. And from a symbol, both the story and the knife became trophies, not of Moishe's bravery, but of God's power. Ceil mounted the knife on a wood plaque as a gift for Moishe, and the attached brass plate was engraved: "Therefore, if anyone is in Christ, he is a new creation; old things have passed away; behold, all things have become new" (2 Corinthians 5:17).

That adventure also illustrated Moishe's idea of courage. To him, courage was not fearlessness; courage meant that he couldn't let circumstances deter him from doing what needed to be done. He would have given the kid his money, but he felt compelled to give him an opportunity to hear and respond to the gospel.

For Moishe, the 1960s were a time of building and rebuilding. His years in Bible school had somewhat dampened his natural tendency to tell everyone he met about Jesus. Yet he had learned much about the Bible and about faith. He'd seen God meet so many needs in unexpected ways. And now he was getting back into the habit of telling people about Jesus, wherever he might meet them.[*]

In Los Angeles, he had a great deal of freedom to put all he had learned into practice. The move to North Hollywood signaled a new and very successful time of ministry for Moishe. Yet that time had begun with a personal tragedy that deeply affected both Moishe and Ceil.

In the late summer of 1961 they were surprised to find out that Ceil was pregnant. Originally they had talked about having four children, but their second daughter's life-threatening condition at birth changed that. Doctors explained that additional pregnancies would exacerbate the RH incompatibility and could result in fetal death. Despite conscientious birth control, Ceil was expecting. She could tell by comparing it with the first two pregancies that something was wrong. Moishe kept reassuring her that everything would be okay, but in the beginning of her ninth month, Ceil went into labor and their little boy was stillborn.

---

[*] He later described this as "Witnessing on the Way" (WOW).

In this excerpt from a letter that Moishe wrote to his friend Paul Liberman, he explained the event and its aftermath more than four decades later:

> Both of us went numb. I backslid. I didn't run around and get drunk. I didn't do anything different at all. It's just that I emotionally shut down. I threw myself into the work. I stopped praying. I didn't read the Scripture. When it came to sensing any presence of God, I was just numb. But the day after [the baby died] I preached in two different churches.
>
> Here's the surprise: that [backslidden state] lasted most of that year, and it was my most successful year in ministry. I prayed in public like I had always prayed. I preached what I'd always believed. But I didn't have any strength, or to use the Yiddish word, *coyach*. It was like sleepwalking. I just went from one thing to another. . . .
>
> Then something happened, I became spiritually awakened. . . . I feel that God reached down and lifted me. I feel that the many achievements were just due to the fact that I did my duty. And God spoke through me, even though [for that period of time] I was not acquainted with Him.

The baby boy, who would have been named Jonathan Edward Rosen, was born and died on April 7, 1962, a day before Ceil's birthday. Moishe and Ceil never saw the baby. Friends arranged an unattended burial in a nearby Burbank cemetery. Ceil never ceased to regret the lost opportunity to say good-bye. Weeks later she visited the small grave—alone—without ever telling Moishe.

The tragedy affected husband and wife very differently; they had opposing theological views concerning the death of a newborn. That, along with the difference in their personalities, resulted in their need to mourn in separate ways. And like many couples who lose a child, their contrasting ways of managing the shock and grief put them at somewhat of a loss for how to comfort one another.

Devastated by the loss, Ceil comforted herself with the thought that the child she would never hold was not hers but God's—and that though he was in heaven, he was still an instrument to work God's will in her life. Her great sadness was very apparent for more than a year, though she did not talk much about it. Moishe, as indicated in his letter, went on outwardly as though nothing had changed, while inwardly, nothing remained the same.

For Moishe, the tragic experience was almost the polar opposite of his joyous discovery of God's care for him during Bible school. Having experienced such wonderful provision and protection, Moishe was shaken by the firsthand knowledge that truly terrible things not only can, but do happen even to those who trust God. He had known it intellectually, but now he knew it personally and was shaken to his core.

There was no single event that reconnected Moishe's emotions to his intellect, no particular revelation that restored his spirit. What he described as "God lifting me" others might call healing. Even so, he never again responded to an impending crisis by assuring himself or others involved that everything would be okay. Eventually the tragedy enabled him to minister in a deeper way to those who were grieving.

Moishe's personality was not charismatic in the traditional sense of the word. His mild stammer disqualified him from being a "smooth talker." But his genuine interest in people, combined with his sense of duty and enthusiasm for his work drew people to him.

For the most part, the San Fernando Valley years were very good to Moishe and Ceil. During the Pico years, Ceil had never complained about the weekly meetings that took precedence over their home life and privacy or of Moishe's being "at work" whenever he happened to go into his little office or whenever the phone or doorbell rang. But after the move, even though she was happy to entertain guests, she loved having a home life that was distinct from her husband's work.

The house had a large backyard with a peach tree, a fig tree, and an apricot tree. The front yard had numerous rose bushes, which Moishe learned to tend. Describing his interest in roses he said,

> There were lots of things growing at the house in North Hollywood, including the roses. I got a book on roses and how to train them and make them grow. It wasn't that I planted so many things; it was mostly that I kept things growing that were already there. This reflects on my creativity in general—I tend to develop what is already there, or what I find happening around me.

In keeping with his interest in "whatever was at hand" Moishe made a brief foray into the world of art—because he happened to have an artist living in his garage. The artist, unlike the roses, had not been there when the family moved in.

His name was Darwin Dunham, and Moishe met him at First Baptist Church of Hollywood. An artist from childhood, Darwin wanted to use his talents for God but wasn't sure how. The following is an excerpt from a 2009 e-mail sent by Darwin:

> I went to Art Center School in Los Angeles to become a successful illustrator. My whole life was aimed in that direction. [Then] one Sunday . . . Rev. Martin Rosen [taught] our Sunday School class. He spoke from John 4—the woman at the well. I had never heard of a Jewish believer in Christ. Nor had I ever heard the Scriptures expounded from so Jewish a perspective. He spoke directly and honestly without syrupy spirituality.
>
> . . . I determined to get to know this guy better. I thought that if an intelligent Jewish man like Rosen could believe in Christ, he could answer my questions. My first impression did not change on getting to know him. It deepened. His life was marked by singleness of purpose, steadiness, maturity and sincerity. He had no phoniness about him. As a creative thinker he was bold and willing to try new things. He made ministry look exciting. I've never met anyone quite like him.
>
> Moishe encouraged my artistic pursuits, set my theological sails, encouraged me to attend Talbot Seminary . . . trained me to speak in churches . . . I believe that the Lord used him to draw me closer to Himself and to lead me on to another career path.[*] I saw in Moishe a person with a biblically tough-minded reality about him that I did not often see in others in the ministry.

From the start, one of Moishe's gifts was his ability to encourage others to exercise their own gifts. Part of that encouragement was his genuine appreciation for what others could do.

Although the LA work was going smoothly, strange things began to happen. Moishe's records showed inconsistencies, and rumors sprang up here and there. Moishe felt that people were starting to doubt his credibility, if not his sanity. He could not imagine what had been happening to his files, until, as he later described it, "I was eating dinner in our kitchen when a voice beyond myself came to me, and I heard myself saying, 'All these troubles—rumors, missing bills, and messed-up records—have come because our office is being

---

[*] In 1972, Darwin and his wife, Carolyn, went with Africa Inland Mission (AIM) to fill the need for an artist at Inland Press in Mwanza, Tanzania, East Africa, where they served for thirty-two years.

burglarized, and the burglar is Joe, and tonight he's going to break in for the last time and then burn the building down.'"

Joe (name changed for purposes of this book) was about Moishe's age, and they had first met through Hannah Wago in Denver. Eventually, Joe came to LA and became affiliated with the ABMJ and with Moishe. Moishe didn't know the man well; he did know that he was a tough negotiator and was always looking for angles to receive benefits from the mission.

When Moishe said that Joe was the culprit, it literally came out of the blue, but once the words were out of his mouth, he did not doubt their veracity. He asked Darwin and another man he'd been training, Harry Jacobson, if they would take turns standing watch over the office that night.

Darwin arrived after midnight to relieve Harry, who had been hiding in the closet in Moishe's office. Darwin went to the chapel and stretched out beneath a pew. Sure enough, about 2:00 a.m., he heard a soft thud upstairs as someone came in through a classroom window and dropped to the floor. Then came the sound of footsteps on the stairs. Dar held his breath as he heard the office door open; he waited a few moments, then silently crept out from under the pew and surprised Joe, who was going through the files with a flashlight.

After a brief tussle, Joe became docile. Darwin phoned Moishe, who called the police. Moishe did not press charges, and Joe never returned.

Once again, God had shown himself faithful to reveal critical information in a timely way. These incidents occurred now and then throughout Moishe's life. He never made the knowledge of them part of his public ministry, but they made a deep impression on him and contributed to his trust in God.

God's little intrusions into Moishe's life were like a series of brush strokes. It was as though God were painting a picture, showing Moishe that whatever the circumstances, trust and obedience were key elements in the destiny that God had designed for him.

Ben and Rose at house on Federal Blvd in Denver

Rose Rosen 1927

(above left and above) Moishe and Ceil's wedding, August 27, 1950

(above right) En route to honeymoon

(left) Moishe and Baby Lyn

(above left) Moishe's graduation photo from Northeastern Bible Institute

(above right) Ceil street preaching in Manhattan

(right) Moishe street preaching in Manhattan

(top) Rosens 1960 left to right: Lyn, Moishe, Ruth and Ceil

(left) Moishe in his high priest costume during LA ministry with ABMJ

(above) Moishe and Daniel Fuchs

(top left) Moishe at Jesus Joy Rally at Felt Forum in New York City's Madison Square Garden, 1972

(top right and below) Moishe at one of the early Jews for Jesus demonstrations

Moishe giving a broadside tract to a Berkeley student early 70s

San Francisco's Mayor Alioto receiving a broadside from Moishe in the same era

NINETEEN

Salesmanship is no substitute for a Spirit-led ministry.

—MOISHE ROSEN

It was summer of 1961 and Lyn, not quite eleven, was happily walking with Patti Ryan, her very good friend, and one of six siblings who lived next door. They were on their way to their favorite drugstore—a great place to buy lots of candy without spending much. At the store, they decided that they would each trade half of whatever they bought with the other, but there were so many choices! They carefully studied the shelves laden with colorfully wrapped treats before finally making their selections. Then they decided to browse in one of the five and dime stores before going home.

As they wandered through the aisles of the second store, the girls were having a hard time ignoring their bags of candy. Soon they were huddled together, each carefully transferring half her candy into the other one's bag. Just as they were finishing the delicate operation, the store manager came up from behind.

"Girls," he said in a severe tone, "do you know that there's a word for what you're doing?"

They looked up at him, startled and confused.

"It's called shoplifting" he reprimanded, "which is the same as stealing."

The girls hastily explained that they had bought the candy at another store.

"Then where are your receipts?" he demanded. When the girls produced them, he seemed almost as angry as before and ordered them out of the store.

When Moishe came home Lyn and Patti told him all about the mean man who had accused them of shoplifting, and how it sure was a good thing they had kept their receipts.

Moishe nodded. "And did he apologize when you showed them to him?"

"No," Lyn replied. "He was still mad and told us to leave."

Moishe frowned. "Ceil?" he called out to her in the other room, "How long till supper's ready?"

"About half an hour" she called back. "Why?"

"I need to take these girls to the store," he said, "But we'll be back in time for dinner." Then, turning to his daughter and her friend, he said, "I'll drive you back there. You both deserve an apology."

Patti looked at her friend's father apprehensively. "Um, Mr. Rosen, I gotta see if it's okay with my mom. I'm s'posed to go home now."

Apparently Mrs. Ryan didn't mind because a few minute later Patti met Lyn at the car and Moishe drove them back to the store where he asked to speak to the manager.

If the manager recognized the two girls, he did a good job of hiding it. He focused instead on their rather large, stern-faced companion and asked, "May I help you?"

"Yes," Moishe replied. "Earlier today you accused these young ladies of shoplifting. If you thought they were stealing, I can understand why you confronted them. But when they produced sales receipts you continued to treat them as though they were guilty by asking them to leave the store. Now I think that you owe them an apology."

The manager swallowed hard but didn't flinch as he returned the larger man's gaze. He cleared his throat. "I see." He glanced at the girls. "And I do apologize for the misunderstanding."

His tone was cool and perfunctory, but Moishe had made his point. He nodded to the man then smiled at the girls. "Let's go home." And, as predicted, they were back in time for supper.

———

Regarding the above incident, Lyn later recalled, "Dad's insistence on that apology made us feel important; the incident stands out as a reminder of how Dad respected us and cared for our feelings."

The incident was typical of Moishe's cut-and-dried way of dealing with wrongdoing. Having just gotten home from work he didn't particularly want to go to the store, nor was he fond of confrontations. Still he was compelled to settle the matter quickly and have done with it.

He was protective, not only of his own family, but of any friend. Whether it was a matter of principle or a matter of pride (perhaps two parts of the first to one part of the latter), Moishe was determined that anyone who trifled with those he cared for would have to answer to him.

The confidence and authority to act quickly and decisively seemed to come naturally to him. He had the same confidence and authority in working with people at the mission, but that had developed over time.

The move to the center on Lexington had been a challenge; the new building multiplied Moishe's opportunities as well as his responsibilities. Rooms for additional children's classes meant finding more teachers to expand the program, and there was a large fellowship hall that could accommodate far more people than he'd been used to teaching at the weekly Bible study on Pico. This multipurpose room was adjacent to a large kitchen. Moishe, who always loved good food, enjoyed it even more when sharing it with others. So besides the regular Bible study, he instituted occasional family nights, where in addition to learning from Scripture, people could share food and fellowship.

Now Moishe also had a staff to supervise. When the ABMJ bought the building from the church group, they inherited two of the church's workers. Janice Dundas, who later became Janice Vanderslick, was hired as a secretary. Elizabeth Taylor, a seminary graduate and youth worker, stayed on to help with the mission's afternoon "Sunday school" until she met and married her husband, Pastor Paul Larson. Over the years, the ABMJ sent Moishe four or five people to train. Once again, Moishe became a boss not by choice, but by circumstance.

Moishe's life and ministry were greatly enhanced by many who came alongside to help him. Albert Vanderslick, a graduate of Talbot Seminary, also became an important part of the ministry. When both Janice and Liz married and eventually left the mission's employ, Fay Cohen came to help with the typing. Mama Cohen, as everyone called her, was a Jewish grandmother and a faithful follower of Jesus with a warm smile and an even warmer embrace. Mama Cohen also helped in the kitchen before meetings.*

Eventually Leslie Shapiro (who looked like Elizabeth Taylor—the movie star, not the youth worker) came to work as Moishe's full-time secretary. In those early days at Lexington and Lodi, Leslie helped Moishe build the filing system that he continued to use throughout his ministry. When Leslie married her husband, Harry Wright, in 1966, Moishe co-officiated at their wedding. Linda Caldwell took over the position vacated by Leslie.

Planning and supervising other people's work were never Moishe's strong suit, and he knew it. Correcting what was wrong always seemed the most natural way for Moishe to help people do what was right, stemming as it did from

---

* Mama Cohen's "Easy Brisket" recipe eventually turned up in the *Jews for Jesus Family Cookbook*, available through Purple Pomegranate Productions, http://store.jewsforjesus.org/.

both his upbringing and his personality. Reflecting on his time in LA, he said, "I never liked being a boss. I never sat down with somebody to plan out what they should be doing. I've always preferred to work with people who know what they should be doing. And if they don't know exactly how to do it, I'd rather troubleshoot it. I knew that I was supposed to be regulating them in some way, but I never did get the hang of that." Some might say that later in his career, Moishe overcompensated for that shortcoming by regularizing the work and stressing accountability to the point that people, at times, felt overmanaged. But he never saw himself that way.

On the other hand, Moishe felt that he had much greater success with volunteers. Albert Stoltey and his wife, Muriel, were prime examples of the wonderful people who freely gave their time, energy, and resources to build the work. Moishe met the Stolteys through Bette Jacques while the ministry was still on West Pico. He recalled:

> Al Stoltey called to talk about what we might do together. He was an engineer and a Dallas Seminary graduate. Muriel had a nursing degree from Wheaton College. They had two daughters, Janet and Lynne, about the same age as ours, and the daughters became good friends. They [Al and Muriel] had been Christians for a lot longer than Ceil and I, and both were better qualified to do the work than I was. But they just came alongside and upheld me. Al helped with the outdoor meetings, led the singing at the worship services, and occasionally sang a solo in what was obviously a highly trained voice. Muriel helped with the children's ministry by teaching Bible stories, songs, and memory verses.
>
> So I learned to work with volunteers. I had quite a few. The Stolteys continued to be the backbone in that work—even after we left LA. What I learned about volunteers was, first, you had to give more of yourself to them. And second, they were highly motivated—often more motivated than the professionals.

Despite his mild stammer, Moishe's reputation as a teacher and preacher began to grow. (One friend, Diane Hart, commented years later that whereas Moishe sometimes stammered in conversation, "he never missed a beat" when preaching.) He received recognition and acclaim from the ABMJ and was invited to speak at their conferences. People who came to his Bible classes or who heard him speak in church often invited others to hear him. He estimated that by 1963, he was speaking just about every other Sunday.

The ministry was going mostly well. Of course not everything Moishe tried was a success. Commenting on what he tried that didn't work so well, Moishe said that he knew that the telephone could be used for evangelism, but when he tried to communicate by phone, he did a poor job. Whether it was his stammer or his shyness, he never enjoyed initiating a phone call, even for social purposes.

Perhaps a more significant failure was Moishe's brief foray into the world of counseling. He and Al Vanderslick completed a course of study in counseling at the American Institute of Family Relations. Moishe then put a notice to that effect in the bulletin for the regular Sunday afternoon meeting at the mission center, and he also announced from the pulpit that he would be available for counseling. Three people sought his counseling help. He recalled,

> I appreciated the insights that this course in counseling gave me. But I concluded that all that counselors can give is feedback based on what the client has told them, which may or may not provide an adequate basis for understanding the problem. And I guess I should have a higher view of it,* but I view my own attempt at counseling as one of my failures.
>
> For one thing, I felt that my reasons for wanting to do it were wrong. I wanted to draw people so that I could minister to them, and I felt that the people would be more drawn to a counselor than a Bible teacher.
>
> Of the three people who came for counseling, I only continued to see one, and that was a man who was basically having trouble getting a job, and I found I could be of some help to him. But I discovered that I really didn't want to be involved in any kind of counseling. I got out of the counseling mode and I got into the ministry mode where I could point to the Bible and say, "Thus says the Lord . . ."

One adjunct to Moishe's counseling studies was the battery of analytical tests required of the students. Moishe's test scores confirmed what others had told

---

* The caveat, "I guess I should have a higher view of it," might best be interpreted as Moishe's recognition that some Christian counselors genuinely help their clients. But he felt that the proliferation of counseling degrees rather than theology degrees from Bible schools and seminaries was not healthy, and that the potential for damage in this field was very high.

him—that he had chronic low-grade depression. Understanding this depression sheds significant light on Moishe's outlook and how he operated. He described his depression this way:

> A low-grade depression involves a certain pessimism. It is almost a fear of being optimistic and of being disappointed. I'd rather be pessimistic and be [pleasantly] surprised. . . .
>
> I would not say that I "suffer from depression." People with this [low-grade] condition can smile, can enjoy themselves and other people—the overall outlook is not exactly bleak, but, you know, you go to bed at night and you find yourself thinking, *Thank God, no catastrophes happened today.*
>
> My depression has more to do with expectations than a particularly painful feeling. My enthusiasm is a quiet enthusiasm. My optimism is a "maybe" thing. . . . Depression doesn't keep me from enjoying what is at hand. It keeps me from expecting or anticipating the enjoyment. And many things turn out better than I expect. . . .
>
> That lack of expectation has led me to be cautious in everything. Sometimes it has cost me joy. But in a sense, the depression represents my character or, at least, feeds into my character.

It is easy to equate optimism with faith (God will provide) and pessimism with a lack thereof. Moishe was always optimistic about the big picture. He could enthusiastically proclaim his faith that "Jesus is coming again." He could experience certain joy in knowing that whatever difficulties might come about, "All things work together for good to those who love him [Jesus] and are called according to his purposes" (Rom. 8:28). And if he knew that God was leading him to go here or expand there, he could have faith that God would provide. But though Moishe prayed and sought God's guidance, the times when he knew (and told others) that a particular decision was God's will were few.

Again, what he termed *practical piety* was a far more common aspect in his life and work than the occasional supernatural leadings. The infrequent instances when he knew God was speaking to him were more often warnings than encouragement.

Encouragement usually came in everyday ways, as a result of accomplishing the work that God apparently chose to bless. One of Moishe's greatest satisfactions during the ten years he ministered in Southern California was his part in developing more cooperative efforts among various ministries and ministers.

When Moishe arrived in Los Angeles in 1957, he didn't know what to expect from other ministries. At Northeastern he'd been taught that when a missionary comes to a new place, he or she should meet with others on the field and ask their help in fitting in with the work already being done.

When Moishe began making such visits, he discovered that various missions were in competition. They competed not only for funds but also for the attention and allegiance of Jewish people who might attend their meetings. Moishe recalled,

> One mission invited me to speak, but their representative told me, "I don't want you to take any names and addresses of any people you meet here." If I'd started out with the attitude that everybody should share everything since we're all here to do the same work, I would have been disappointed.
>
> When I saw this competition, I realized that other ministries had interests to protect. My orientation changed, and I looked for ways to cooperate that showed I understood their interests. Instead of being disappointed when some were unfriendly, I was delighted to discover that some were very friendly and received me well.

Moishe was not the only one who was eager to foster a spirit of cooperation. Ron Fleming, a Presbyterian minister whose mother was Jewish, was like-minded. Fleming had been raised as a Jew and was deeply interested in the work of Jewish evangelism. He suggested getting the leaders of various missions together for a joint day of prayer and fasting on Yom Kippur.

So it was that seven or eight men, including Moishe, Ron Fleming, Marvin Jacobs, Emanuel Gitel, and Abe Schneider, got together at South Hollywood Presbyterian Church on the Day of Atonement to pray for the work of the gospel among Jewish people. Hank Vigeveno, then pastor of the church, was a Dutch Jew, and he also participated.

Moishe recalled it as a wonderful time of prayer and unity. It formed the basis for several cooperative efforts. For the next three or four years, this core group brought their constituents together annually for a Christ in the Passover banquet, a youth picnic, a Hannukah/Christmas event, and a high holiday service.

Moishe was doing what he loved best—meeting and sharing the gospel with Jewish people and helping others to do the same. He recalled, "By the middle sixties, I was recognized as somewhat of an expert in the field. If someone wanted to know how to do something in Jewish evangelism, they came to me. I could pretty much tell them what to do and how to do it."

Thinking about whether his experience in sales made him a good missionary, Moishe had quite a bit to say:

> In sales, there is an opener, a presentation, and a closer. There is a parallel when witnessing [telling others what Jesus has done], but there are important differences.
>
> When you go to a car lot, the salesman who presents the car to you is different from the one who closes the deal. Some salesmen are just closers, and they have a whole technique that involves wearing you out. Now maybe not everyone does that, but many do and that's one way that salesmanship differs from ministry.
>
> Basically, you [missionaries] look for people who are open and willing to discuss spiritual matters. You give an opening statement to many different people—"Let me ask you this, who do you think Jesus is?" If somebody says, "I don't care," or "I don't want to talk about Jesus," you don't go any further.
>
> I never had any sense of personal achievement when people received Christ. I never felt that it was because I gave such a good presentation—there was something beyond me that was moving people. Either the Holy Spirit was at work to move them, or he was not at work. . . .
>
> When you present the gospel, the thing that keeps most people from the Lord, even when they are interested, is the belief that it is not possible for them to receive Jesus—If they'll articulate that, the answer is always the same—God empowers us, don't you think God can take care of that? An evangelist can give reassurance and examples from the Bible and personal experience about what God will do. An evangelist can show people the possibilities they would not otherwise see. . . .
>
> It is very important to avoid becoming a spiritual scalp hunter, running up a score, "I got another three souls this week—you know." We didn't get anything. It's God that won the person to himself, and we were there to help.

Moishe always encouraged missionaries to invite people who were tracking with the message and seemed to believe the gospel to pray to receive the Lord.

That simply means that a person declares to God that he or she believes the gospel and trusts God to forgive his or her sin based on Jesus' sacrificial death and resurrection. The prayer usually is brief and includes an understanding that to receive forgiveness in Christ implies a trust and surrender of one's life to become his disciple.

This prayer, or profession of faith, is (or at least can be) the beginning of a new life. But Moishe was always cautious about making such prayers the point at which he would rejoice. He would rejoice whenever he had a good opportunity to explain the gospel, to do the duty God had called him to do, but he did not rejoice any more than usual when someone prayed to receive Jesus. Moishe explained,

> My particular joy has been that people I have forgotten from years and years ago, get in touch with me and say, "Do you remember me, you prayed with me, you led me to the Lord," or "you helped me along." And when I hear that years after I ministered to the person, I always rejoice.

For example, in the year 2000, Jews for Jesus received an e-mail in response to a publication they mail to Jewish believers in Jesus:

> About 35 years ago Moishe, or Martin as I knew him, was speaking at the Bel Air Presbyterian Church. ...[M]y wife-to-be and I met with Martin who led me to believe in Y'shua. It's been a long time and I would look forward to seeing him again. Are there any articles or newsletters written by him? If so I would like to see them. Thanks.
>
> Al & Judy

Even more encouraging than those voices from the past are those of people who remained in contact with Moishe since his ministry to them in the 60s.

Once such person is Sam Hart, who contributed the following descriptions of Moishe as he had known him for decades:

> He couldn't have been more than thirty years old, maybe not even that, but people looked up to him. He just had a wisdom and a feeling of being approachable and being spiritual. I think that I could discuss anything with [him and] get an answer that had both wisdom and was godly but never "holier than thou." . . .

I knew where I stood with him, he knew where he stood with me, you know. If he disagreed with me about something, he would tell me—and I would tell him, too! He was concerned for me and the family as a dear friend and when I shared concerns, he would contemplate, and then say, "Let's pray about that."

Sam and his family were among many people who felt they had greatly benefited by Moishe's ministry. Daniel Fuchs, recognizing Moishe's success in Los Angeles, wanted to bring his vision and expertise back to the mission's headquarters in New York City. He felt that Moishe could organize, even revolutionize, the training program and the general missionary work. Ceil recalled with some embarrassment, "Daniel Fuchs came out from time to time to see how the work was going. And one time he sat down with Moishe and me and talked with us about the possibility of moving to New York. I remember being a little nonplussed about it. And I actually had the audacity to say to him, 'Wow, that's a big step. You can't move people around like you move chess pieces.' I was probably overstepping myself to say that to the boss. But he wasn't *my* boss; he was Moishe's boss."

Nevertheless, Ceil had determined long before then that she would never stand in the way of Moishe's calling. Once she saw that the plans were in motion, she acquiesced, though she was heartbroken to leave LA, along with the friends and the life she had built there over ten years.

Moishe also had reservations, but for different reasons, as will be seen in the following chapters. Yet the promotion that Daniel wanted him to take in 1967 was not one that Moishe could easily refuse without appearing to be disloyal or disinterested in the mission that had invested so much in him.

TWENTY

A good friend is one that tells you that you need to zip your fly or,
if you're a woman, that your slip is showing.

—MOISHE ROSEN

Moishe was enthusiastic about the Fellowship of Christian Testimonies to the Jews. (FCTJ), an organization of professionals concerned about Jewish evangelism.* As he prepared for their biannual convention, held that year at Nyack Missionary College, he wondered what would come of the day's deliberations.

He'd been asked to chair the program committee for the conference, a first for him with this group. He'd met with the program committee many months prior to the event and particularly appreciated the way everyone wanted to work together to have the best possible program, even if it meant that none of them would be on the speaking platform.

During those planning stages, one young man, Lyle Murphy, had suggested: "You know, it would be very good for us to hear from a rabbi. I would like to see us invite one to speak on the image of the missionary in the Jewish community."

Moishe had quickly glanced around the room to see if someone would voice the obvious truth—that any rabbi who allowed himself to be announced as a speaker on that program would be committing professional suicide. Even if such a rabbi stood up and berated the group, the fact that he had dignified their existence by coming to speak would be a perpetual black mark against him. Moishe felt certain of that and would have almost guaranteed that no rabbi would accept such an invitation.

Knowing looks on the other committee members' faces confirmed that they had similar thoughts, though no one said it aloud. When the silence began to grow uncomfortable, Moishe cleared his throat and said, "Uh, I think it's a good idea, but I don't know of a rabbi who would want to do it. If you can find such a rabbi, I'll reserve a good place for him on the program."

Even though Murphy had been unable to procure a rabbi, he'd come

---

*In Moishe's opinion, it was a precursor to the Lausanne Consultation on Jewish Evangelism, which came together in the 1980s.

surprisingly close. So, as Moishe strode down the campus path toward the conference, he was looking forward to meeting Dr. Sidney Lawrence, director of the Jewish Community Relations Council of Kansas City. Dr. Lawrence had attended a yeshiva and studied to be a rabbi, but apparently had never accepted ordination.* Nevertheless, he was an exemplary servant of the Jewish community, a man with the courage of his convictions—and he'd accepted the challenge to speak to this conference of missionaries and missionary leaders.

Moishe was conversing with some colleagues outside the meeting room when he was struck by an aroma alien to the carefully regulated alcohol- and tobacco-free campus. Cigar smoke. Dr. Lawrence had arrived.

Moishe introduced himself, remarking that he had been born in Kansas City, though raised in Denver. Dr. Lawrence nodded and easily engaged in good-natured small talk. His personality was such that everyone he interacted with would have been happy to call him friend. He circulated among the conference participants, always enveloped in a cloud of smoke and continuously wondering aloud where the ashtrays were. No one explained that to him, though someone made sure he had a paper cup into which he could tap the ashes.

At last the meeting was called to order and the room grew quiet as people took their seats. More than a little curious about Dr. Lawrence's thoughts regarding the image of missionaries in the Jewish community, Moishe was glad when the preliminaries were finally over.

Moishe was not surprised when Dr. Lawrence asked that the recorder used to tape the sessions be turned off. Then he began what was probably the briefest address ever given to the FCTJ. He thanked the group for inviting him. Moishe immediately sensed that he had done quite a bit of public speaking and knew how to use his voice. He leaned forward, eager to hear what would come next. The essence of Sidney Lawrence's message was as follows:

> You seem to be nice people, but I'm afraid I'm going to have to disappoint you. The topic you gave me is one that's impossible for me to address, and furthermore, I don't think anyone else could tell you much about it. You want to know about the image of the missionary in the Jewish community. *You don't have an image!* I remember years and years ago that at every major

---

* According to Moishe's recollection, Dr. Lawrence had not gone through with the ordination because he was not certain that God existed.

conference I attended—and there were many—there was an occasional workshop on "the missionary menace." But in the past twenty years, there have been no such workshops. If you had any image at all, you would be seen as a threat. There would be all kinds of committee meetings, task forces, and discussions about how to deal with the missionary menace. I don't say that to hurt your feelings but to tell you the truth.

The rest of his comments were equally brief:

So far as missionary work is concerned, I think of two Yiddish words. The first one is *narishkeit*, which means "foolishness." That you should attempt to come to us Jews and tell us about our Messiah is *narishkeit*. That you should tell us that somebody died for our sins and rose again from the dead is *narishkeit*.

But it's not only *narishkeit*, it's *chutzpah*. *Chutzpah* means "effrontery," and I must ask, Who are you to tell us anything? Believe me, if there were anything to it, the rabbis would have told us that Jesus was the Messiah. I'm sorry to disappoint you, but I have nothing further to say.*

With that, Sidney Lawrence left the podium.

The audience was stunned. Moishe found it difficult to listen to the rest of the proceedings. Lawrence's words, spoken without hostility had hit him hard.

After the conference, the program planning committee met to discuss the speakers, how people had responded and what to present to the next program planning committee. Moishe presided over the dozen or so missionaries, keenly aware of the murmurs that signaled the discussion had unofficially begun before he called the meeting to order.

If Moishe had been hit hard by what Lawrence had to say, he was even more discouraged by how many of the missionary leaders responded. It seemed as though each had his own way of denying Dr. Lawrence's assessment.

Doesn't anyone else realize that Sid Lawrence was right? Moishe wondered. *Most Jews are not hearing the gospel from those of us who have been called to tell it!* It was a painful truth, but now he realized that he had suspected it for some time—on the whole, Jewish missionaries didn't count for much. Even in LA,

---

* The session was not recorded; this is not a transcript nor is it intended to represent a direct quote. It represents Moishe's best recollection of what Dr. Lawrence said, which so impacted Moishe that he repeated the gist of the message countless times throughout his ministry.

where he'd hit a good stride and was seeing results, Moishe did not consider himself wildly successful. Yet apparently that moderate measure of success was greater than most were seeing. Why else had Daniel given him this promotion?

Moishe appreciated and liked his colleagues, but he was startled and repulsed to hear the leaders deny Lawrence's statement. He was aghast at their intransigence and shocked by the realization that he was headed down the same path.

Why can't they see the truth? Why can't they admit that we are failing? They can't bring about the necessary changes, he thought. *They are mostly serving as custodians of something begun by others. And what makes me think that I am any different?*

———

These events might not have affected Moishe in quite the same way had they occurred within his first year back on the East Coast. He arrived in New York with some sense of optimism. He had built the work in LA just as Daniel Fuchs had hoped he would, and in 1965, he was named director of recruiting and training. Presumably it was Daniel who had convinced the mission's board of directors to transfer the entire training program to New York City, a decision that precipitated Moishe's move to New York in the summer of 1967. In addition to recruiting and training, Moishe was appointed missionary in charge of Headquarters District.

Moishe viewed his promotion with a combination of eagerness and uncertainty. He was excited about the prospect of returning to New York, the best possible city for reaching out to Jewish people as far as he was concerned. And he was nostalgic regarding the place and people he'd met as a Bible school student. Daniel's enthusiasm and confidence were also gratifying. But Moishe was a cautious person and would not take much for granted. Before he agreed to the transfer, he pressed Daniel to tell him more about his future role.

Daniel responded somewhat vaguely, and this discomfited Moishe. In New York, there were a lot of bosses and a number of staff with more seniority than he had, and Moishe wondered if he, as a veteran yet unmistakably less senior missionary, would have the authority to carry out his new responsibilities. Accordingly, he asked Daniel if the board of directors had approved his appointment to the position. Daniel assured him that it had and, at Moishe's request, showed him the minutes of that meeting. Moishe saw a line about moving the training operations to New York; it didn't mention him by name, and it didn't convince him that he would be given a free rein in his operations.

He had met a number of wise and godly people in his travels, particularly among some of the pastors whose pulpits he had shared. One was Warren Hultgren, pastor of First Baptist Church in Tulsa. "I explained my concerns and asked his advice about taking the position," Moishe recalled, "and he advised that if I could, I should avoid going—but he didn't think that I could. I was starting to realize that the administration in New York was complicated, and Dr. Hultgren's advice made me wonder more than ever if I was getting myself into something that was over my head."

Moishe secured a promise from Daniel Fuchs: if the position in New York did not work out, he could move back to California and resume his efforts in the field. The agreement was that in that event, he would not return to LA, but would go to the San Francisco Bay area. *If* his new position didn't work out. Certainly Moishe hoped that it *would* work out, and he arrived in New York ready to dig in and do all he could to make it work.

It was a big move; the distance from home and friends in LA could hardly have been greater. His older daughter, a high schooler, was attached to a close circle of girls whose company she would miss. However, she was outgoing, and Moishe knew that she would make friends easily. The younger was in a pre-adolescent funk and not very happy with school. While Moishe was unaware of this, he did know that she could be perfectly content curled up with a good book in a room by herself, so he was not too concerned.

The move was probably hardest for Ceil. Though shy and reserved with those she didn't know, over time she had formed deep attachments. She did not want to leave the friends she'd come to love and was not thrilled at the prospect of meeting new people. But when Moishe reminded Ceil that she would be within three and a half hours of her family in Boston, she was consoled and even excited by the prospect.

Daniel Fuchs had encouraged the Rosens to look for a home in a suburb called New City. He and his wife, Muriel, lived there, and Moishe liked the idea of settling in the same town, though not in the same neighborhood. He and Ceil found a lovely split-level home in an upper-middle-class neighborhood consisting largely of families whose children were similar in age to their own.

Despite his uncertainties, Moishe arrived at his new job with zeal and determination. In addition to training, his assignment involved preaching at the Sunday afternoon services whenever he was in town, teaching Tuesday night Bible study, and visiting Jewish seekers. It also included the remodeling of the West Seventy-second Street property.

Daniel Fuchs wanted Moishe to oversee the project, but Harold Pretlove made it clear that he was ultimately in charge of the remodeling and that Moishe was to work under him. More than ten years after taking what had begun as a temporary position, he was still the boss. However, that chapter in the mission's history was drawing to a close—due in part, Moishe felt, to something he later regretted.

Moishe had known that the remodeling would require a renewal of the building permits. He mentioned this to Daniel, who told him to have the architect take the matter directly to Harold Pretlove, who, after all, had instructed Moishe not to speak directly to the architect or to say anything to him that he had not first cleared with Pretlove.

Moishe felt it was obvious that Pretlove would drop the ball. He was not surprised when Harold Pretlove's neglect of this matter and the ensuing cost to the mission proved to be the "last straw." The board of directors eventually appointed Daniel Fuchs, who was already in charge of the missionaries, to lead in Pretlove's place.

In retrospect, Moishe felt that leaving the matter between Pretlove and the architect had proved treacherous, and that both he and Daniel were to blame. *Treacherous* might seem a harsh word for what others may describe as "letting nature take its course." But in Moishe's thinking, even if technically it was between Pretlove and the architect, morally it was his duty to inform the boss that the building permits had expired. Moishe concluded, "If you know that [not saying] something will hurt the organization in which you serve, and you decide not to say it, then you've done something wrong."

Reflecting on the incident, Moishe also said, "Treachery, when given a foothold in an organization, eventually becomes the usual way of doing things." Years later, Moishe felt that both he and Daniel eventually faced certain consequences for the way in which the situation had been handled.

When the remodeling was complete, Moishe was especially pleased with the sanctuary. Attendance for the 3:30 worship services increased to about 120, the maximum the chapel could hold. While Moishe usually gave the sermon, every few weeks he asked Rachmiel Frydland, a true scholar of the Bible and of rabbinical writings, to preach.

Moishe had never lost his childhood sense of reverence for holy places or holy books and how they were set apart from ordinary things. Accordingly he was upset to find that the chapel was doubling as a "warehouse" (his word) on a regular basis. The mission mailed out a publication called "The Chosen People" to some 60,000 of their constituents every month. Whoever was in charge of the mailing had been accustomed to piling the mailbags full of magazines into the chapel until it was time to bring them to the post office.

To Moishe, this was a matter of great irreverence. He complained about the dirty gray canvas mailbags filling up the aisles of the little chapel, and in some cases, being deposited on top of the brand-new chapel seats. He pointed out that there was plenty of room to store the mailbags in the basement. He complained of this three months in a row. When, during the third month he came in one Sunday to see the mailbags still there not long before the service was to start, he threw them all down the stairwell. Bags burst open, bundles that had been put in zip code order broke apart, and it was quite a mess.

Daniel Fuchs roundly scolded Moishe over the incident. It seemed that the person who had put the bags in the chapel had never been told that it was wrong. Moishe recalled, "The authority structure was like a maze—I had to tell so-and-so who then told so-and-so and eventually the person concerned would hear it from so-and-so." But sometimes things fell through the cracks. This frustrated Moishe who believed that the purpose of authority is to facilitate things and to see that the standards and quality are maintained. He felt that some people were using authority as a means of dominance—not Daniel Fuchs, but some of the people under him.

Apparently the concerns Moishe had had about bureaucracy and authority before he left Los Angeles had not been misplaced, and that was discouraging. However, as unpleasant as the entire incident was, it did put an end to the use of the chapel for warehousing magazines and mailbags.

A bright spot in Moishe's ministry with the ABMJ in New York was the training program. The mission was already conducting many good classes when he arrived. Dr. Henry Heydt, founder of Lancaster Bible College, taught Hebrew and was the resident scholar. Rachmiel Frydland also had great academic stature. Charles Kalisky taught Hebrew, and veteran Coney Island missionary Hilda Koser taught child evangelism. Moishe respected these people and considered them tremendous resources. However, he added a level of practical experience to the largely academic course work.

His first training class included such notables as Arthur Katz, a Brooklyn-born Jew who was as controversial as he was charismatic. Katz finished his training and did well with the mission; however before long, he began his own evangelistic ministry. Another candidate was Eliezer Urbach, a Jewish believer who, after barely escaping Poland in time to survive the Holocaust, came to faith in Jesus in Brazil. Eliezer served with the ABMJ (later Chosen People) for years. He pastored messianic congregations, mentored Jewish believers in Jesus, and is considered a patriarch of the messianic Jewish movement.

Dan and Arlene Rigney, graduates of Moody Bible Institute, took part in the training program in the fall of 1968. They recalled,

> He [Rosen] taught us street boldness and how to do street preaching on Broadway in New York City. He was also influenced, although he didn't know him directly, by Joseph Hoffman Cohn . . . Moishe would teach us principles that he thought that Joseph Hoffman Cohn would have used as well.
>
> He loved to keep us awake in class by shooting his cap gun off, particularly if he spotted someone who'd fallen asleep. He had us eat schmaltz herring* and he said we probably wouldn't like it. But everyone did like it.
>
> Sometimes during class we would sit at the window on the sixth floor and look at people walking by and Moishe would say, "Now, try to imagine what this person might be thinking today."
>
> He was the first to introduce us to Japanese food, he was the first to take us down to Katz's deli on the Lower East Side.
>
> He also enjoyed teasing people. But if he ever said anything outrageous and you asked if he was for real, he'd always confess if he was teasing.

Despite his mischief making, Moishe took the training very seriously; yet some in the mission did not regard all of his practices favorably. Moishe was aware of the disapproval and looked for someone who could be a sounding board. Avi Brickner, a colleague and close friend, was ministering in Boston with Israel's Remnant during those years. Moishe invited him to see the training program for himself. Avi recollected:

> The exercises that day were aimed at preparing the group for the emotional aspects of intense opposition that they would face in street evangelism.
>
> Moishe tried to stimulate the trainees to express their own extreme anger . . . but the trainees had a very hard time expressing anger spontaneously.

---

* The herring was part of training for purposes of acculturation—there were many non-Jews in the class and Moishe wanted them to be able to eat what might be served to them in a Jewish home without hesitation.

Suddenly Moishe arose from his seated position, took his chair in hand, and with heated angry words began to smash the chair to pieces on the floor. The intensity of his expression shocked most of those in the group, and one woman burst into tears and fled from the room.

A second exercise that day involved dealing with harassment when one was giving a street testimony. Moishe acted as the opposition, and several were asked to give testimonies. Moishe was very effective in unsettling those who tried. He asked me to step in and give it a try. He became particularly vociferous with me, and the louder he got, the softer I got. This response tended to wear him down, while I remained fairly calm. It was the very response, it turned out, that he wanted to demonstrate. We had not really devised this beforehand. . . .

I learned later that . . . Moishe wanted to use my presence and observation to verify the psychological soundness of his methods of training to meet opposition because of my then present involvement in graduate work in psychology and counseling. Moishe told me later that he thought it far better that missionaries were conditioned beforehand to face opposition and anger rather than to have it come upon them suddenly and be unprepared.

Avi Brickner's relationship with Moishe spanned more than four decades, but they were never closer than during those three years that Moishe served with the ABMJ in New York. Years later Avi recalled,

Moishe always had a desire to effect creative and positive change in both the organization with which he was working and also in the entire field of Jewish evangelism. Therefore, he always seemed to seek ways and channels through which he would be an influence for such change. He did this through personal networking with individuals, through seeking to influence the direction of the FCTJ and through a willingness to lend a helping hand to boost the ministries of other individuals and organizations that he thought worthy of assistance. I had the impression that he never sought to guard what he thought valuable and keep it for himself or his own organization, but to share it with others and other organizations so that they might benefit.

He had been trying to recruit me to join the ministry of the ABMJ. I began to share with him how discouraged I was . . . and how unfruitful I felt myself to be in the ministry of Jewish evangelism. I told him that I had decided to leave the field and that I had received an offer to become a teacher in a private school in Connecticut when I had completed my graduate work. . . .

He quietly remarked (these may not be his exact words), "I think that the poorest efforts of some people who may think themselves failures are better than the best efforts that some other people can make." Those words went deep into my heart so that I never forgot them. I felt that I was hearing not just the words, but the heart of a friend who truly valued me.

Avi was the kind of quality friend Moishe truly did value, as were many others he met through the work in New York. Yet even as new friendships were developing, his relationship with Daniel Fuchs seemed to have cooled, and Moishe did not know why. He thought there might have been some disappointment on Daniel's side concerning their social life. From Moishe's perspective, "The Fuchses led a quiet life and socialized quietly," whereas "the Rosens tended to have a younger, more energetic circle of friends." As time went by, he perhaps did not seek out Daniel's company as much as he might or ought to have done.

Moishe was also less and less content with the status quo. The large variety of gospel tracts that were available included a few that Moishe found worthwhile, but he dismissed most of the literature as too syrupy, too preachy, or just too far-fetched to engage the interest of most modern Jewish people. He knew that a more current style of literature was needed, but it was easy to sideline his concerns when there was so much to do. His schedule had grown so busy that by his second year in New York, he rarely met with Jewish seekers anymore. Most visits he scheduled were in conjunction with the training. He also served on numerous boards and committees of other organizations and was in demand as a speaker at churches and schools. It is not surprising, then, that some feelings of self-importance were in play during this time.

Three things happened to shock Moishe out of his complacency and orient him toward the ministry that eventually became Jews for Jesus. One was the scenario with Sidney Lawrence, described at the beginning of this chapter. Something changed in Moishe the day that Lawrence spoke, but it was only one turn of the screw. It took two more painful realizations to turn Moishe completely around and and orient him toward the ministry that eventually became Jews for Jesus.

The second turn that helped to shake Moishe loose from his seventh-floor office was the death of his mother, Rose Rosen. His last visit with her was painful, to say the least. Moishe deeply regretted his old promise not to bring up religion, a promise both his parents held him to for the rest of their lives. As he grieved for his mother, he wondered if the Jewish identity he'd grown up with had become somewhat diluted—and that was disturbing.

The third thing that helped launch Moishe into a new stage of ministry was an encounter at Columbia University. Moishe had been asked to address a regional meeting of InterVarsity, a strongly evangelical organization dedicated to helping Christian college students grow in their faith and share that faith with others. Moishe's topic was "Hippies, Radicals, and Revolutionaries."' Moishe got a lot of laughs when he repeated a joke he'd heard defining a hippie as someone who "talks like Tarzan, walks like Jane and smells like Cheetah." But when he finished speaking, Bob Berk, a Jewish social worker who also believed in Jesus as Messiah, confronted him:

"Did you ever smell a hippie?"

"No, I never got close enough" came the wry retort.

"Do you know that a lot of hippies are Jewish? Do you know what they're saying, how they feel? What are you doing to try to talk to these people?"

"I don't want to talk to people who don't want to talk to me." Moishe rarely found himself on the defensive, and he didn't much like it. Who *was* this guy who was challenging his position as the expert on Jewish evangelism? It's not unusual to feel testy in the face of criticism, especially when it's given with zero tact. But Bob Berk seemed oblivious to the testiness and pressed on.

"Well, you're making fun of a group of people you should be trying to reach." And with that accusation, his point hit home.

So began Moishe's long-standing friendship with Bob Berk. Berk—abrasive, unmannerly, and often unkempt—was considered offensive by some, but Moishe valued him as a man whose blunt truthfulness helped to change the course of Jewish evangelism. Moishe's willingness to accept the truth wherever or from whomever it might come had brought him to faith in Jesus to begin with—and now that same willingness was about to radicalize his ministry.

Moishe knew a young Jewish believer in Jesus, Susan Alexander, who was familiar with the hippie counterculture. He told her what Bob Berk had said and how it had troubled him. Susan told Moishe that if he would go to Greenwich Village and "just sit around," he'd find it easy enough to meet and talk with hippies.

Moishe, now considerably overweight and still sporting a crew cut and a skinny tie, began to frequent Manhattan's Washington Square Park on Wednesday afternoons. Most hippies did not judge him by his appearance and would talk to just about anyone who wanted to engage in meaningful conversation. As he interacted, he found that while some simply wanted to enjoy life unfettered from the establishment, many had deeply spiritual values and aspirations.

Next, Moishe began writing his own gospel tracts (he called them "broadsides") to communicate what the traditional tracts could not. He handwrote and illustrated his first broadside, "A Message from Squares," with a simple figure of himself, made up of bulky squares, on the front. Here is its message:

Hey, you with the beard!
We think you are Beautiful.
God likes long hair and beards, too.
He didn't want the Israelites to trim their beards.
Can you just imagine Moses or Elijah with a crew cut?
You are brave to do your own thing.
Most of us don't have the heart to make the scene.
We both want LOVE but we settle for either sex or sermons.
All want Life. Most get a kind of living death called existence.
We try to be the saviors of the world, and we just end up sinning against
    those we want to save.
Maybe Jesus, the real Savior, can save us, give us peace and help us come
    alive, to live and love.

He then quoted John 3:16.

Daniel Fuchs was reluctant to have the mission associated with literature that departed so radically from its conservative image. He didn't want the name of the mission on the pamphlet, though he gave Moishe permission to use the address in case anyone actually responded. Moreover, the mission would not print the tract, but if Moishe wanted to reproduce it, he was welcome to hand it out as an experiment. Moishe decided to use his Yiddish name rather than Martin on the back of the tract, and he instructed the receptionist and secretaries to send anyone who asked to see Moishe Rosen directly to his office.

He wrote more broadsides and handed them out in Greenwich Village.

Before long, Moishe's office had become a gathering place for, as he once put it, "wall-to-wall hippies."

Moishe was energized! Once again he was doing what he liked best: telling people directly about Jesus. Daniel had charged Moishe with revolutionizing the ABMJ staff. He didn't realize that Moishe himself was in need of a personal revolution. How could he? Moishe hadn't realized it when he accepted the position. And when that revolution came, it was not what anybody expected.

TWENTY-ONE

History is written in terms of conflicts and resolutions.

—MOISHE ROSEN

It was January in San Francisco and still dark outside at 6:00 a.m. Moishe was prepared for rain, but surprisingly, there was none—nor was there much traffic at that time of day. Just fog and lots of it. He was on his way to Golden Gate Seminary for a speaking engagement. As the director of recruiting and training, he was frequently scheduled to speak at colleges and seminaries around the country, usually during their chapel hour. It was a way to expose aspiring ministers to the importance of Jewish evangelism and to meet prospective missionaries.

Harold Sevener, who'd once lived in the Bay Area with his wife, Grace, had set up this trip. Sevener had been Moishe's right hand during the latter part of his time in Los Angeles, and they continued the relationship following Moishe's move to New York. Harold was well organized and had a confident, cordial manner that made him pleasant to be around. Moishe trusted him, not only with his California travel schedule, but also with some of his more serious concerns.

As he made his way onto Highway 101 North, Moishe tried to clear his mind of those concerns, but it wasn't easy. He'd been feeling defeated, training missionaries to do the work, only to have them sent to help people who either didn't understand or couldn't appreciate their skills. *So here I am, looking for new recruits, but if I find them, what will become of them? When the old-timers ask for help, all they seem to want are people to do errands and administrative work.*

But it hasn't all been bad, he reminded himself. Eliezer Urbach had remained in New York after his training and was doing a fine job. Though he was older than most who had joined the ABMJ, he was energetic and enthusiastic. In fact, he was one of the best of the bunch when it came to handing out those new broadside tracts. Art Katz had done a good job starting up a work in Kansas City, and so had Terrell Delaney, one of Moishe's LA trainees, starting a branch in Denver.

But those two did well because they were on their own in those cities, with no other staff to stifle their initiative and creativity, Moishe mused. *You can't put a*

new patch on an old garment, and you can't keep on opening up more branches just
because people in the existing ones aren't properly utilizing the new missionaries.

He quickly braked as the lanes narrowed on the approach to the Golden Gate
Bridge. It was still foggy but Moishe could see the halo of lights, forming a grace-
ful outline of the suspension cables. He crossed the bridge and before he knew it,
was heading up the steep road to Strawberry Point, where the Seminary nestled
on a hill high above the Bay.

At last the road leveled out into a parking lot. Moishe eased himself out of
the rental car to search for signs of campus life, but he'd arrived much earlier
than expected; no one was in sight and no buildings seemed open. Spotting a
bench under a streetlamp, he sat down, and Bible in hand he began to pray—
not about what he would say or do for the chapel—he was all set for that. As
he stared out into the darkness he sought God's direction about the troubling
situation in New York.

Around 7:00 am the pre-dawn darkness began fading to grey, and before
long it had melted away before the rising sun. As Moishe continued to pray
and watch, he had one of those rare experiences he would never forget. In the
darkness, he'd been completely unaware that he was facing the city. Now as the
light struck San Francisco, the low lying fog obscured only the bottom half of
the city while the skyline remained, so it looked like the city was floating on
an enormous cloud. The fog also reflected the bright morning sun, lighting up
the buildings like nothing Moishe had ever seen. He gazed in wonder at the
gloriously golden city floating before him.

Had God arranged for him to see this amazing sight as an answer to prayer?
After all, Daniel had agreed he could take the post in Northern California if things
did not work out in New York. But as awestruck as Moishe felt, he did not want
to convert those feelings into a conclusion concerning God's direction for his life.

Moishe gave a last lingering look at the city and headed off to meet Francis
Dubois, the seminary's head of missions who was to introduce him as the guest
speaker for chapel. After exchanging a few pleasantries, Moishe began to tell the
professor some of what he'd been discovering in New York—that many hippies
were open to discussing spiritual things and that people who were protesting the
war in Vietnam seemed ready to hear about the peace that Jesus could bring. To
his surprise, Dr. Dubois nodded his head in agreement. He proceeded to show
Dr. Dubois samples of the broadsides. There were now six titles, one of which
had been written by a new Jewish believer, Vicky Kress.

Dr. Dubois looked at the literature with interest and said, "I'm glad to see what you've been doing. I'm going to introduce you to some people who've been involved in outreach to people immersed in counterculture. You'll see that what God is doing in New York, he's also doing here in the Bay Area."

That was exciting news for Moishe, and he was glad to meet, among others, Kent Philpot and Paul Bryant. Both confirmed what Dr. Dubois had said.

After the chapel service, which went well, Moishe was eager to hear more about "the Jesus Revolution" that Paul and Kent had talked about. "You gotta go to Berkeley," Paul announced. "That's where things are really radical. These pamphlets of yours would go over great there."

"You know any good places to eat in Berkeley?" Scoping out good food was always high on Moishe's list of priorities.

"Yeah, sure, there's tons of places," Paul assured him. "I'll come with you and introduce you to some good people and some good food."

That's how Moishe met Jack Sparks of the Christian World Liberation Front (CWLF). *Wow, these guys really are radical,* Moishe thought as he heard about ministry communes, demonstrations, and more. *Nothing I'm doing would seem strange or off the wall to them.* He couldn't help feeling excited at the thought that if he did transfer back to California, there'd be people he could learn from and who could learn from him. Not only that, but Jack introduced him to a couple of Jewish Christians.

To Moishe, all this was absolutely wonderful. As far as he could see, the "happening" was even greater on the West Coast than it was back East. However, he was distracted from these thoughts by a rumbling in his stomach.

"Hey, ever hear of Cody's?" Paul asked.

"Is it a restaurant?" Moishe replied hopefully.

"No, it's a bookstore," Paul laughed. "C'mon I'll show you."

Moishe had never seen such a huge bookstore, except perhaps the big Brentanos in Manhattan. Everyone seemed to be wearing blue jeans and either tie-dyed tee shirts or sweatshirts with anti-war slogans. Some sat on the floor reading. Moishe was still in his speaker's attire, tie and all. A few looked at him with curiosity but most ignored him.

"What's that smell?"

"Oh, you mean the patchouli oil? Yeah, a lot of people wear it to mask the smell of pot" Paul said nonchalantly.

Cody's had a place for posting bills, and Moishe found it interesting to peruse the different rallies and demonstrations that were taking place. There were also numerous posters for saving trees, saving various animals and of course, a myriad of ads for concerts, free and otherwise.

"Cody's is kind of a hub for the Berkeley community," Paul explained, as they left the store.

Moishe was fascinated by the whole Berkeley scene. There were street vendors everywhere. He picked out a couple of pairs of dangly earrings for his wife and older daughter, and a beaded headband for the younger one. "Okay, I'm hungry," he told Paul as he stuffed the small paper bag containing the gifts into one of his pockets. "What's to eat around here?"

"C'mon, the campus is right over there."

"What about a restaurant?" Moishe pressed.

"Cheaper to eat by the campus. C'mon. It's good."

Paul pointed to a row of sidewalk vendors selling shwarma, falafel, kebabs as well as hot dogs, hamburgers and pretzels. Moishe aquiessed, and pronounced the food, "Not bad."

"Oops, got a little on your tie there," Paul pointed out. Moishe wiped his tie with a napkin but a trace of the shwarma juice remained. That was why he favored the cheap polyester ties to the fancy silk ones.

"Yeah, here too," Paul gestured to the side of his mouth. Moishe liked the fact that Paul wasn't afraid to mention these things. He looked around at his colorful surroundings; in fact, there was a great deal to like about the place and the people.

That night as Moishe prepared for bed, he couldn't help wondering if all that had transpired that day was a confirmation of what he sensed God might have been revealing through that amazing sunrise.

Yet he felt torn. He was preparing to begin training a new class of missionary candidates. He couldn't abandon them. But neither could he ignore the problems that were plaguing him back East or the opportunities that seemed so ripe in California. *I'm not going to decide anything tonight,* he thought sleepily. *We'll see what happens when I get back.*

———

Whether or not the trip to California confirmed Moishe's future, it certainly confirmed his conviction that outreach to hippies ought to be a primary focus of Jewish evangelism in New York—and that the organizational skills and methods of the antiwar organizers were an effective way to communicate.

Moishe observed, "They could take five hundred mimeographed sheets and hand them out in the morning, and at noon have five thousand people gathered in a given place. I studied the way they communicated and it was not fancy, it was not slick. They spoke in slogans."

The name "Jews for Jesus" began as a slogan during Moishe's time with the ABMJ in New York, and he did not originate it. In a 2009 letter to some friends, Heidi and Scott, Moishe explained how it came about in the late 1960s:

> I was finding out a lot of exciting things. One young lady came to one of our meetings. She was twenty-three years old. Her name was Alice [the afore-mentioned broadside writer, who changed her name to Vicky, short for Victorious]. Miriam Sleichter (formerly Mary Anne Sleichter, now Miriam Nadler) actually led her to Christ. Alice had zeal! I was worried that that zeal was going to get us into trouble.
>
> At any rate, in those days, I traveled a lot. . . . When I returned one Monday, I prepared for my Bible study on Tuesday. But, that particular Tuesday, there were several new people . . . and they explained that they came because of our advertisement in the *Village Voice*. I knew that I hadn't advertised in the *Village Voice*. Afterwards, I asked what happened. Alice, with a big, beamy smile, said, "I paid for that myself!"
>
> Was I grateful? No! I was angry at her. I said, "You could have gotten me in trouble. What does the ad say?" She showed it to me: "We are a group of Jews for Jesus, and would like to invite you to come and study the Bible with us," and [it] gave the details. Well, there was nothing wrong with the ad, but it was in the *Village Voice*, which was known as alternative media. The *Village Voice*, where they could publish dirty words and discuss subjects that wouldn't be discussed in the *New York Times* or *Tribune*, etc.
>
> Well, I grumbled and mumbled, but nobody [in the mission] really complained. A couple of more [new people] dropped in the following week, and so on.
>
> It got me wondering, and it occurred to me that the people who were communicating best were using slogans. But, "We are Jews for Jesus" was just too long, so I cut it down to "Jews for Jesus."

Actually, when Moishe first saw the phrase "Jews for Jesus" he didn't especially like it. However, he soon realized its value; it communicated a big message

quickly and easily. People remembered it and responded to it. Moishe intensi-
fied his efforts to reach the counterculture, trying as he did so to get others
excited about the possibilities.

Avi Brickner recalled,

[Moishe] invited me to accompany him to Greenwich Village late one
Saturday night (actually staying there until early morning) to view the people
on the street and to listen to him as he tried to communicate with them in
the parlance of the street. Though I didn't really "get the message" then, I
later came to see that Moishe was seeking to communicate to me, in the
most effective and impacting way possible, the changes taking place in the
society that called for a change in the way the good news was to be effectively
communicated.

Moishe wanted to bring Daniel Fuchs in on his ideas, but could not rely on
him for encouragement to move forward in the direction he wanted to go. He
always received affirmation from Daniel in the more conventional work that he
did. But it remained a stretch for Daniel to affirm some of the less conventional
means that Moishe was using to communicate the gospel.

Daniel thought the first broadside seemed silly and would embarrass the
mission and its donors. Ironically, later, when Moishe had written several
broadsides and brought them to a meeting of the FCTJ, a number of members thought the tracts were brilliant and congratulated Daniel on the work
that Moishe was doing. One can imagine how awkward that might have been
because Daniel still did not feel comfortable with that style of literature.

Yet, despite his discomfort, Daniel made efforts to see what Moishe saw.
When Paul Bryant accepted Moishe's invitation to come to New York, he had
Moishe, the trainees, and some staff members demonstrating in front of porn
theaters in Times Square. Moishe asked Daniel if he would join them. "It's not
a protest, so much as it is an attestation of Christ and his love, versus what these
guys are selling," he explained to his boss. And Daniel did come to one of those
demonstrations.

Moishe remembered: "He came. He carried a placard for a couple of minutes, and then handed it back, and said, 'I think I'll just pray.' He stood there
and prayed silently, but he saw the action. My life was becoming so radicalized
at that point that he no longer understood me. Nor did I understand myself."

Moishe considered Daniel Fuchs his mentor and one of his best friends and was unhappy that the tensions and distance between them continued to grow.

When Moishe was floundering in LA, Daniel's leadership style had given him exactly what he needed. Daniel had taught him a great deal, but since that time, he'd also learned a great deal from many others. And the more Moishe learned, the more he felt what was lacking.

For example, toward late 1969 he heard a management lecture that stressed the importance of balancing responsibility with authority and accountability. No sooner had Moishe heard that than he saw how it applied to his situation, as he later explained:

> In 1967 I was charged with reinvigorating the mission but I had no real authority. And I might say that that's one reason why, when Jews for Jesus got going, I always tried to balance those three things in every assignment that I gave, so that each person would have enough authority to manage the responsibility. And the more authority that I gave them, the more accountable they were to me.
>
> So, I found that I couldn't change anything and what was worse, I was training missionaries and sending them to branches that were not prepared to have assistance. All these things that I was teaching them to do, how to visit Jewish people, how to start a children's work, how to do outdoor preaching, were counting for nothing in most of the branches.
>
> Each branch had a different structure; each one had a different emphasis. Some had a good work, but it was based on the leader's personality and how he or she chose to do things. And when some of the older ones retired, often the work they had built fell apart.

Since his boss expected Moishe to revolutionize the mission, why did Moishe believe that Daniel didn't prepare the existing missionaries to do anything differently? Moishe explained,

> Daniel didn't understand revolutionary ways. I believe he thought I would come in, and they [existing staff] would be so taken with me that they would immediately want to follow me and do what I suggested. But Daniel had a mistaken idea of leadership and what leadership could do.
>
> Whatever Daniel set his hand to, he did well. But he didn't recognize

that not everybody is equally competent at everything that they do. So, in a sense, the mission developed a "one size fits all" attitude, rather than looking to carefully match people in places where their strengths would balance the weaknesses of others, and vice versa. The places the people got sent had little to do with either the situation or the individual's level of competence.

I strongly suggested to [Daniel] that the new missionaries who were Jewish Christians might do well in branches where the head of the branch was a Gentile Christian and they needed a Jewish Christian testimony. He thought that was a wonderful idea. But when it came to balancing things the other way [deploying Gentile missionaries where there was already a strong Jewish testimony], I could not convince him. It was up to me to make deployments, but I had to get his approval. . . .'

[And] Daniel had resigned himself to working around the preferences of some of the senior staff.

These details have not been included for the sake of airing old grievances or critiquing a good man with whom Moishe had long since been reconciled. They are included because understanding Moishe's frustrations over these matters is foundational to understanding many of the principles and policies he insisted upon later as the executive director of Jews for Jesus. They explain some of his attitudes and actions when he faced similar situations and decisions that Dr. Fuchs had faced.

Moishe voiced some other things that troubled him during his New York years:

I had this ideal that every ministry should help every other ministry. And to a degree, that was happening through the Fellowship of Christian Testimonies to the Jews. Ruth Wardell, who was in charge of the ABMJ's Long Island work, was very much involved at her own expense, and she was the first one to suggest that I get involved [with the FCTJ]. But in general, the attitude of most of the established missionaries seemed to be that . . . we were the largest, we had each other, and we didn't need the others. And nobody openly criticized anything. We had the best literature, we had the best this, we had the best that . . . I wasn't always so sure that we had the best of everything. But not only that, I felt that if we did have the best of anything, then we had something to give to the others.

In addition he said:

> There were many things I did not realize when I was in Los Angeles. When
> I went back to New York, I saw that instead of the administration working
> to uphold missionaries, the missionaries were treated [by some of the head-
> quarters staff] as an unwanted appendage.
>
> I began to see my team [candidates and missionaries] as being separate
> from the administrative team. In my team [particularly the missionaries who
> worked out of the Manhattan branch] I had people who, like myself, were
> willing to work all night. We did what we did, not because it was duty, but
> because it was fun, and we liked to see things develop. The administrative team
> arrived on time and left on time.

Moishe did not recall making his complaints or concerns a matter of discourse
within the mission: "I've always expressed myself in hyperbole—too often saying, 'always' or 'never.' But, for the most part, anyone could have seen that I
was very supportive of the ABMJ." Yet there was at least one person who was
not so certain of Moishe's support. And his suspicion finally convinced Moishe
that he could not succeed in New York. That person was his mentor, friend,
and boss—Daniel Fuchs. This came as a painful shock to Moishe, as did the
manner in which he learned of it.

Because he often worked long hours, Moishe frequently ate at his desk.
He also made a big batch of chili at least once a year, and there were always
leftovers. One day he decided to share some of that chili with a few coworkers,
including a man named Bob. Moishe recalled,

> I seldom drink alcoholic beverages, but with chili, I usually drink a beer. I
> had bought myself a can of beer and shared the chili with Bob and others
> but I found out later on that he had gone and told Daniel Fuchs that I had
> brought beer into the building. I don't remember if I got beer for anybody
> else—I tend to think not, but I might have. But there was no rule that you
> couldn't drink and most people drank wine occasionally.
>
> . . . I later learned that Daniel had told Bob to keep an eye on me and to
> report back to him. And Bob didn't really know what he was supposed to be
> looking for, but he figured it must be some wrongdoing.
>
> The way that I found out was that Bob came back to me afterward and

explained that he was told by Daniel Fuchs that he'd been assigned to the training program to find out what I was teaching and what I was doing because Fuchs had become suspicious of me. At that point, I knew that I would never teach another training class.

Academic freedom might mean little until you start teaching. But once you find yourself teaching, you know that you need liberty to teach. You need the liberty to express yourself—even if some of your opinions are negative. And so far as I knew, I was not expressing any negative opinions toward either Daniel Fuchs or the ABMJ.

Well, much later I found out that what Daniel Fuchs was really looking for was proof of something he had heard: that I was trying to take over the mission by developing loyalty to myself instead of to the organization.

No doubt many trainees and missionaries *did* feel a loyalty to Moishe. That loyalty could have been seen as a benefit and not a liability to the mission because it came with a sense of enthusiasm for the work. Moishe tried to anticipate the needs of those he supervised, involving them in things he thought they'd be good at and, when possible, keeping them away from those things that they would not be good at. He invested in them, which not only made them loyal to Moishe, but also made them better missionaries.

Would Daniel have responded differently to the rumor/allegation that Moishe was seeking his position if the two of them had not played a part (at least from Moishe's perspective) in unseating Pretlove? Possibly—there's no way to know. But years later in a private conversation during a conference in Baltimore, Fuchs told Moishe whose comments raised those suspicions.*

Sadly, it was a trusted friend. But by the time Daniel disclosed it (within a year or so prior to his death in 1988), Moishe knew two things. First, he could not claim to be so innocent when he reflected on the incident with Pretlove and the building permits. And second, had Fuchs' suspicions not arisen, Moishe probably would not have felt compelled to leave New York—a move that was necessary to fulfill his destiny.

When Moishe found out that Daniel had asked someone to spy and report on him, he was heartbroken and once again felt that he was failing. He'd already experienced feelings of failure with regard to the actual work of evangelism,

---

* By the time of that conversation, the person Daniel named had long since replaced him (Daniel) as president of the mission.

but that had turned around with creative new literature and a determination to relate to people who were open to the gospel: namely, the countercultural group known as hippies.

Moishe had also struggled with feelings of failure over his inability to accomplish Daniel's mandate to revolutionize the work. He simply did not have the necessary authority—nor would Daniel exert his authority on Moishe's behalf—to make it happen. Moishe couldn't find a solution to that one, but had continued doing his best to train the missionaries anyway. Now, how could he teach a class if he had to censor his opinions and observations?

The choice had become simple. He could stay in New York and fail, or take the successes he'd begun to have in New York to another place where they could flourish. Knowing that this class of candidates was going to be his last, Moishe met with Daniel, reminded him of their agreement, and made plans to transfer to California that July. It was 1970.

Moishe still felt invested in the candidates and was particularly concerned about Miriam Sleichter, a dynamic personality whom Moishe often referred to as "a spark plug." He was afraid she would languish in one of the branches. He arranged with Daniel Fuchs for her to go to Israel where she would continue studying and learn Hebrew for a year.

In a sense, by taking the transfer, Moishe had demoted himself. But it was a carefully negotiated demotion. As he later observed, "Even though I've joked that I assigned myself to San Francisco, that had been a prearranged option. What had not been prearranged was that I also assigned myself two cars, an executive salary, and a secretary."*

---

* That was Marcia Black, another trainee who'd graduated from Moody Bible Institute. Whereas Marcia did secretarial work, she was also very active in evangelistic endeavors that Moishe employed on the West Coast.

TWENTY-TWO

Reality lies somewhere between our highest hopes and
our deepest fears. We live in the light of the victory or
in the defeats that we anticipate.

—MOISHE ROSEN

Neon lights flashed competing claims that theirs was the hottest show in town. The three-block strip of Broadway in San Francisco's North Beach was packed with tourists, sailors, and even some lonely locals lured by the promise of the most outrageous and exciting "adult entertainment" imaginable.

A place calling itself "The Garden of Eden" featured one of the most prominent signs on the strip: a voluptuous figure of a naked woman, a palm tree and a leering serpent—all promising "a taste of Paradise."

Now Moishe was no crusader and he didn't feel it was his place to try shutting down all the sex shops in the city. His calling was to point to Jesus as the solution to sin for Jews and Gentiles. So he wasn't so much railing against those who were "selling" sin as he was pointing out that God was freely offering forgiveness, reconciliation, and a better way to find fulfillment.

Nevertheless, this sign galled him. To trade on the Bible as a ploy for advertising cheap thrills was deplorable. This exploitation of humanity's fall from innocence epitomized the whole North Beach scene. And it made the Garden of Eden the most obvious place to stage a gospel demonstration.

He was leading a group of twenty or so demonstrators clad in denim jackets embroidered with "Jesus Made Me Kosher" and "Jews for Jesus." About half the group carried colorful, hand-calligraphed placards with slogans such as "God's Love Lasts," "Love, Not Lust," and "Jesus Is Coming Again."

"Get them started with 'love, not lust,'" Moishe said to Baruch Goldstein, who nodded his assent as he stood at one end of the group. Meanwhile, Moishe had joined the picketers.

As people raised their signs and began to march, Baruch said, "Stay close together, keep moving, and get ready to chant, 'Love, not lust.'"

After a few moments of silence, someone called out loudly, "Love, not lust," and the group joined in the rhythmic chant. Everyone looked straight ahead, carefully keeping pace with the person in front of them. There were to be no gaps, no stopping or lingering, nothing that would block the flow of foot traffic on the sidewalk, nothing that could be used as an excuse to curtail the group's right to free speech.

Many passersby stopped to stare at the group. When one drunk tried to join the line, some tourists laughed, figuring this was all part of the evening's entertainment. But others looked at the signs proclaiming God's love in contrast to the tawdry signs offering sex for sale and seemed to realize they had someplace better to be and better ways to spend their money.

Then one woman suddenly stepped up to the picketers and screamed, "That's my religion you're ridiculing!" Shouting obscenities, she began alternately trying to tear up the placards and kicking several of the girls in the group. Finally, she pulled out a pair of scissors and started stabbing at the marchers. It was unclear whether she was trying to get to the placards or to the hands holding them.

No one in the group responded to her. Their commitment to nonviolence was not optional, and the obvious intention not to fight back often prevented the escalation of violence. But this half-crazed woman was working herself up into a more and more violent state, so Moishe sent Bruce Skoropinski, one of the group leaders, to get the police.

The attacker was focusing her rage on a young woman holding a placard that proclaimed: "God Loves You!" When Moishe grabbed the placard in an attempt to redirect the woman's fury, she tried stabbing Moishe's arm repeatedly, but the thick denim sleeve of his jacket protected him. At last she succeeded in inflicting a deep wound on his right hand.

Blood rushed from Moishe's hand, down his arm, and onto the sidewalk. Bystanders began to scream and call for help as the woman continued her efforts. Moishe was frightened, but he and the others had a predetermined strategy, and he now focused all his attention on that strategy as he began to yell, "They're attacking me because I'm a Jew for Jesus! This bar condones violence because they don't like Jesus!"

Moishe tried not to notice how the blood was streaming down from his arm—he held it up high, hoping that would slow the bleeding, not even realizing that the blood from his raised hand together with the sign proclaiming God's love appeared highly symbolic, if not heroic, in this context.

A bystander managed to get the woman off Moishe. Someone procured a clean towel from a nearby restaurant, and Moishe wrapped it around his hand and managed to stop most of the bleeding by the time the police arrived. He picketed as long as he could, bloody hand held high, but was scheduled for a radio interview that night.

Steffi Geiser (later Rubin), one of the earliest Jews for Jesus volunteers and one of the strongest creative forces in the group, helped Moishe get to the interview. Moishe had lost a lot of blood and knew he should not get behind the wheel alone. Before leaving, he made a request to those who stayed behind: "Do one thing for me. Demonstrate here an hour longer than we usually would, to show them that a little blood's not going to stop us."

As he rode to the radio studio, Moishe fought the lightheadedness that was starting to creep over him. He prayed that God would give him the strength to get through the show.

He arrived at the studio looking like quite a character. A middle-aged man, six foot two, he was sporting a leather cap, blue jeans, and an army surplus denim jacket embroidered with Jews for Jesus on the back while the front was plastered with campaign buttons proclaiming "Free Soviet Jewry" "Torah is Good for the Soul" "Jesus is a Jew" etc. Add to that the blood-soaked towel and jacket sleeve. If the talk show host had any doubt that he'd be interviewing a colorful character that night, all such doubts went out the window the moment Moishe walked in.

Once again, God answered prayers and Moishe made it through the program as though nothing had happened. It wasn't until after the show, when a doctor at a nearby hospital stitched up his hand, that he began to feel really weak and somewhat woozy. After he'd been stitched up, Steffi and Moishe drove back through North Beach just to make sure that the others had left safely. It hardly seemed possible that there had been a dramatic disturbance on the site. He looked at the stitches on the back of his hand. *It happened all right,* he thought sleepily. *I wonder if I can wait till morning to explain this to Ceil.*

––––––

Moishe's hand healed well, but a scar remained—like the knife on the car seat in Gila Bend—to remind him of what had happened. Did he see himself

---

* The opening section is based on pages 11–13 of the book *Jews for Jesus*, by Moishe Rosen with William Proctor, published by Fleming Revell in 1974.

as a role model of courage? Yes and no. He clearly stated, "I saw myself, in the early seventies anyway, as being an example of courage. Someone who could show others what to do. A bit of a way-shower. And I wasn't so much a father to all of these volunteers as a big brother. And that's the role that I like best."

Yet he also said, "Some of the things that gave me a larger-than-life reputation were just a matter of sticking to a schedule. When I got stabbed, I wasn't being heroic. . . . I was trying to hold things together as best as I could. Oftentimes, that was my reason."

In this case, holding things together meant preventing the demonstration they'd planned from dissolving as well as sending a message to the opposition that violence was not going to bring about any desired result. Moishe communicated many times that backing off from violence or threats of violence would only encourage more violence. Also holding things together meant not losing the opportunity for that radio interview. He always had a strong sense of the value of the media.

Was this the life he'd envisioned for himself when he told Daniel Fuchs that the time had come for him to take that transfer? No. He knew that he was on an adventure, but there was no way he could have imagined the situations that awaited him in California or the amazing people who would join him to become the group known as Jews for Jesus.

When Moishe first told Ceil that it was time for another cross-country move, she was predictably upset about being uprooted again. But there was one phrase that Moishe didn't use often, and when he did, his wife would follow. That phrase was, "I believe that God is showing me . . ."

Moishe was convinced that the move was God's will for him and for his ministry. He'd learned some hard lessons in New York, lessons he could not have learned in LA. So while he felt the move to New York had been necessary and right, he was also convinced that it was time to move on.

As for the mission's response to the transfer, Moishe said,

I have no doubt that Daniel Fuchs felt put off by the move, but he had promised and he was a man of his word. I wanted to settle in Berkeley, but he received an objection from someone on staff with another mission agency in Oakland. Though Daniel didn't necessarily pay any attention to objections from other missions when it came to deploying his staff, I believe he felt a need to, as he put it, "clip my wings." So, I was not allowed to live in Berkeley where I wanted to settle. Instead, we headed for Marin County, just north of San Francisco.

The trip from New York to San Francisco turned out to be relaxing and fun.

What should have taken us six straight days of driving ended up taking us about 18 days because we were in no hurry. I was entitled to a month's vacation, which I hadn't taken—ever. So I was entitled to take as long as I wanted to get there. It was like a pilgrimage, because in addition to my wife, two daughters and the family dog, we brought five other women.

We had Vicky [previously mentioned]. She was employed for a time as a secretary for someone on the ABMJ staff, but that hadn't worked out. She remained part of the group and I brought her along because she was a new believer and she just needed someone to look after her. And the same thing was true of Lana Korotkin, a new Jewish believer from Philadelphia. But Lana had also taken a shine to Paul Bryant when he came to New York and that's partly why she wanted to come to California.

Well, we stopped in Philadelphia because Lana said she was going to get some things. She didn't tell me that one of "the things she was going to get" was her younger sister. She came back to the car with Terry, and I'd never met Terry before; but like her sister Lana, she was very artistic and a little kooky. So Lana smiled and said, "I told Terry that she could come with, is that alright?" and Terry smiled and I smiled and said, "Sure."

Then there was Marcia Black (later Goldstein) who had been in my last training class. I asked her to come and be my secretary. Marcia had the schooling and training to be a missionary but confrontation was difficult for her. She was willing and able and did come out with us to hand out tracts, but what I liked about her was that she emanated a sense of order. Pat Klein was her friend and had graduated from Moody at the same time and she came along, too.

Even the dog was a girl dog. I don't know why I didn't feel uncomfortable surrounded by all these females.

Once they landed in Marin, the summer passed quickly. Lyn went off to college. Before long, Lana and Paul Bryant were engaged. (Paul had a house ministry in

San Anselmo.) Terry went back to Philadelphia to finish high school. Pat found a job, and she and Marcia rented an apartment in Mill Valley. Vicky found a place to settle in as well. Moishe continued handing out his broadside tracts with Marcia and the close-in volunteers. He began teaching a weekly Bible study in Berkeley in conjunction with the CWLF.

He said,

> Different people came alongside from time to time. The first that really "stuck," other than the people who made the trip out with me, was Mitch Glaser whom I met on December 31, 1970. Through Mitch, I met Baruch Goldstein, Jhan Moskowitz, and others.

Mitch was part of the Jewish counterculture that Moishe felt he was called to reach. A fairly new Jewish believer in Jesus from New York, he'd been sitting by the water in Sausalito, asking God what he was supposed to do next. When a piece of paper drifted up, he pulled it from the water. It was a gospel tract . . . and it had Moishe Rosen's name and address on it.

Mitch accordingly showed up on the Rosen's doorstep. Ceil answered the door, and told him that "everyone" (Moishe, Lyn, and Ruth) was in the back-yard. Lyn, who was home from college for winter break assumed that Mitch was one of her father's interesting new friends, and Moishe assumed he was one of Lyn's friends.

At some point, Mitch asked Moishe what it was that he was supposed to do. Somewhat surprised, Moishe replied, "Why are you asking me?" Then Mitch explained about the tract on the water and Moishe realized that his family had been entertaining—or failing to entertain—a stranger.

Meeting Mitch and his friends was a turning point for Moishe. They all had an eagerness to tell others about their new faith. They were talented, smart and determined—and most of them were from New York. Then there was Steffi, mentioned at the beginning of this chapter. Like many of the others, she was from the Bronx. In January, 1971 she came to one of the Berkeley Bible studies that Moishe was teaching, and weeks later, came to believe in Jesus. Susan Perlman, a Jewish believer from Brooklyn, had experience with writing, drama, and media and had a way of "getting the job done."

Stuart Dauermann, whom Moishe had met in New York, left the East Coast to be part of what was now becoming a movement in its own right. Stuart brought musical genius to the group, a brilliant mind and, like several in the group, a rather cutting sense of humor. Sam Nadler was yet another highly intelligent, creative Jewish hippie from New York who was now seriously "into Jesus." Moishe had said that he was coming to San Francisco to learn how to reach Jewish people in New York, and it seemed as though half of New York had moved to San Francisco!

Miriam finished her year in Israel, came out to visit, and liked what she saw. She recalled,

> There was lots of energy and excitement so when Moishe invited me to move out and be a part of what was happening I felt . . . that it was definitely the right move for me to make.
>
> . . . I was handed a phone, given part of a desk to use in what I remember to be a pretty crowded and bustling office, and told by Moishe to "start calling churches and make meetings for the music group." I think this was sort of the beginning of the church ministries department. It . . . seemed there were new believers everywhere, new songs being written, performed, and recorded, new tracts being written, [and] outreach constantly.

Tuvya Zaretsky was another of the "originals." He was a Jewish believer from Northern California, whom Miriam had met in Israel. Still in Israel, he had exchanged letters with Moishe and asked whether Moishe had a job for him if he returned to the States:

> He wrote back and explained that he couldn't employ me, but I was welcome to have meals at his house, [and] sleep on his floor until I could find a place to live and secure a job. However, right in line with his priorities, he added "All I have to offer you is an opportunity to serve the Lord."
>
> I finally did return to the United States in the fall of 1972. He struck me as incredibly thoughtful, intense when engaged in conversation but with enough mirth and mischief about him to keep you on your toes.
>
> He was true to his word. That fall in 1972 I slept on the floor of his living room for a few nights and shared meals off and on with his family, until I found an apartment of my own and the means by which to support myself. He also made good on the promise to give me an opportunity to serve Jesus.

The group was certainly not limited to East Coasters. Moishe met Amy Rabinovitz, a Jewish believer who was working for Campus Crusade, at a Christian rally in Dallas. Amy was a talented writer and organizer, eager to use her skills for the cause of Jewish evangelism.

While this is a biography of Moishe Rosen and not a history of Jews for Jesus, it is impossible to discuss the one without the other. Moishe's life and identity were inseparable from the birth of Jews for Jesus. The two books already written on the history of Jews for Jesus* describe the early group as a tribe, not an organization. There was a great sense of belonging; though the people came from diverse backgrounds, there was a common purpose that helped to forge a common culture. Moishe did not see himself as the creator of that culture. He saw the talent and the determination of many young people who had more or less gathered around him, and he did his best to pull the personalities and the talent together and keep the group on track, whether they were working hard or playing hard, and sometimes it was difficult to determine which was which.

Amy Rabinovitz observed,

As far as I knew, Moishe's idea of fun was a great idea—executed well. He set incredibly high standards for how to nurture a good idea, and I think it is one of the things I took with me when I left [Jews for Jesus]. . . . He definitely looked for ways to make communication interesting and in that I think he broke the mold of what was happening in Jewish missions. In retrospect, if I were to gauge his style, it would be more Bill Gates than Steve Jobs. Jobs was an inventor, creating his vision. Gates saw what Jobs was doing and looked for ways to take it to a wider audience, to shake up what existed. This Jesus people movement was already happening—Moishe recognized the importance of it and looked for ways to shake up Jewish missions and utilize what he knew to reach a wider audience.

I remember Moishe as a person who took a lot of delight in discovery . . . little things like an odd fact or a new restaurant . . . and an equal amount of delight in sharing those things with others. I also remember that delight disappearing as he struggled to build the organization.

Anyway . . . he discovered a very good restaurant . . . Swiss, French,

---

* *Jews for Jesus*, previously mentioned, and *Not Ashamed: the Story of Jews for Jesus*, by Ruth Tucker published by Multnomah Publishers.

something like that . . . and he took a copy of their menu, put a $20 bill with it (plenty for dinner for 2 in those days at that restaurant), and gave it to someone else in the group. Whoever went to the restaurant did the same thing and so on and so forth. Pretty soon all of us had been there to eat. Because of the way we had done it, we each had our own experience, but it was a group experience also.

Tuvya Zaretsky had similar recollections:

I think Moishe found learning to be a form of recreation. He seemed to take such delight in hearing about an experience or discussing a thought with other people. That wouldn't be everyone's form of recreation, but he wasn't exactly a skier. . . .

I was always amazed at the sense of humor that Moishe evidenced in his lessons and messages. It came so naturally. The style of humor was self effacing, wry, and often with deep irony. He would use hyperbole and understatement as a form of humor. He seemed to pull it off naturally. I don't remember him telling jokes. His humor seemed to be knit right into the fabric of life and the rest of his ministry.

No doubt there is material enough to fill an entire book of other people's impressions of Moishe.* And there were certainly many more who were part of those early days. Suffice it to say, all whose names have been mentioned in this chapter were at the core of the living, breathing, sometimes quarreling community that became Jews for Jesus. Each of these people was significant to Moishe, and many remained so throughout his life.

It would be difficult to overstate what a diverse, headstrong, talented, bright, and altogether unlikely group this was. Moishe had no doubt that God had called them together for a purpose: to let the world know that Jesus is the Jewish Messiah, and that no Jew ought to be ashamed to follow him. They were unconventional people, following an unconventional leader, to perform an unconventional task.

Ceil recalled,

---

* A couple of the original Jews for Jesus mentioned in this chapter preferred not to contribute to the research for this book, and others were not contacted. This does not diminish their importance to Moishe or to the early days of Jews for Jesus.

Moishe was very comfortable with these young people. He related to them very well and liked to discuss philosophy. He could sit on the floor and talk to them—something he couldn't do in a suit and tie in New York. He enjoyed it. I think he felt liberated to do what he knew how to do best, which was evangelism.

It took Ceil a little time before she felt comfortable with this crowd of hippie believers, who, at first, seemed very strange to her:

Moishe explained some of their thinking to help me understand. I didn't run away from them, but they were not *exactly* the kind of people I would have chosen to relate to. But I learned rather easily that they were nice people.

Though Ceil came to value the people who had become such a major part of Moishe's world, she would have preferred a life in which Moishe's time in ministry was more clearly delineated from his free time or time with family. She explained,

It was like he was living, eating, breathing Jews for Jesus all the time. I let him know that I didn't like it. He let me know it wasn't going to change. So it was an impasse. But then you go on.

I felt that whatever he was doing was what God wanted him to do— and one thing I had decided early and never went back on was that I would never interfere with his talking to people about the Lord. So whatever that entailed—and there were a lot of people he had to talk to once we went to San Francisco—had to be okay by me. . . .

He had this much respect for me that he never tried to make me do anything. But then on the other hand, I was not to make him do things either. So, I think we both knew our limits.

There was a bit more delineation (though not much) between home and work once Moishe set up his first office in Corte Madera. One room was Moishe's office/library, and the other room served as space for the weekly Bible studies, staff meetings, and day-to-day operations.

All of this activity was still under the auspices of the ABMJ, where it was referred to as "the project" or "Rosen's project" and for a while "the Jews for Jesus branch in San Francisco." It was a truly wonderful time for Moishe, who later said,

The three years before Jews for Jesus became an independent mission were a very happy time for me. I was delighted with the young people I was meeting and influencing, and we were finding courage to try things that other people couldn't do.

And toward the beginning, Daniel Fuchs was very happy with the work we were doing . . . and said it was the best work that was being done in the mission. And I was glad that he was happy. I always liked Daniel Fuchs.

When Dr. Fuchs came to visit, Moishe took him to Berkeley where Daniel observed him handing out broadside tracts to a crowd of protesters. Moishe knew by then how to be in the right place at the right time, how to avoid being stuck in the ensuing "riot," and when and where to exit. Daniel had a front row seat, so to speak, to some of the current events things he'd been reading about and seeing on the news.

It was not only success in the work and his boss's approbation, but the relationships and group dynamic that made this such a memorable time in Moishe's life. He recalled,

> Even though we worked hard, we did a lot of playing. Some of it was mischievous. We pulled pranks on one another. In those early days, the relationship was not a professional relationship. We were a family in the best sense of that word. We looked out for each other; we provided for each other. If somebody needed money, we all worked together. Just getting together—even Bible studies—there were constant jokes and laughing and having fun with one another, and I miss that.
>
> Often I would say, "We take God seriously, but we don't take ourselves too seriously." But we did our work, and nobody had to remind us to be serious about getting out the gospel.

Certainly there were days that were ordinary. But for the most part, the 1970s were packed with adventures for Moishe and the people involved in the Jews for Jesus project.

TWENTY-THREE

I could not get people to do things because of their devotion to me.
What they did, they did because of their devotion to God.
I was only showing them a path that they could take.

—MOISHE ROSEN

Hey, Goldstein, what are you doing with that broadside?" Moishe frowned. It wasn't like Baruch to waste gospel literature.

His curly headed, barrel chested cohort grinned mischievously. "You'll see." Within seconds, Moishe saw that Baruch had made the tract into a paper airplane. "Okay, watch this—" Baruch said, as he opened the window of their sky-high Sheraton hotel room on 35th Street and 8th Avenue.

Before Moishe could protest, Baruch had sent the paper airplane gently sailing down to the street below. Both watched as it glided over the traffic and across the street. It continued to glide up the street, then down the street, as if it were looking for somebody. A man stopped and reached up to grab it. Moishe and Baruch watched in wonder as he unfolded what must have seemed like a strangely contorted leaf from a mysterious gospel tree. The magical moment passed as Baruch hooted with glee. "Didja see that, Moishe? The guy's reading it!"

For the next ten minutes the two of them took turns launching gospel missives out the window, watching eagerly to see what would become of them. Nearly all the pamphlets were picked up and read by curious New Yorkers.

Moishe and Baruch Goldstein were in New York City for the Jesus Joy Festival, set to take place on Labor Day. Baruch, who received a disability check from the army, was practically a full-time volunteer with his own means of support. He had come along as Moishe's bodyguard.

Moishe could still hardly believe it was all happening. Originally, he'd been asked to fill a ten-minute speaking slot.

"You're going all the way to New York to talk to a bunch of people for ten minutes?" Ceil was dubious when he first mentioned the opportunity.

Moishe explained, "It's the venue—New York City and the Felt Forum! Imagine 3,500 New Yorkers—plus they're bringing in all these Christian folk rock artists. Even if it is a Christian concert, a lot of the young people who'll want to come to hear them are going to be Jewish.'"

Ceil nodded appreciatively. "Okay, I can see why you're excited."

Moishe grinned. "You should have seen Susan Perlman's eyes light up when I told her about it. She started putting together a press release right away. 'I think she's sent one to just about every local radio and TV station plus every newspaper in every borough of New York. If there's a plumbers' association of Staten Island and they have a newspaper, you can bet she's sent them a press release too."

Susan's work had paid off; she'd been able to line up numerous media opportunities before the event. As soon as the Jewish newspapers picked up on the fact that Moishe Rosen was coming to New York, the flurry of articles and interviews had snowballed and the festival organizers decided to change his original ten-minute slot to a twenty-minute keynote speaker spot.

He smiled as he recalled how Susan had practically shrieked, "Moishe, you gotta see this!" Then she showed him a copy of the *Jewish Press*. There on the front page was the decree that all Jewish organizations had forbidden their members to attend the Jesus Joy Festival because "an apostate who calls himself Moishe Rosen" was to be a speaker!

"So who," Moishe asked in his most ironic tone, "is this new 'Jewish pope' that thinks he can forbid every Jew in New York from coming to a concert?"

"Exactly!" Susan replied, brimming with satisfaction. "Who *wouldn't* want to come to the concert after this?"

Susan was right. Not only was the prohibition bound to roll off the backs of a strong-minded, independent, think-for-themselves community of New York Jews, but it turned the event into a matter of great curiosity.

The festival itself was quite an event. Intense Christian rock music and several dynamic speakers electrified the crowd. As Moishe stepped up to the podium, his adrenaline pumping, cameras flashed to capture images of the denim-clad forty-year-old. He had a palpable feeling that the crowd was with him. They punctuated his most passionate points with applause—whereas if he paused to create suspense, there was silence as the crowd waited eagerly to hear what he would say next.

And then it was over. He'd gotten his message across. Jesus was not some namby-pamby figure portrayed in so many religious paintings. He was a radical, relevant Messiah who came first to the Jewish people, but would bring purpose and meaning to the life of any Jew or Gentile who would turn to him.

Moishe was well aware that some very angry people were awaiting him near the exits. The police had suggested that he and his four-person entourage leave the Forum incognito since they were going to walk back to the hotel. But Moishe felt it would be wrong to show fear or compromise their visibility. He told the young men with him,

"We've got to double time it out of here and keep it up all the way to the hotel. Don't run. Don't lag behind. Keep in step. And whatever you do, don't answer back or engage in conversation no matter what they say. Now is not the time. If we stick together and stay focused, I don't think anyone will get hurt. Got it?"

On the city sidewalk the small band of Jews for Jesus was met with shouts and jeers, and perhaps a shove here and there. For the most part, the group tried to follow Moishe's instructions. But one man turned to answer a particularly provocative remark from the hostile knot of protesters. His brief reply was enough to make him a target, and as he turned back to continue pace with the rest of the group, he received a hard kick in the behind.

Despite the hostilities, the overriding emotion back in the hotel room was excitement bordering on euphoria. Moishe called the rest of the group back in California. His blow-by-blow description of the events helped to expend some of his adrenaline. Yet in the days that followed, Moishe reflected that for the good of his own soul, he would prefer not to speak in front of a crowd of thousands again.[*]

———

The media coverage of Moishe Rosen and the early Jews for Jesus catapulted the issue of being Jewish and believing in Jesus into the public arena. In June 1972, *Time* magazine published the article "Jews for Jesus" in the religion section. The article covered the phenomenon of Jewish people as part of the Jesus Movement (already waning by 1972), which was far broader than Jews for Jesus. The phrase "Jews for Jesus" was already being applied to all kinds of Jewish Jesus-believers, partly because it was so catchy and simple to say, and partly because under Moishe's leadership, Jews for Jesus was highly visible and very colorful. That same month a clip of Jews for Jesus aired on network TV.

---

[*] Moishe said that he had experienced a "rush" from the crowd's response to him and had realized that it would not be healthy for him to indulge in that feeling. The influence that Moishe sought was always one of individual reasoning; he found the idea of sweeping large crowds into a fervor frightening and repulsive.

While the *Time* article was objective and fair, and the TV clip allowed the group to speak for itself, that was not always the case with the publicity that swirled around Jews for Jesus. But though the coverage was often unflattering and sometimes inaccurate, for the most part, Moishe saw it as beneficial to the cause.

Nevertheless, the publicity had a downside. Early on, Moishe had numerous opportunities to talk to Jewish groups but once the press picked up on Jews for Jesus, helping to make the group into a phenomenon, the Northern California Board of Rabbis issued an edict forbidding Jewish organizations from inviting Jews for Jesus to speak to their groups.

The prohibition against inviting Jews for Jesus to speak did not prevent individuals from agreeing to meet privately with Moishe, who frequently took his young volunteers to observe how he shared his faith in one-on-one situations.

To Moishe, the crux of ministry was always the opportunity to relate to people as individuals. However, he believed that because most Jewish people are taught automatically to dismiss the possibility of Jesus being the Jewish Messiah, the public needed to be continually challenged to reconsider that response. That is why visibility and a high profile were indispensable to the Jews for Jesus project.

That is also why Moishe eventually embraced the slogan "Jews for Jesus" after originally dismissing it as too unsophisticated. When people used the phrase to try to dismiss the group, saying, "You can't be Jews for Jesus," Moishe realized the slogan was invaluable and had it copyrighted. No other phrase and no other name brought the issue to the forefront so succinctly.

The Jews for Jesus project presented a creative and determined band of obviously Jewish people who not only raised the image of Jesus as a Jew, but also insisted that there was absolutely nothing un-Jewish about embracing him as the promised Messiah. Jews for Jesus challenged the cardinal "rule" that being Jewish and Christian are mutually exclusive. That challenge was (and is) seen as a threat to Jewish identity and survival.

Suddenly, the Jewish community felt it had a war on its hands, and it was mostly a war of words. Many Jewish newspapers labeled Jews for Jesus a cult and warned parents about soul-snatching missionaries. Ironically, Moishe had made it very clear that no one was to approach a minor with the gospel or make a nuisance of himself or herself when offering the message.

None of the unfounded accusations came as a shock to Moishe. His response was to educate people about what constituted a cult, the characteristics of cult leaders, and the dynamics of brainwashing.[*]

He never desired to antagonize the Jewish community, but he recognized that anything that made Jesus an issue to Jewish people would be considered antagonistic. He therefore did his best to prepare the group to take the heat. He continued to adapt some of the revolutionary tactics of the antiwar movement to suit the group's purposes.

Moishe said, "I learned something from my father. He used to say, 'Either people threaten or they strike.'" Jews for Jesus did take its share of "strikes." A bullet through the Corte Madera office window, for example, was cause for a police investigation.

Some of the strikes were predictable, as when Jews for Jesus showed up at an event to let people know that they were not going to be intimidated, despite the rumblings of the Jewish Defense League (JDL) about how they would "defend" the Jewish community from the missionaries. The only missionary "attack" was a handful of smiling people who, identified by their clothing as Jews for Jesus, might offer gospel tracts. The public was always free to refuse the literature, and no one was forced to talk to the pamphleteers. The "defense" the JDL spoke of seemed to consist mainly of attempts to scare off the Jews for Jesus and/or prevent Jewish people from seeing and interacting with them.

Some in the Jewish community recognized that the Jews for Jesus were interested in Jewish causes and were also some of the best volunteers when it came to a good rally or demonstration for causes like freeing Soviet Jewry. Susan Perlman recalled,

> We had, as individuals, gone to different Jewish events—some attended local synagogues, some went to Hillel on the campuses. We were always marginalized and Moishe knew and accepted that. But that didn't deter him and the rest of the tribe from wanting to identify and support the Jewish community.
>
> I remember when the Munich Massacre happened; Steffi silk-screened red circles for the Olympic symbol onto black armbands. And we wore them, you know, as a badge of identification.

---

[*] Years later a former employee interviewed for an article that appeared in the March 2010 edition of *Charisma* magazine reminisced about a leadership meeting in which Moishe joked about one such article, saying, "If we're a cult, how come I can't get you guys to do what I want you to do?"

We had "Free Soviet Jewry" buttons; we worked with Hal Light, who headed up the early Soviet Jewry demonstrations in San Francisco that really were a precursor for the Jewish emigration out of the former Soviet Union.

Jews for Jesus lent a strong presence to several Bay Area demonstrations, and they came without the Jews for Jesus T-shirts and jackets because that would have been counterproductive to bringing attention to the plight of Soviet Jews. But some of the organizers and community leaders knew Moishe—had actually met with him—and appreciated him and the group, though they could never publicly acknowledge it.

While opposition was mounting, Moishe sensed that something even bigger was about to happen, but he did not know what. In January 1973, in a staff meeting—though most of the "staff" were volunteers—he asked the group to make a commitment to one another to keep working together for the next eighteen months, whatever might happen. And they did. No one, not even Moishe, realized how vital that commitment would soon prove to be.

Meanwhile, the ABMJ home office in New York was not particularly pleased about the publicity. After all, who was to say that some of their Christian constituents might not believe the accusations against the Jews for Jesus? Daniel Fuchs had been happy about much of what Moishe was accomplishing, but he also had concerns. As previously mentioned, somebody within the mission had sowed seeds of suspicion regarding Moishe's supposed aspirations to take over the mission. Moishe found this ridiculous because, as he put it, "The fact of the matter is, the second man in charge has the most fun. I never wanted to be the top man, because the top man has to be a figurehead, has to go around, has to nod politely and be seen in the right places and affirm everything and be a diplomat. The second man usually gets to plan and lead operations, and that's the position that I liked."

Nevertheless Daniel had, for a time, spoken to Moishe about becoming his successor. Apparently now he feared that Moishe was eager to see that come about sooner rather than later. The truth was, even though Moishe did not covet the position of top executive, he wanted the freedom to do everything as he saw fit. When the home office refused to sanction some of his plans, Moishe complained and didn't think until years later how some of his behavior must have come across to his boss.

Moishe did recall an issue that seemed to bring his relationship with the

ABMJ to a crisis point, though he later saw that there had been much more leading up to it:

> A woman from Pacific Grove called our office. She had heard about what we were doing in the Bay Area and wanted to help with a significant donation. . . .
>
> At that time, we needed a house [not for the Rosen family but for some of the volunteers]. We had been using the parsonage at the Baptist Church in Mill Valley, but they called a new pastor who needed the rooms for his family. The amount this lady wanted to give would have met that need. But we had a procedure that was proper. . . . That was, we referred generous donors who had inquiries to our headquarters in New York. It was Daniel Fuchs' purview to decide how to spend such a large gift. Well, he decided it would be better spent elsewhere. And actually, I think the project he used it for was a good project. The point was, the woman seemed amenable to helping us first, and, in a sense, I felt she got talked out of it.
>
> That was within Daniel's rights. But I grumbled about it. He felt that I was rebellious. We spoke on the phone during a trip I had taken to the Toronto branch of the ABMJ. He said, "Really, the way things are working out, you're the kind of person that has to be in charge," which I felt was not true. I just wanted the things that I wanted to do to happen, that's all. And I argued that I had just completed something like seventeen years of working under him, which didn't seem too persuasive to him at the moment. He said, "I'm afraid you're going to have to leave the mission, but we've got a lot to talk about."
>
> I wanted to be able to see Daniel's face when we talked because I've never been able to measure what is happening by someone's voice alone. That was fine with Daniel. "You're scheduled to be in New York to speak at the Summer's End conference," he said. "We'll discuss it further then."
>
> It was July 1973. Now, you've got to appreciate that it had been a decade since I'd seen anybody dismissed for anything less than personal immorality. I was in shock—I never expected to be fired.
>
> There was a whole lot more to this [dismissal] than the one incident. Some of it involved our music group, the Liberated Wailing Wall. It seemed like everything I proposed was seen as an attempt to put myself in the leadership position. The fact of the matter is, I've always regarded leadership as a nuisance. I didn't particularly like the responsibility.

Let it not be said that Moishe ever felt he was victimized or blameless in the matter of his dismissal. After the initial shock, he could see that Daniel was right to fire him because as he later explained,

> I was difficult to manage. I would be with the ABMJ today if I had practiced the kind of humility that I believe in. But I was arrogant. First, I boasted a lot about the Jews for Jesus project. I thought it had been handed to me by God himself, and I believed I was boasting about what God was doing, not what I was doing. But there was a certain arrogance that went along with it that I didn't see in myself.
>
> The second thing was, I had come to the point where I knew more about Jewish evangelism than anybody else, and I didn't hesitate to say it. I did not treat him [Daniel] with the proper respect. I was a hot item, and when people called to interview me, I should have deferred to him. My attitude was that he didn't know how to do it and it was better for the cause if I did it. . . .
>
> The third thing is that I presumed on my relationship with the American Board. I came to New York in 1967 with a romanticized view of the mission and reality. When I found things weren't exactly as I'd thought they should be, I didn't take the time to build and affirm relationships, particularly with Daniel, that I should have. I didn't maintain what had been a good friendship and fellowship. And when I moved to California, I thought that the mission ought to continue supporting me because I was doing these terrific things and they were gaining from the work that I was doing. But my standards and their standards were very different, and I didn't shrink from letting people know that I felt my standards were correct.

Another factor was Moishe's struggle with understanding the nature of authority. Before he came to New York, he imagined the proper response to authority was a "Yes, sir" salute and do-what-you're-told compliance. He said,

> When I found out that things were far more flexible than that, and that every decision involved right and wrong and standards, I started getting confused. And I suppose that my confusion was part of a battle between the ideal and the real, and how to reconcile the two, since I could not make the real live up to the ideal. I'm not saying that I always lived up to my own ideals. But it was a struggle because I felt that if I ever gave up my ideals, I'd be in profound trouble.

Part of Moishe's struggle had to do with a public face that seemed to be expected of him. The nature of that public face was to express more affirmation and enthusiasm than Moishe was comfortable expressing. He explained,

> Daniel was filled with praise for the staff, and he would talk publicly about the great dedication and all the wonderful work that was being done. But when we were alone, privately he would express reservations. I know that he would have liked it if I had been the same kind of person, praising the staff and the organization publicly. But I didn't raise my kids with too much praise, and I didn't treat anybody else with too much praise. And if somebody would start repeating these praises, if I didn't think they were justified, I would start contradicting by saying what I knew to be true. He would rather that I kept my mouth shut.

Ceil reflected,

> I don't think he [Moishe] expected to be fired and I certainly didn't expect him to be fired. I remember that he was shocked, but not angry. He said Daniel was probably right to fire him. He knew that he had too many ideas that didn't go along with where the mission was heading. And he was very outspoken and openly critical of things he disagreed with.
>
> After they fired him, he was ready to be a salesman or go do anything he needed to put food on the table and he would hand out tracts and talk to people in his spare time if he had to. He just knew that he had to continue preaching the gospel, and if the ABMJ wouldn't support him, he would find another way.

Did Moishe regret the time that he spent with the ABMJ? He said,

> No, because they were the best mission out there . . . their ideals were the basis for my own ideals.
>
> I do regret that I didn't take the time to avail myself of some of the great men who were part of the staff. Just to sit and listen to them, to apply myself to them. I feel that I could have, number one, learned a lot; number two, been blessed by their experiences. But I was so eager to get experience on my own that I went off on my own too quickly, too early to try things.

As shocked as Moishe was by the dismissal, he had already begun to form a somewhat separate identity from the ABMJ. In old correspondence, some of his letters to supporters talked about the ABMJ "allowing us" or "helping us"—delineating "us" (the Jews for Jesus project) from the rest of the mission. He presented the mission as the sponsor of Jews for Jesus. Moishe was trying things that no one else in the organization was doing, and in that sense, Jews for Jesus had been sanctioned as something that *was* separate from the rest of the ABMJ. In hindsight, it is difficult to see how either Daniel or Moishe could have overlooked the ramifications of that separation and how eventually it would become untenable for Jews for Jesus to remain part of the ABMJ.

While he never saw himself as being disloyal to the mission, Moishe later stated, "My first loyalty was always to those I ministered to and those I ministered with." But he'd had to remove himself as far as possible from mission headquarters in order to minister to and with those he felt he was supposed to reach. The success of the Jews for Jesus project could not have led to anything other than an eventual parting of the ways.

When asked to identify his greatest success and failure during his years with the ABMJ, Moishe replied,

> My greatest success and my worst failure was the same thing; it was the Jews for Jesus project. It was the greatest success inasmuch as I discipled more people, mobilized more people, and got out the [gospel] more than at any other time I served with the mission. But it was the greatest failure because all of this "more" served to disconnect me from the ABMJ.

Daniel had prepared Moishe for the dismissal by phone, but made it official and worked out the details of the severance in person. Moishe recalled, "He wasn't unkind; he let me keep one of the cars and saw that we were paid through the end of November. He'd initially told me in July, so he gave plenty of time to find a means of support."

In parting, Daniel Fuchs reiterated that he was doing Moishe the biggest favor of his life and that one day Moishe would tell him so. Neither of them realized just how soon that day would come.

PART THREE

Challenging the
Status Quo

TWENTY-FOUR

Don't let your friends happen to you; don't let life happen to you;
don't let *things* happen to you. Make the kind of friends and
the kind of life that you believe you ought to have.

—MOISHE ROSEN

Moishe pulled up to Susan Perlman's apartment in the oversized red Dodge Polara that the ABMJ had allowed him to keep after his dismissal. Susan, looking very much the fresh young professional in her suit and high heels was outside waiting. As usual, the bench seat of the "the boat" (as Moishe's family called the big sedan) was pushed all the way back to accommodate his height and girth. Susan clambered in, bracing herself for the arctic blast. Regardless of the outside temperature Moishe generally kept the air conditioning on full force because he was easily overheated. When he was overheated he tended to grow logy, and today's visit to the JCRC (Jewish Community Relations Council) demanded nimble, clear thought.

He considered telling Susan his entire plan, then decided, *No, it'll just give her more time to be nervous if I tell her the details—but I do need to tell her enough to be able to count on her help.*

Moishe had made more than one call to the JCRC regarding members of the JDL, who were not only suspected of slashing tires on the groups' vehicles on more than one occasion, but were making a habit of roughing up the Jews for Jesus staff and volunteers when they encountered them on the streets.

"These guys are claiming to defend the Jewish people by making aggressive attacks on peaceful citizens," Moishe had said in his first call to the JCRC, "and their behavior reflects poorly on the Jewish community. I don't expect you to agree with our message, but I think you'd agree that their tactics don't represent the values of most Jews in the community, or how we want to be viewed by non-Jews. If you tell the JDL that this is not the right way to deal with things, I believe they'll listen."

The JCRC had little to say in response, but the head of the local organization did agree to a meeting. After thinking through the various people he could bring along, Moishe had decided to ask Susan. She appeared younger than her age—and few would guess the kind of mettle that lay beneath that doe eyed, sweet exterior.

"Should I come in colors* or regular street clothes?" Susan had asked.

"Neither," Moishe had replied. "A suit. Cognitive dissonance, remember? They have us pigeon holed with that hippie street image. Anyway, we want them to see by how we dress that we are showing respect."

Now as Moishe pulled away from the curb, he phrased his words very carefully. His speech still gave way to an occasional stammer. "Uh Susan, we might not have another opportunity to get our point across to this group. So during this meeting, I'm going to ask something of you that is hard for me, and it will be hard for you. It's something I'd rather not ask, but I need your help for the sake of the whole group. Do you trust me?"

"Yeah, I trust you Moishe," Susan replied. She didn't say it lightly. She might look young for her age, but she was no pushover.

They arrived at their destination and Moishe stood before the group to receive a brief introduction. It was not a large group, and he was close enough to make eye contact with each person.

First he outlined the recurring incidents as he had already done over the phone, and reiterated that this was not a Jewish way of handling disputes. "Up until now, we haven't talked to the media about the kinds of physical opposition we've been facing," he added. "As Jews, we don't want the public to judge the Jewish community by these roughnecks any more than you do." Some of the members exchanged glances. Was this a veiled threat? Would Moishe go to the media if they were unwilling to help? Pausing for a few moments, Moishe thought, *Let them wonder.*

"We've come to you because these guys will listen to you in a way that they won't listen to us—and I uh, I hope you'll agree that it's in everyone's best interest for them to listen. So here's the message I'm asking you to get across. Violence is not the answer. Our people are trained to handle it. They will not run from it."

Moishe paused again and took a deep breath. "I'd like to show you something that I—uh—think will carry more weight than I can convey in words."

And then he said, "Susan, would you come here?"

Susan's high heels clicked across the hardwood floor as she joined Moishe

---

* Meaning a T-shirt or jacket bearing the words "Jews for Jesus."

in front of the group. "Susan," Moishe said, "would you allow me to slap you to demonstrate something for these people?"

"Yes." Susan responded without hesitation.

Moishe extended his right arm as far back as it would reach, and with his hand open, he took a powerful swing at the pretty young face before him.

As the group let out a huge corporate gasp, Susan was knocked off her feet and literally slid across the floor. Taking only a brief moment to compose herself, she picked herself up, straightened her suit, and smiled. Half her face was beet red, but her smile was just as bright, as she said, "It's okay, Moishe." Moishe swallowed hard. Then he turned to the group and said in a measured tone, "All of our people are like that. They're not going to be deterred. I hope that we can count on you to get the word out."

Moishe wished it could have been one of the guys—but he'd thought it through and knew it would do no good to choose someone with a tougher exterior. If the opposition heard that someone they might see as vulnerable could handle a blow like that, they could be pretty sure that the others would not respond to bullying, either.

The local JDLers didn't stop opposing Jews for Jesus, but soon after that meeting there was a marked decline in the level of harassment. It seemed clear to Moishe and the other Jews for Jesus that the JCRC had indeed passed along his message.

———

Susan was able to help Moishe make his point, not only because she trusted him but also because she, like the rest of the group, had received training before converging on New York City for what was to become the first of their annual Summer Witnessing Campaigns.

Everyone who wanted to participate in that campaign agreed to what was then referred to as "pain training." During the training, each person received one hard slap across the face. In addition, Moishe gave a serious lecture about pain, fear, and depersonalizing the hostility that they might encounter.

Once in New York, the group divided into smaller teams and passed out their gospel literature four times a day. In addition to these sorties and the specialized music and drama, Moishe encouraged the group to think outside the box with parades, processions, and colorful placards.

Moishe never had a five-year plan or a ten-year plan for his life or for Jews for Jesus. He believed that Jesus might return at any time, and he treated each big opportunity as though it might be the last. He was thrilled to be leading a band of bright, creative people who would let all of New York City know that there were Jews who believed in Jesus. By that time there was a drama team, the New Jerusalem Players (NJP), as well as the music team, the Liberated Wailing Wall (LWW).

Creativity and camaraderie were integral elements of the summer project. It was fun, but strenuous and demanding. All of them worked harder and longer than they ever thought possible. Standing for hours in oppressive summer heat produced sore muscles and blistered feet. As objects of spitting, swearing, and occasional slapping or shoving, the group experienced emotional fatigue. But Moishe was convinced that by God's grace they could handle it. And they did. Moishe participated in many more such campaigns, but after the first one, he nearly always put someone else in charge.

No longer under the auspices of the ABMJ, Moishe realized that while his primary goal was to further the gospel among Jewish people, he must also concern himself with training leaders so that the operation would be able to continue without him. He expected the others to recognize him as the primary leader, but more and more he began to see Jews for Jesus as a leadership cadre.

That is not to say that the moment Moishe was fired by the ABMJ, he swung into action and formulated a myriad of plans. The underlying depression that had been his constant companion for years deepened. He became emotionally numb and for a time allowed himself to be moved along by others. Moishe recalled, "In the beginning, being on my own in ministry was really more responsibility than I thought I could handle. I liked being accountable to another person."

Once other missions heard that Moishe was a free agent, he received more than one employment opportunity—and the thought of working for another organization had its appeal. Yet Moishe did not consider himself a free agent because he was part of the covenant he'd asked the group to make just six months before he was fired. With a full year of the commitment remaining, Moishe explained to other mission leaders that unless their ministries could offer positions to the whole group, he did not feel at liberty to accept a position for himself.

Moishe credited three people and one project with keeping him going during those difficult days. There is more about the project later in this chapter, but the people were Amy Rabinovitz, Susan Perlman, and Steffi Geiser. Moishe also credited his wife:

> I should mention . . . [Ceil]. She took a part-time job in a law office, and for several months, hers was the only paycheck that came in. When it came to . . . ethics, she encouraged me to do the highest good. For example, there was something that we needed for the house (I can't remember what it was) but because we had so many guests, I said that we could have the ministry buy it. But she wouldn't hear of it.

While Moishe credited various women for "keeping him in line" and seeing to it that Jews for Jesus moved forward, he was very much aware that several men also had key roles in building Jews for Jesus into an organization, including Sam Nadler, Baruch Goldstein, Mitch Glaser, Jhan Moskowitz, Tuvya Zaretsky, and Stuart Dauermann. Moishe said, "We became a wonderful team and got a lot done in a short time."

In terms of the actual birthing of Jews for Jesus as an official nonprofit missionary organization, Moishe realized that he needed outside help, and he turned to Byron Spradlin, an energetic young Christian who was passionate about seeing the gospel proclaimed in creative ways. Byron, a musician and youth pastor, was affiliated with the Conservative Baptist Association, the denomination that had ordained Moishe. Byron was also a seminary student with a quick mind. Moishe asked him to help draw up the articles that would officially incorporate Jews for Jesus. Together they hammered out the details of the official documents at the Rosens' dining room table. Byron agreed to serve as the chairman of the board of directors, a post he held for some three and a half decades.

Moishe found that he had a new responsibility that weighed rather heavily on him. He needed to ask people to help support the organization. In the ABMJ, he and others had prided themselves on not asking their constituents for money. But now, unless he made the need known, there was no way that people would be able to help.

Ceil recalled,

> I typed addressograph labels with names and addresses of personal friends, mostly from our Christmas card list. . . . Some were Gentile believers; some

were Jewish believers who also had other ministries. We started with something like two hundred names. Moishe sent out a letter explaining that we were no longer under the auspices of the ABMJ, and we needed support. Our friends responded almost immediately. We not only received funds, but pastors donated reams of paper for our literature, and sent volunteer helpers from their congregations. We felt as though the Lord was certainly taking care of us.

While Moishe hadn't had much experience with ministry fund-raising, the business classes he had taken decades earlier as well as his retail experiences provided useful principles and insights. He said,

> One principle that I learned long before Jews for Jesus was "If you don't have it, don't spend it." I've always been reluctant to buy things on credit.
>
> We say that we live by faith, but when we contract—take out a mortgage—we're saying, in effect, that we have some knowledge that the donors are going to give this [certain amount], and I've never been comfortable with that. I feel that God has set a limit on the size of every organization and what he was going to provide by way of people, what he was going to provide by way of resources, what he was going to provide by way of a task to be done.
>
> I've never seen a ministry or a mission that I felt had a permanent destiny, even a local church. I feel there might be a need for a church in a place now, and that need might not exist at a future time. [In which case] I thought that an institution should be allowed to die a graceful death. But, as long as people had a pecuniary interest [in said institution], they would keep it going because it put food on the table. That sounds cynical but [it's part of the reason] I didn't want to build a super-big organization, and I didn't want to incur debts.

Although Jews for Jesus was the most visible and most publicized group of Jewish believers in Jesus, there were many other Jewish, Jesus-believing individuals and groups who were not affiliated with the missionary organization. Many recognized that Jews for Jesus had been a slogan before it was the name of an organization. Since the words described a movement of Jewish people who were following Jesus as the Messiah, they had no qualms about being called Jews for Jesus.

Moishe addressing students at University of California at Davis

Rosens, early 70s (back: Lyn and Moishe, front: Ceil and Ruth)

Moishe on the Lee Leonard show; host is reading one of the early Jews for Jesus broadsides

Moishe Rosen and Jews for Jesus senior staff members, 1987
Front row left to right: David Brickner, Stuart Dauermann, Steve Silverstein,
Alan Bond; middle row Avi Snyder, Baruch Goldstein, Susan Perlman, Jhan
Moskowitz, Efraim Goldstein, Steve Wertheim, Tuvya Zaretsky, Mitch Glaser;
back row Moishe Rosen, Steve Cohen, Bob Mendelsohn

1980 Consultation On World Evangelism in Thailand Moishe is back row center
David Harley to Moishe's left and Jhan Moskowitz to his right; also pictured
front row third from left, Ole Kvarme, fourth from left, Susan Perlman)

(above) Moishe with Jews for Jesus board members, spouses and guides in Israel, 1991: top row left to right: Susan Perlman, Steve and Chris Lamos, Vernon Grounds, Jhan and Melissa Moskowitz, Steve and Janie-sue Wertheim, Moishe and Ceil Rosen; bottom row left to right: John and Marilyn McDonald, Warwick and Annette Cooper, Jerry and Del Karabensch, tour guide Miriam Vanosh, Pam and Byron Spradlin, Tuvya Zaretsky

(left) Moishe given honorary doctorate from Western Seminary Commencement

Moishe attending his grandson's bar mitzvah

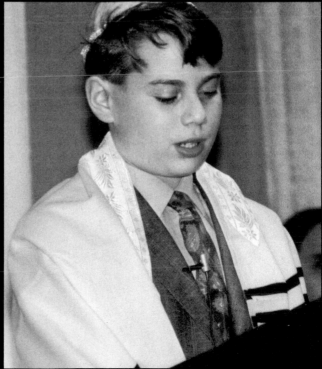

Grandson Asher chanting the prayers at his bar mitzvah

Moishe addressing the senior staff—including the nine-member Jews for Jesus for Council—after the nomination of his successor in 1996

December 2008 at the Rosen home: Moishe seated, left to right, Lyn, Ruth, Asher, Bethany, Alan and Ceil

Moishe knew it was unlikely that he would live long enough to attend his granddaughter's wedding, but wanted very much to have a part in blessing them and celebrating their engagement. Gary and Bethany agreed to an informal "betrothal ceremony" put together at the Rosen home in December of 2009.

Moishe and Ceil
Taken on Thanksgiving, his favorite holiday, 2009

Others, however, really chafed at being lumped together with the group of radical young missionaries. After all, many of the things said in the press about Jews for Jesus were untrue, even for those who *were* part of the organization. And many things that *were* accurate concerning the missionary organization were not necessarily applicable to all Jesus-believing Jews.

It should be no surprise then that a number of those who wanted to remain distinct from Jews for Jesus had no great love for Moishe and his somewhat flamboyant, often controversial methodologies. Such people seemed to view him as personally responsible for the unwelcome assumption that they were part of "his group."

For the most part, Moishe showed no interest in alleviating those hostilities. Maybe he felt that whatever undesirable connotations others had to bear as a result of being associated with Jews for Jesus fell under Jesus' teaching: "Blessed are you when they revile and persecute you, and say all kinds of evil against you falsely for My sake" (Matt. 5:11). What was Jews for Jesus, other than a group of Jewish people drawing attention to the name and person of Jesus? And hadn't Jesus predicted that this would bring false accusations? Moishe had little patience for any Jewish believer in Jesus who chafed at being called a "Jew for Jesus" because he saw it as a badge of honor (as did many who were not part of the organization). To him, anyone who saw it differently wasn't seeing things straight. Of course, this frustrated and offended those who *did* see things differently.

The very name Jews for Jesus seemed to be an affront to those who held the view that they should never say Jesus, but only say Yeshua, the Hebrew pronunciation of his name. They also refused to identify with any term that included the word *Christian*—in favor of *messianic Jew*.

Reasons for emphasizing terminology were in part due to the need to reiterate the fact that belief in Jesus did not negate one's Jewish identity. To that degree, Moishe was happy to use the terminology. He often talked about Yeshua (later Jews for Jesus chose to spell it Y'shua). However, he objected to the insistence that some terms be used exclusively and others rejected or disallowed as inappropriate.

Moishe firmly believed that the only way to truly counter the visceral reaction that words like *Jesus* and *Christian* evoked in many Jewish people was for individuals to discover for themselves who Jesus really is, what he did and what he taught. Only then would people understand that Jesus was not responsible for the deaths of millions of Jews and that those who committed atrocities in his name were acting contrary to his teachings.

Moishe understood that many chose not to describe themselves as Christians because being Jewish and Christian are commonly considered mutually exclusive. But he "refused to refuse" to allow his Jewish identity to separate him from Gentiles who were following the Jewish Messiah and who, as a result, loved the Jewish people. He made his feelings known both privately and publicly, which did not endear him to those who saw things differently. One can only imagine the chagrin of those who believed it necessary to say "Yeshua," not "Jesus," when they were continually referred to in the press as "Jews for Jesus."

The world of Jewish believers in Yeshua (Jesus)—as relatively small a world as it is—has its share of divisions, just as the larger communities of Jewish people who don't believe in Jesus do. Within the world of Jewish believers in Jesus, Moishe did not see himself as either the cause or the potential solution to these divisions. Some, no doubt, would disagree.

In any case, it is not unusual for people of influence who see things differently from one another to butt heads. That certainly seemed to be the case with Moishe and certain other influential people in the movement of Jewish believers. Yet he was also an encourager and supporter of many in the movement and was quick to recognize the talents of others, including the music group Lamb. Accordingly, when Moishe was invited to speak at the Chicagoland Messianic Rally, he let the rally organizers know that he thought a concert by a music team called Lamb would enhance the program and that he would like them to share the platform and sing before he got up to speak. Further, he respected the group's abilities enough to employ their help in producing the first Liberated Wailing Wall album. (The album was the project noted earlier that helped lift Moishe out of his depression.)

Moishe felt that the Liberated Wailing Wall (a mobile evangelistic music team) was one of the most valuable assets that Jews for Jesus had brought to the ABMJ while the group was still under their auspices. Most of the team's songs were written by Stuart Dauermann, though many others in the group contributed music and lyrics. Because *Fiddler on the Roof* was very popular at the time, most people, whether or not they were Jewish, could immediately recognize the Jewish sound of the Liberated Wailing Wall. As for the lyrics, they were from Scripture, whether from the Psalms, Hebrew prophets, Gospels, or Epistles. The Liberated Wailing Wall raised Christian awareness, not only of Jews for

Jesus but of the need for Jewish evangelism. It also spoke to the hearts of many Jewish and gentile seekers—who began following Jesus as a result. And so, at a time when his income was still rather precarious, Moishe used his own money to produce the first Liberated Wailing Wall album.

Some may wonder how Moishe's relationship with his daughters fared throughout the 1970s when he was investing so much time and energy in Jews for Jesus. Children of visionaries may feel overlooked or left out, as many biographies and autobiographies attest. Moishe never pushed either of his daughters to do what he was doing, but he welcomed both to be as involved in the world of Jews for Jesus as we cared to be. This was true both before and after the mission became independent.

As a speech and drama major, Lyn was particularly interested in the evangelistic street theater the group was pioneering. Eventually she became part of the New Jerusalem Players. She recalled,

> When Dad lost his job he never made me feel like there was anything I needed to do without. I really enjoyed the four of us around the [dinner] table. He often brought home a dinner guest and there was always enough [to eat]. He never acted like he expected me to be part of his ministry, but whenever I wanted to be part of what he was doing, he was always happy to have my participation.

As for me, I was fairly strong and outspoken in my beliefs and went on several of the demonstrations. However, I withdrew for almost a year, during which time I was not interested in anything connected with God. This had nothing to do with my relationship with my father—it was just normal teenage "stuff" that included dating a boy my parents did not approve of.

Later, when I was once again strong in my faith, Moishe asked me if I would like to join the Summer Witnessing Campaign in New York. "No, not really," was my reply. Eventually I agreed to go—not because I was interested but because that year (and it was the only year) the New York campaign was only two weeks, and I felt it would make him happy. It turned out to be a life-changing experience that led me to transfer from a liberal arts school to a Bible college and eventually join the staff of Jews for Jesus. This seemed as unexpected a turn of events to Moishe as it was to me.

By that time, Lyn was fully involved with Jews for Jesus. Moishe was surprised and delighted that both of his daughters felt God leading them into the ministry that meant so much to him.

Not only that, but shortly after Lyn's graduation, a young Oklahoman made his way out to California. Alan Bond had been dating Lyn during her last year of school. Knowing that he had been president of his church youth group, she had assumed that he was a Christian. As their relationship became serious, however, Lyn realized that for Alan, Christianity was simply part of his culture, not a life-changing belief in Jesus.

Lyn was miserable. Feeling that she could not marry a man who did not understand or share the faith that was such a central part of her life, she had prayerfully determined to break off the relationship after six months unless he had a change of heart. Totally unaware of Lyn's decision, for the first time in his life Alan began to think seriously about what it meant to be a Christian. Before the six months ended, Baruch Goldstein had led Alan in a prayer of faith in Jesus. Alan and Lyn were married in June 1974, and in September 1975 both joined the staff of Jews for Jesus.

Lyn recalled,

> When we asked Dad if he would perform our wedding ceremony, he [declined and] said, "I want to be the father of the bride and enjoy the wedding." But he did write the wedding service for us.
>
> I will never forget how, before the service on our wedding day, Dad disappeared with our best man, Tuvya, to collect the mail. I couldn't figure out if the mail was really that important—or if Dad was just a tad nervous, and didn't quite know how [else to] wait for the service.

Ceil, already in her mother-of-the-bride dress, tending to last-minute details, was totally unaware of Moishe's brief disappearance. It was just as well.

TWENTY-FIVE

*The way that I understand anger is that it's a God-given emotion,
and its purpose is to energize us to do the right thing;
one's temper is something that one uses, not loses.*

—MOISHE ROSEN

Over the hum of an old air conditioner and the muted yet audible din of street traffic and sirens, a loud voice burst from the other side of a closed office door. The words were muffled, but the tone was unmistakable. Raising a worried eyebrow, Susan Perlman winced and held her breath, straining to listen. The loud voice belonged to her beloved Great Uncle Gutel, who was engaged rather heatedly in conversation with Moishe Rosen.

Gutel, a regional director for the Jewish National Fund, had spent much of his adult life raising money to reforest Israel. A devout pillar of the Jewish community, he was very upset that Susan had come to faith in Jesus, and worse yet, was associated with the nefarious Jews for Jesus that he'd read about in the *Jewish Press.* He blamed Moishe for Susan's move from New York to California and for changing her life. When Uncle Gutel had learned that the notorious Moishe was coming to New York (for the first ever Jews for Jesus Summer Witnessing Campaign), he had asked for an appointment with him.

Now the two were alone in the room that served as Moishe's temporary office, and who knew what might happen next? Uncle Gutel was not only elderly, but very excitable. Susan feared he would get so agitated that he would have a heart attack.

Her worry only increased when a second loud voice interrupted the first, its cadence punctuated by the stutter that sometimes invaded Moishe's speech when his mind moved faster than his mouth—or when he was trying to get a word in edgewise. But to Susan's great relief, the shouting only lasted a minute, before both voices suddenly decreased in volume. Could they actually be having a calm, civilized conversation? The two were in there for a long time while Susan sat in the other room, alternately worrying and trying to concentrate on her work. At last the door opened, and Uncle Gutel came out.

Moishe's bulky six-foot one-inch frame appeared in the doorway, his expression thoughtful.

"So, Moishe, what happened?" The tightness of Susan's attempt at a light tone betrayed the concern underlying her curiosity.

Moishe smiled reassuringly. "You know, Sue, I learned a lot from your uncle. After he calmed down, I asked him how he went about raising money for the Jewish National Fund. He said he always tried to let people know personally how much he appreciated their support and encouragement. That's something I've always felt was important, so I asked what he did to express his appreciation.

"I guess you know that since your uncle doesn't drive, he's always taking trains and buses to visit people and make presentations for the cause. Well, he told me how he put those travel times to use. He'd buy postcards, and while he rode along, he'd write personal notes thanking donors he'd met in previous places. It became a regular part of his routine, sending those handwritten, personal postcards. I think that's a great idea, don't you? Maybe we should be writing personal postcards to our donors."

"Yeah, okay, but . . . you two . . . you parted as friends?" Susan was pleased that Moishe liked her uncle's postcard idea, but she was a lot more interested in how her uncle had responded to Moishe.

"Well, I don't know that your uncle would appreciate being referred to as my friend, but I think he would agree that we are now at least respectful and cordial acquaintances. Your uncle is a wise man who understands how to relate to people. I think I'd like us to try out that donor postcard thing."

Susan smiled with relief. "I guess it went well. That's a real answer to prayer. And . . . about the postcards, Moishe . . . , I think you're right. It just might work for Jews for Jesus, too—*if* you can get people to do it."

———

One of Moishe's strengths was his ability to recognize when people had something worthwhile to teach him, regardless of differences in age, experience, or belief. Throughout the 1970s, Moishe not only taught, but continued to learn many lessons.

Some of his sources of information proved controversial. Early on, Susan Perlman brought Saul Alinsky's book *Rules for Radicals* to Moishe's attention, when a friend showed it to her with the suggestion "some of this might apply to what you guys are doing." Moishe read the book, saw its value, and shared it with the leadership team. All agreed that while much of it must be discarded as inappropriate for followers of Jesus, some of the "rules" could translate well into the group's strategies, particularly in responding to opposition. These principles, such as "make your opposition live up to their own standards" and "de-personalize hostility" were perfectly ethical. However, the fact that they were found in a book that also contained objectionable ideologies and practices became a matter of controversy among Moishe's critics.

Some of the lessons Moishe learned were serendipitous, coming when he least expected them. It was his personal policy to meet any relatives of the early Jews for Jesus who were willing to see him if they came to town, or if he was traveling to their area. He always parlayed such meetings into opportunities to commend the staff person to his or her parents or other relatives. He knew that many had grave misgivings about family members being involved in Jews for Jesus, in large part because of the outrageous claims made in the press by anti-missionaries. Moishe wanted to give relatives an opportunity to meet him and ask questions, balancing what they had read with firsthand experience so they could draw their own conclusions. He also wanted to be available to discuss Jesus, knowing that many people find it easier to discuss such matters with nonfamily members.

And so it was that Moishe had met and learned something from Susan Perlman's great uncle. As Susan recalled, "It wasn't all that long after [Moishe's meeting with Uncle Gutel] that we started writing personal communications on postcards to our donors."

As Moishe continued to learn and teach, Jews for Jesus grew. By 1976, the work had expanded from the San Francisco Bay area to Los Angeles, New York, Chicago, and Boston. For that year's New York Summer Witnessing Campaign, Moishe thought he could use the increased ranks for an expanded evangelistic outreach that would cover more places on the eastern seaboard for a longer period of time. Since it was our nation's bicentennial celebration, someone suggested the name Operation Birthday Cake (OBC) for a Jews for Jesus witnessing campaign. That year, approximately eighty staff and volunteers participated.

Moishe later said,

> I learned a whole lot from my mistakes. For example, in '76, we just had too many people to run a really good campaign. This was a mistake I could easily recognize [though after the fact] because of what the military had taught me: you never take more people or equipment than is necessary to get the job

done, particularly equipment, because you have to haul it there, use it, then haul it back. . . .

So I was in Philadelphia, as well as Boston and New York that summer. The ABMJ was also in Philadelphia that summer with a big conference. And I went to see Daniel Fuchs, and what was apparent [to him] was that we [Jews for Jesus] looked huge and we were. I met with Daniel and made a point to say, "You told me that one day I'd come and thank you, and I'm here today to thank you." He replied a bit wryly, "But I didn't think it would be so soon."

Whereas Daniel might have been impressed by the growth of Jews for Jesus, Moishe recognized a problem. The organization had become too big for its stage of developmental leadership. One of his primary responsibilities was to develop that leadership to a point where they could continue without him. As far as he was concerned, that meant teaching them to follow certain nonnegotiable principles that he felt were crucial for leading a ministry properly, and he pushed hard to get that message across.

No biography would be complete without exploring issues that have caused contention and controversy. Of course the conviction that all people, including Jewish people, need to know Jesus is the central controversy. Moishe and all the Jews for Jesus bore that as part of their calling. But among the more interpersonal controversies we find such things as leadership style, particularly issues of control and anger. The former is addressed in the next chapter, but we turn now to the latter.

Moishe could react harshly when he felt his authority was being ignored or challenged, particularly if he felt someone was intentionally undermining a principle of the ministry he had worked so hard to build. In such instances, he could display great anger, reprimanding the offending party in front of the group.

Moishe had thought through his reasons for making such reprimands very loud and very public. He wanted to make the reprimands memorable, so they would serve as lessons not only to the person receiving the reprimand, but also to the other hearers. He wanted staff to be accountable to him and to one another.

Yet Moishe never regarded himself as an angry person. He often stated—and semed convinced—that his displays of anger were calculated to make a point and that he was not inwardly angry. At times, this was believable; at other times, these displays appeared to be a genuine show of temper and personal frustration that would have better been kept under control.

Some people simply did not listen if he didn't yell, according to Moishe. And, at times Moishe seemed to use volume to compensate for his slowness of speech. He often felt others who could speak far more rapidly than he could were cutting him off before he could finish a thought.

Part of Moishe's mystique was that his perceptions were razor sharp; not only could he assess people and situations quickly and correctly, but he could recall with alacrity and accuracy countless details he had learned from books, magazine articles, observation, and personal experience. Being so often right made it difficult for him to see when he might be wrong.

There were also areas in which his self-awareness was surprisingly lacking. But one can argue that this is inherent in human nature. In later years when he told me on numerous occasions—and in all sincerity—"I could never figure out why people said I was so intimidating," I was simply amazed. On one such occasion, I reminded him, "I've been in the room many times when you've yelled at people, and even when I wasn't the one being yelled at, I found it quite intimidating. Don't you remember those times?" He began to explain why he had yelled, but when I reminded him that we were discussing how others felt and why people were intimidated, he nodded his assent.

In fact, Moishe never considered yelling at people a big deal. He was well able to compartmentalize. He could read someone the riot act during the day and invite him for a friendly dinner that night. And some to whom the riot act was read were also able to compartmentalize these interactions. Moishe's son-in-law, Alan Bond, was one of them. He seemed to have no problem leaving his professional life behind him when he came to see his in-laws. However, in my estimation, that was and is a rare ability—a fact that Moishe did not seem to realize.

Moishe had made the lecture on depersonalizing hostility part of missionary training. He'd taught the staff and volunteers to deal with hostility by remembering that the opposition did not know them—it was not the individuals but what they represented that was the target of the insults. But when anger came from Moishe, it was different. He knew these people. He cared for these people and they regarded him as an important person in their lives. What he perhaps failed to see was that when *he* displayed anger, regardless of how he meant it, it was quite naturally felt as personal hostility. If he said something hurtful, no lesson had been given in how to depersonalize it, short of people convincing themselves that he really didn't know or care about them.

So it was that people who had shared with Moishe a sense of adventure and even play in their common purpose to creatively proclaim the gospel now found he was often questioning, criticizing, correcting, and disciplining them. Regardless of whether Moishe was acting correctly, one can understand how natural it would be for some to feel disappointed and hurt.

Perhaps the disappointment and hurt was, at times, proportional to the depth of the relationship that people had enjoyed with Moishe. When a leader helps a person discover how to do things previously unimagined, and works alongside that person to achieve a common purpose in ways that bring out their very best, it's natural to ascribe great importance to that person. That typified Moishe's relationship with many of those he mentored.

Miriam Nadler, when asked what she saw as Moishe's greatest strength said, "To give vision and encourage others to go beyond what they think they can do."

Susan echoed this in describing his role in her life: "He [Moishe], for whatever it was worth, believed in me, that I could do things that I didn't think I could do. And I was willing to believe him believing in me. So I did them."

Susan and many of those whom Moishe mentored not only became leaders in Jews for Jesus, but beyond Jews for Jesus, serving on numerous boards and steering committees.

As Moishe found his circumstances changing, his role in the lives of those who had looked to him primarily for support and encouragement also changed. These changes occurred in a somewhat unsystematic way that was neither mutually understood nor mutually accepted by Moishe and those under his authority.

Through it all, Moishe very much wanted to maintain the fun and adventure of Jews for Jesus. He continued to encourage creativity, affirming and encouraging people's gifts, and reaching out to the staff in many ways and on many occasions that demonstrated high levels of kindness and caring.

Unfortunately, painful incidents often leave stronger, longer lasting impressions than positive and pleasing experiences. Few people are likely to memorialize each act of kindness as clearly as they remember negative interactions. This, too, is human nature, and it takes a special grace to keep a balanced perspective on any person who has caused pain. Fortunately, Moishe retained, or in some cases regained, many wonderful friendships throughout his life through the grace that he both gave and received.

TWENTY-SIX

Some people think I'm an ogre, others think I'm a genius, but I am neither.
—MOISHE ROSEN

I watched as several hundred students pressed into the gym, filling the bleachers. I took a deep breath. Thanks to Jews for Jesus, I'd already had substantial experience with public speaking. Still, this was one of the largest groups I had ever addressed. I approached the microphone, smiled briefly, and greeted the student body, who responded warmly. Then I began, "You know, a lot of people ask me, 'What's it like to be Moishe Rosen's daughter?'" I usually reply, 'Compared to what? I've never been anyone else's daughter.'" A small undercurrent of amusement rippled through the audience. I went on to describe my father as an ordinary person God had used to do extraordinary things. It took about three minutes to complete the introduction. The longest round of applause I could remember hearing for a chapel speaker ensued as I left to take my seat. My father, still able to carry his considerable weight with relative ease, came briskly to the podium.

As Moishe spoke, he seemed to create his own culture, so different from the students, yet so able to connect with them. He didn't work at being relevant like some speakers who used vernacular terms they were not really comfortable with to show they could "relate." I listened with pride as my father captivated his audience with a combination of humor, wisdom, and genuine interest in his listeners. The gist of his message was that God uses ordinary people to accomplish his extraordinary purposes. We had not coordinated my intro to match his message; we were just on the same wavelength.

Moishe understood his listeners and knew how to cast a vision they could somehow make their own. It wasn't the vision of Jews for Jesus. It was a vision for how anyone could make a difference by stepping out in faith. He used a bit of self-deprecation to make the point: "I'm overweight, overbearing, and over forty" he pointed out, not for the first or last time, "and not the most likely candidate for God to choose to lead a group of young people in a mission like Jews for Jesus."

The students loved his candor. They smiled and laughed, but mostly, they listened. Afterward, a knot of students surrounded him, and I stood a few feet away, awaiting my turn. One student approached me.

"I noticed that you refer to your dad as 'Moishe.' Can I ask why you don't call him your father?" he said.

"Sure," I replied. "He asked my sister and me not to." Noting the student's shocked expression, I quickly continued, "Oh, at home if it's just family, I call him 'Dad' or 'Daddy.' But he prefers that we refer to him as Moishe when we talk to or about him around the Jews for Jesus staff and volunteers, so I'm used to calling him that most everywhere. You know, because he's the boss. As far as he's concerned, we don't get any special treatment, and he'd rather not draw attention to the fact that he's our dad."

The young man nodded. "That makes sense."

"Yeah, I think so." I smiled inwardly. Not many kids could call their parents by their first name without seeming disrespectful.

———

The side of Moishe that Biola students saw that day was very much a part of his persona, in one-to-one interactions as well as when he spoke to groups. But in addition to the "relatability" factor, there was a toughness that Moishe felt responsible to maintain in his role of executive director.

Once Jews for Jesus became an organization, standards, goals, and accountability became a primary focus of the ministry and of Moishe's leadership. He not only had to raise funds to support the missionaries, but he also felt responsible to ensure that he and the other missionaries were worthy of that support. He was never content to trust that things were happening as he thought they should. He always felt that people, including himself, had a tendency to do less than they ought if left to their own devices. So he looked for principles and procedures to keep himself and others on track. He explained,

> You don't invent principles; you discover them. And principles really don't help you get things done; they keep you from doing what's wrong. They keep you on target, but you have to propel yourself forward. It takes a personal application of energy to do what you know you ought to do. And it is procedures by which you accomplish things, not the principles.

When Jews for Jesus became an organization in 1973, I had to set standards. . . . And I had all of these volunteers who were now professionals, and I had to move their attitudes from being volunteers to understanding that there were professional standards. When I use the words *professional minister*, I'm talking about somebody who has standards. There is a big difference between a missionary and a witness. A good witness tells [about Jesus] as much as he can and whenever he can, but a missionary schedules his life so that he's available to tell people [the gospel].

You give yourself to volunteers—and all that they give back is appreciated because they don't have to. You still give yourself to staff, but mainly to train them to give to others. What they give is expected, and they are to be accountable for maintaining a standard of professionalism. If they only do what is expected, they are considered minimalists.

Moishe added,

The role that I never liked was that of being an enforcer. But the problem is that once you have principles, once you have policies, once you have procedures, if the top man is not willing to be the enforcer, then, everything collapses. And one of the big problems I've seen in other missions was that the enforcer got caught up in the "Nice Guy" complex. On the one hand, he was expected to keep the rules, and on the other hand, because he was a nice guy, he made excuses for people when they did not do their duties. I must admit that was a temptation I also had. But the head of any organization has to set up rules of enforcement to see that the principles, policies, and procedures are followed. If you don't do that, you're not the head of the organization.

Add to this an excerpt from one of Moishe's leadership lessons to the senior staff: "A leader does not enjoy discovering a subordinate in a mistake, but a leader must continually test subordinates for errors. For, if you fail to test, then you fail to strengthen." As far as Moishe was concerned, continual vigilance, testing, enforcing, and the expectation of accountability were aspects of his responsibility as a mission leader.

In holding people accountable for their work, Moishe never based his assessment on people's word alone. He therefore believed it his duty to check up on staff because not checking would encourage them to slack off—which he believed most people, including himself, were inclined to do at times. If Moishe suspected (rightly or wrongly) that someone was slacking and/or exaggerating or falsifying the amount of work done, the level of accountability he required could become painstaking and meticulous. Some former staff felt deeply wounded because, they pointed out, Moishe seemed to believe the worst and to regard people with whom he had once been so close with suspicion and mistrust. In certain cases, his suspicion and mistrust proved to be well founded. However, in other cases, there never was a meeting of the minds about what had or had not happened—and as a result, before the decade was over, one of the founding couples of the ministry left feeling that they had been grossly misjudged.*

Years later Amy Rabinovitz noted, "There were a lot of subtle changes when he [Moishe] left the ABMJ, both in terms of his personal fears and his personal strengths. Later, for a period of time, he grew very self-protective, but it's been too long since I've seen him to know if that was just a phase or if that became part of him. I suspect that it was a phase and considering all the kinds of pressures coming at him, [it was] probably predictable."

Part of that self-protection probably reflected Moishe's ambivalence about what he felt was necessary in his role as executive director. As he later explained,

> Unfortunately, once we became an organization, I felt some strange sense of accountability that I had to be much more serious, much more demanding than I had been up to that time.

In the 1970s, Moishe frequently used the word *control* in dealing with the staff, yet he never considered himself a controlling person. One of Moishe's sayings was that he wanted "to control little but influence much." He often added that he wanted that influence to be through his ideas and his humor, and it often was.

When Moishe talked about control, he meant to make sure the staff adhered to principles, policies and procedures. Adherence could only be measured through accountability, and means of accountability often overlap with means of control. Moishe saw such control as an objective necessity, not a personal hunger for power.

In a discussion about structures of leadership and what he learned from the military, he said,

---

* Some three decades later, this couple returned to the Bay Area to celebrate their wedding anniversary and visited Moishe in his home following one of his chemotherapy treatments. Moishe was thrilled to see them after so many years, and they seemed equally happy to have the opportunity to share fond memories with him.

One kind of structure is hierarchical: the chief approves everything; nothing happens without the chief. If a chief insists on being that much in control, boy, he'd better not try to do too many things. If he goes to war, maybe he can train archers and swordsmen, but he can't train archers, swordsmen, and catapult operators and sappers, etc. You are very definitely limited when you have that kind of autocratic leadership.

Although many would equate Moishe's leadership with that description, somehow he never saw himself as being as much in control as others did. He did his best to train leaders who could be in authority over those in their branches. But while the level at which the branch leaders were accountable to Moishe may not have seemed so great to him, it loomed very large to those under him. That made it difficult for him to be friends with anyone he supervised, including Avi Brickner, who had joined the staff of Jews for Jesus in 1976. Avi had looked forward to having Moishe as a mentor and he also looked forward to continuing the collegiate type of relationship they'd had for so many years, but sadly that was not to be the case. While the two remained friends long after Avi left the staff of Jews for Jesus, the relationship was never as close as it once had been.

An interesting aside is that Moishe had many friendships that were not only sustainable, but grew deeper over the decades. Herb Links, a Jewish believer in Jesus and a Presbyterian pastor was one such friend—perhaps in part because he was never interested in Moishe's overtures to recruit him to work with him.

At any rate, while Moishe continued to see himself as Avi's friend after Avi left Jews for Jesus, Avi recalled, "I know that he still had regard for me, but . . . that regard was expressed in ways that were not easy to take."

Avi also observed that whereas Moishe had been such a good listener in the earlier years of their friendship, it seemed that in their latter conversations, Moishe did most of the talking.

Nevertheless, Avi concluded, "Even with the regrets I have about the negatives [in the later years of the relationship], there is also a lot of appreciation and gratitude for the way the Lord has used Moishe to bless [my wife] Leah and me. [As for] what I think about his [Moishe's] contribution to Jewish evangelism, it is immense and seminal."

Avi's observations and feelings certainly did not characterize all of Moishe's friendships, but neither were they unique. When it came to conversations, Moishe always enjoyed listening to others as long as they engaged his interest, but if he heard something that set off his instinct to solve a problem or teach a lesson, he would jump in and sometimes lose track of the other person's part in the conversation. Moishe joked more than once, "I'm always interested in what I have to say." But then, most people prefer to hear themselves talk. If Moishe had a problem in conversations, it was usually not an issue of control. He was either trying to "fix" or solve something or forgetting that he was not the only one who liked to hear himself talk.

Moishe was not unaware of his faults; he mentioned and occasionally apologized for them in council meetings. In one such meeting he stated that he realized how, at times, he had been a trial for the leaders of Jews for Jesus because of his impatience and anger, adding that these were qualities that he didn't admire in himself or in others. Pride and ego were present in him, as they are in any human being. Yet he believed strongly in the importance of humility and openly acknowledged that his attitudes were not as far along as his convictions and ideals in that area.

Between 1976 and 1978, Moishe had a growing sense that the ministry was lacking in certain areas. One was training. Another was the sense of community that he felt was dissipating as the staff grew larger and people were spread farther apart. By 1978, Moishe had introduced a radical idea at one of the Jews for Jesus council meetings: close down all the branch operations for the better part of a year and bring the entire staff back together in San Francisco.

He explained that he felt the group was lacking not only in community, but also in the godliness promoted by community and having to put others first. He wanted to bring in some of the very best pastors and Bible scholars* to teach the staff and to be with them for a minimum of a week, so that the staff could learn by observing how to have a stronger spiritual life. Members of the staff were alternately excited, skeptical, and once again excited. They agreed on *Avodah* (a Hebrew word pronounced "ah-voh-*dah*" that embodies the idea of work and worship as one) as a name for this special time.

As Moishe explained it back then,

> We have been leaders so long that we don't have peers, and we are a group who needs peers. It [Avodah] will also be a blessing for those who are not leaders or not yet leaders. It will be a blessing for those who need a supportive

---

* Such notable pastors and scholars as Chuck Smith, Chuck Swindoll, and Walter Kaiser took part in Avodah.

community. It will be a help to married people. It will be a help to those who are single. It will be a help to those who have children. Community can give many things to many people. . . .

Avodah is to be a time of growing together, a time of sharpening our techniques, and a time of innovating in evangelism. Avodah is not a time when we will try to relive 1971, but it is an attempt to foster the same spirit and enthusiasm we had back then.*

Moishe lived and learned far more than he could have ever imagined between 1970 and 1979. Avodah was a transitional period that closed out that era—not just for Jews for Jesus, but for the one who was changing and developing along with the ministry he'd begun.

---

* These goals were not restricted to one period of Moishe's ministry. He continued to feel the importance of bringing the staff together for times of retraining and strengthening community, though never for an extended period like Avodah. Seven years after Avodah, he gathered the staff for retraining at a retreat center in Northern California and then again in another seven years.

TWENTY-SEVEN

If mistakes could sink our ship
we would have gone down at the beginning.
—MOISHE ROSEN

This way, Moishe!" Jhan pointed to some small boats on the river. He then darted to the other side of the road before his boss could reply.

It was a small town in Thailand, but even so, Moishe looked both ways to be sure it was safe to cross. He paused as a Vespa whizzed by. The riders, catching sight of Moishe, pulled off to the side of the road as they screeched the motor scooter to a halt. Two diminutive men quickly dismounted and came running back to Moishe. Smiling shyly, first one, then the other, reached out to rub the large, American tummy. They laughed—not derisively, but with delight—ran back to their scooter, and quickly rode away. Jhan, watching from across the street, stood shaking his head in disbelief. Moishe, hands aloft and both eyebrows raised, shrugged his shoulders as if to say, "Who knows?"

Once on the other side of the road, Moishe allowed himself to be steered by Jhan (or Moskowitz, as he was more commonly called) who negotiated a trip upriver to see one of the local sights.

Moishe generally suffered from severe motion sickness on the open sea, but this little river ride proved quite pleasant. He stared at the scenery in wide-eyed wonder. "And it's not just the place that is beautiful, but the people," he commented. "They are not only outwardly attractive but so friendly."

"Well those guys who rubbed your belly certainly were friendly."

"I wonder what that was about?" Moishe's expression was somewhere between thoughtful and bemused.

"Well, you know how they say it's good luck to rub the Buddha's belly?"

"You mean the laughing Buddha? Well, I know I'm fat, but do I look like the laughing Buddha to you?" He pulled his face into a caricature of a glower.

Moskowitz laughed. "No, Moishe, I don't think anyone could ever mistake that face for a laughing Buddha. But you're probably the closest thing they've seen to those statues, you know?"

Moishe shrugged his noncommittal response. He acted as though he didn't care about his weight, but of course he did. He'd lost quite a bit in the early 70's—perhaps a hundred pounds. But eventually, he'd regained all the weight he'd lost, and more.

Before long, the small boat arrived at the dock and Jhan and Moishe clambered out.

"This looks like a multipurpose river," Moishe observed, looking up and down the shore.

"No kidding. Those people are bathing, those guys are swimming, and that guy over there—what's he doing? Ugh, I don't want to know." Jhan wrinkled his nose in disgust.

"I wonder what they are cooking?" Moishe nodded his head to indicate people who were squatting next to small grills.

"I dunno, Moishe, c'mon, we want to go that way." He pointed to an elaborate structure in the distance. But Moishe was still focused on the barbeque.

"Whatever it is, it smells pretty good."

Jhan sighed as his boss made his way to the closest grill. The owner smiled up at him. Moishe pointed to the meat on the grill, then to himself, held up the requisite number of fingers and said, "Two."

The man, still smiling, gave Moishe two portions of whatever it was in exchange for the bats Moishe pulled from his pocket.

"Here," he said, offering Jhan half the grilled meat.

"C'mon Moishe, you're not really gonna eat that." But Jhan knew that he would.

"Moskowitz, where's your sense of adventure? Wasn't it just yesterday that you rode an elephant?"

"Yeah, well riding an elephant is one thing. Eating monkey guts is another."

"Monkey guts?" Moishe repeated scornfully. And he stuffed the mysterious piece of barbequed something into his mouth.

"Are you crazy man? How can you eat that?"

To which Moishe replied through a mouthful of BBQ, "If it won't kill him," (gesturing to a Thai man who was eating with obvious relish) "it won't kill me."

Jhan watched with concern to see if the food would have any adverse effects. It didn't.

After their sightseeing excursion, they headed back to the hotel.

"It's so much cheaper to get a tailored suit here than back home," Moishe commented. "I think I'll get measured for some shirts and a couple suits at the hotel."

"No, no!" Jhan protested. "They'll rip you off. Look, I found a place downtown where the guy's making me shirts for five dollars each. It's just a two-dollar ride downtown."

Soon they were in a taxi, heading for the tailor. It was a small shop. High above the bolts of material was a shelf and on it sat a picture of the king and queen of Thailand, as well as a small statue of Buddha, with a few pieces of fruit set by as an offering. This seemed standard in most Thai businesses.

Moishe appreciated the people's loyalty toward their royals, but the ubiquitous altars for Buddha made him uncomfortable. Nevertheless he approached the proprietor and smiled. "My friend tells me you're making five-dollar shirts."

Horrified, the tailor looked at Moishe and said, "No, no, no, no!"

"No? Are you telling me that you didn't agree to make my friend shirts for that price?"

"Yes, yes, for your friend, five dollars. For you, big man, I'm sorry, seven dollars and fifty cents."

"Oh, I see," Moishe replied, realizing that a shirt for him would require considerably more fabric than Jhan's. "Well, that's still a very fair price." The tailor smiled, obviously relieved, and Moishe ordered several items of clothing.

When they left the shop, Moishe pointed to a tuk-tuk, "Want to try one of those?" he said. "It looks like it would be cooler than the taxi we took on the way here."

"Yeah, sure," Jhan agreed. The taxis were not air conditioned, and while the tuk-tuks had a roof overhead, they were pretty much open on the sides and back.

The ride back was cooler and considerably more exciting as the two Americans held on for dear life to avoid being shaken loose from the tuk-tuk. Moishe looked at Jhan and said, "Whoever would have thought that you and I would be here, sharing this adventure?"

———

It was 1980, and Moishe was in Pattaya to participate in a conference called COWE, the Consultation on World Evangelism. To understand COWE, it's necessary to backtrack. In June 1974, a group of evangelical Christians met in

Lausanne, Switzerland. Their purpose was to revitalize an international fellowship of missionaries who could encourage one another, share insights, and keep the cause of bringing the gospel to all people moving forward.

Moishe was invited to that conference, but was reluctant to leave the country because Jews for Jesus was still less than a year old as an independent mission. He asked and received approval to send Tuvya Zaretsky in his place. Tuvya met a great many people and did not realize until years later that Moishe had relinquished to him a front-row seat from which he witnessed a significant moment in the history of world missions.

The 1974 group named themselves the Lausanne Committee on World Evangelization (LCWE) and purposed to meet again. The 1980 conference in Pattaya was the second meeting of that group. The conference included seventeen mini-consultation groups to focus on specific areas of world evangelization. Jews for Jesus was part of the group for reaching Jews with the gospel.

David Harley, then the principal of All Nations Christian College in England, was the COWE coordinator of the miniconsultation group on reaching Jews. He had met Moishe in the late 1970s when Moishe talked with people from CMJ, one the Jewish missions in the UK. To give his first impressions of Moishe, Harley named four things:

His size. He could barely fit into our car, which he described as a typical British missionary car—i.e., it was too small!

His warmth and friendliness.

His dislike of British food. He said he now understood that the British built an empire because they could not stand eating at home.

His passion to reach Jewish people around the world with the good news [of Jesus].

The last item made enough of an impression that when Harley was asked to organize study groups for COWE, he wrote to Moishe suggesting that some of the Jews for Jesus staff present papers on Jewish evangelism.

It was 1979, and Jews for Jesus was in the year of Avodah. Moishe required everyone to write a paper for the conference as part of the assigned studies. This was no small contribution to the preparations that Harley was making.

Susan Perlman had accompanied Jhan and Moishe to Thailand, and she recalled,

Moishe cemented relationships with other Jewish missions leaders in a way that only time away from the usual responsibilities could provide. Most of the miniconsultation groups had a minimum of fifty people; the Jewish consultation group had seventeen. But I think we were one of only two groups that actually had finished what they called an LOP—a Lausanne Occasional Paper—because we had done so much prep work.

The group for Jewish evangelism finished their paper the first day, and with more than a week left of the conference, Moishe and the others brainstormed, strategized, and got to know one another. Some participants decided to form a task force, so they could continue meeting for mutual encouragement and the added stimulus of cross-pollinating ideas and experiences. They called themselves the Lausanne Task Force on Jewish Evangelism, which later became the Lausanne Consultation on Jewish Evangelism (LCJE).

Commenting on Moishe's role at the conference and subsequent development of LCJE, David Harley recalled,

> Incalculable! LCJE would never have come into existence but for the enthusiasm and support of Moishe. If I remember correctly, a small group [which included Moishe] met over a meal during the conference in Pattaya and discussed the possibility of forming an international task force on Jewish evangelism. Moishe was very enthusiastic about the idea from the start, and his subsequent support in terms of advice, encouragement, and financial commitment was invaluable. LCJE would never have . . . continued as one of the most significant products of the Lausanne Movement without Moishe's wholehearted involvement.
>
> [Yet] he tended to keep more in the background because he was aware of the divisions within the USA among those who were engaged in Jewish evangelism and he did not want to put some people off because [he knew] they thought the group was dominated by Jews for Jesus.

Moishe played a key role in the LCJE not only because of the commitments David Harley mentioned, but also because he made many of the Jews for Jesus staff available to attend meetings and to do prep work for them. Soon the LCJE met internationally three times a year and regionally once a year.

The history of the LCJE helps demonstrate that whereas Moishe's identity was inextricably linked to his founding and leading the ministry of Jews for Jesus, his influence stretched far beyond that mission. He was an international force for the cause to which he devoted his life: making Jesus known to Jewish people.

At the meeting in Pattaya, Moishe read Ole Christian Kvarme's paper and commented that Ole was capable of great things. He was certainly right. From 1975 to 1981 Ole was a Lutheran pastor in Haifa and executive secretary for the United Bible Societies in Israel and the West Bank. He held other significant posts before returning to Norway in 1986, first as general secretary of the Norwegian Bible Society, then as dean of the Oslo Cathedral. In 2005, he became the bishop of Oslo in the Lutheran Church of Norway, a position he still holds at the writing of this book.

Offering his recollections of Moishe, including first encounters, Bishop Kvarme said,

Some of us Europeans came to our first encounter with him with great skepticism, critical of [what we'd heard concerning] the Jews for Jesus approach in reaching out to Jewish people. But obviously we had not been properly informed. The JFJ material in the preparations for the Pattaya conference had made us curious and prepared us for better things. Simply meeting Moishe together with Susan and Jhan changed everything, almost immediately. Obviously, the first impression was the size of the man. But it did not take long before I discovered a different kind of greatness, his spirit of mind. Here was a person who was deeply anchored in the gospel and evangelical theology, combined with a deep love for his people and Jewish tradition.

We could not help but listen to Moishe when he spoke, we sensed in his voice a spirit of wisdom and gentleness, but also a strong and creative mind. I also discovered a friend who was generous, who wanted the best for his colleagues and friends, and who gave of himself. . . .

Without Moishe LCJE would not have come into existence, or it would not have become the significant network it has been through these thirty years. I am thankful for his enthusiasm and creativity, thankful for his wisdom in leadership, sometimes exercised backstage, sometimes in front, always building bridges across organizational barriers and relationship with many churches for the sake of the Gospel to Jewish people. . . .

I regard getting to know Moishe in 1980 and having the privilege of working with him for almost two decades in the context of LCJE as a tremendous blessing and a high point in my own life and ministry. I am convinced that for many years to come we will see the fruits of his visions and enthusiasm, his creativity and gentle spirit.

Moishe's influence extended not only beyond North America, but also beyond the relatively small field of Jewish missions. He was particularly concerned about maintaining what, in evangelical circles, is referred to as a "high view of Scriptures" (that is, both Old and New Testaments of the Bible are inspired by God and without error). He was very interested in Bible colleges and seminaries that taught students to regard the Bible as the Word of God and to examine with a critical eye popular trends that viewed the Bible as anything less than what it presents itself to be.

One of the seminaries Moishe regarded most highly was Western Seminary, based in Portland, Oregon. Formerly known as Western Conservative Baptist Seminary, the school had a claim on Moishe, first of all, because he was loyal to the denomination that had first ordained him for ministry. Moishe also had a high regard for the seminary, its faculty, and its president, Earl Radmacher. He served on the board of directors of the seminary, and in 1986 the school conferred an honorary degree (Doctorate of Divinity) on Moishe.

Parallel to his strong support of the seminary, Moishe was a member of the International Council on Biblical Inerrancy (ICBI). The group was founded in 1977 to clarify and defend the doctrine of biblical inerrancy.* Moishe first read about the ICBI in *Moody Monthly* and *Christianity Today*. He became a supporter, not only financially, but with letters of encouragement and suggestions on how to gain more popular support for the cause. In 1979 he was invited to address the group. Soon after, he was asked to fill the spot of a charter board member who had died. This put him in close contact with well-known Christian theologians—pastors, scholars, and authors.**

David Brickner and Rich Robinson, two staff members of Jews for Jesus, were invited to one of the meetings. Brickner recalled,

> I was excited to be there. [There were] all of these rock stars of evangelicalism, and Moishe seemed to be known to everybody. And he had this amazing reputation. It wasn't just Moishe. It was Jews for Jesus [that] had that reputa-

---

* A simple definition of inerrancy is the view that when all facts are known, they will demonstrate that the Bible in its original text is entirely true.

** A small sampling of those in this group included James M. Boice, Edmund P. Clowney, Gleason Archer, Harold Hoehner, Walter C. Kaiser Jr., D. James Kennedy, J. I. Packer, and R. C. Sproul.

tion. It was an excellent reputation, but it was partly because of his genius. People recognized it.

He [Moishe] said [the ICBI] is an organization that exists for one purpose, and when its purpose is completed, it needs to go out of existence. It doesn't need to be self-perpetuating. And he spoke with a voice of authority that everybody . . . acknowledged [and saw] that Moishe was the organizational genius [of the group]. He had very strong theological convictions that he could articulate and questions that probed and prodded the theologians to get it right, but he never wrote any of those statements.

Moishe felt strongly that no group should outlive its usefulness. He was immensely pleased that the ICBI chose to disband in 1988, satisfied that they had completed their task by clearly defining and bringing public attention to the issue of inerrancy.*

By 1982 Moishe had contributed his own cache of writings that was not so much scholarly as practical and useful for laypeople. In addition to his articles in the Jews for Jesus newsletter and his broadside tracts, Moishe wrote articles for many Christian magazines.**

The 1980s, perhaps more than any other decade, show that throughout his career, Moishe's life greatly affected many individuals and groups beyond Jews for Jesus. Nevertheless, Jews for Jesus remained his passion, so much so that it is difficult to write a biography that, from the 1970s onward, does not focus primarily on his role within and his concerns regarding that organization.

Moishe feared that Jews for Jesus had grown too fast. One of his purposes for the Avodah year was to ascertain who would stay or leave the ministry. He also wanted to see natural leadership emerge, so he half jokingly and half seriously required all who had been leaders prior to Avodah to wear special buttons for the first few days. The buttons said, "I am not a leader."

---

* They had produced major statements in 1978, 1982, and 1986; some of their work appeared in Carl F. H. Henry's book, *God, Revelation and Authority,* vol. 4 (Waco, Tx.: Word Books, 1979), on pp. 211-219 as well as in *A General Introduction to the Bible,* by Norman L. Geisler and William E. Nix (Chicago: Moody Press, rev. 1986), at pp. 181-185. R. C. Sproul wrote an official commentary on the ICBI articles in the *ICBI.*

** He also wrote a modest collection of books and booklets, including *The Sayings of Chairman Moishe* (a simply illustrated compilation of his aphorisms published in 1972); *Jews for Jesus* (a history of the mission's earliest days, written jointly with William Proctor, 1974); *Share the New Life with a Jew* (a handbook on understanding and overcoming barriers to sharing one's faith, coauthored with Ceil Rosen, 1976); *Christ in the Passover* (also coauthored with Ceil in 1977); and *Y'shua: The Jewish Way to Say Jesus* (a prophecy primer of passages in the Hebrew Scriptures that point to Jesus as Messiah, a collaboration with Rich Robinson, 1982).

Over the course of the Avodah year, Moishe hoped to see more emphasis on community and a renewal of godliness and evangelistic fervor among the staff. But he also wanted to see a new level of consistency in ministry.

Jhan Moskowitz reflected,

Avodah did a lot of good things. It did professionalize us. It really taught us how to be good missionaries. Gave us a standard to work by. But in some ways you know, it moved us away from that spontaneous "tribe." And I think the eighties were reflective of that, and I know that Moishe bemoaned that loss.

As someone who took part in Avodah, I agree that the regularizing and professionalizing of ministry made spontaneity more difficult, but I also think that the changing demographic of the staff would have seen to that anyway. As people married and had children, life would naturally become less spontaneous, and people would naturally become more focused on their spouses and children and the routines necessary for family as well as professional life.

Moishe was a great proponent of marriage and had suggested that Avodah would be a terrific time for single people to marry and for married people to have children—and he rejoiced whenever those events occurred. But he also recognized that entering these stages of life could create natural tensions in how people would want to spend their time. He expected missionaries to realize that theirs was not a nine-to-five job because missionary work does not take place in an office. He insisted that everyone set weekly goals and have a shared understanding of what it meant to meet those goals.

There is no doubt that Moishe saw his role differently in the post-Avodah era. Comparing his function in the 1980s to that of the 1970s, he said,

In the 1980s, I feel my role was to be a discerner, to figure out what kind of music, outreach, and branches we needed. [And] because we had resources, I found [some] people coming to us [mostly] because they wanted to get a job, and I needed a great deal of discernment because a highly dedicated, "called" person and a clever job seeker sound the same.

The other thing between the seventies and the eighties was this: in the seventies we were the revolution, and in the eighties Jews for Jesus wasn't a novelty; we were the establishment. . . .

And so, it was a period of establishment. . . . A lot of it was building up the distribution for things that we have done and services we have provided—going nationwide.

Probably the task I prayed and thought about most was the deployment of personnel and the utilization of resources, to get the right person in the right place or at least the place where they could work. And one of my regrets is that we tried to cover too many fields and thus used some of the less qualified people in leadership.

Of course all the creativity did not dry up during the 1980s. Moishe never regarded professionalism and creativity as either/or propositions. He believed that within the framework of principles, policies, and procedures, there could still be freedom and creativity. In fact, in 1982, Moishe, with his talent for timing, spurred the group into one its most creative periods. As was often the case, the burst of creativity came in response to opposition.

One morning, Moishe and the rest of the headquarters staff were devastated when they arrived at the office to be greeted by a blasphemous misuse of the name of Jesus scrawled across the front of the building. Not content merely to paint over the offensive graffiti, Moishe called the staff together to discuss how to heal the deep hurt they felt over the obscene statement. Moishe concluded that since someone had attempted to soil the name of Jesus, the best way to "counter the attack" would be to lift up the name of Jesus, to honor it, and to draw attention to who Jesus really is. Together, the group brainstormed how to do this, and from that came the Y'shua campaign,* which included writing new songs, gospel ads, and even the book titled *Y'shua: The Jewish Way to Say Jesus* that was offered to those who responded to the ads. The burst of creative communications once again seemed to prove Moishe's aphorism that "every knock is a boost." But much of the Y'shua campaign came from Moishe's sense of timing.

One matter of timing that Moishe did not seem to address quite as consciously was his shifting role in the lives of many whom he had mentored. By the 1980s, it became clear that aspects of Moishe's leadership style that had helped to keep the group together in the 1970s were at the point of diminishing returns. He did work at relating differently to the staff as they grew older, got married, and had children of their own; nevertheless, adapting his role in

---

* Much thought and discussion went into how the group would spell *Y'shua*. Moishe was concerned that those unfamiliar with the word would have trouble pronouncing it when they saw it in print. He thought that Yeshua would be too easily mispronounced as Yeeshua.

the lives of the maturing staff was not his forte. It therefore remained for others to deal on a somewhat unilateral basis with the changing relationships that are natural between mentors and their maturing mentees.

Three people who can provide insight into this are Tuvya, Jhan, and Susan. Each of them was part of the original group who remained with Jews for Jesus "through thick and thin." Each saw Moishe as a mentor.

Tuvya Zaretsky recalled:

In 1971, I prayed specifically asking God for a mentor. There is no doubt in my mind that the Lord brought me into Moishe's sphere to fulfill that longing.

Tuvya went on to explain one of the most memorable times when he received encouragement and affirmation from Moishe.

In the summer of 1977, I was 30 years old. I had completed a 25-month itinerary with the Liberated Wailing Wall. While it was a pressure-packed, character-stretching, life-changing experience, I wasn't prepared for the transition off of the tour.

I had given my all for the ministry and I was a little too eager to settle down. I met a young woman who happened to be serving at our headquarters. It was infatuation at first sight. In spite of my impetuous inclinations, Moishe spoke to me with an expansive, almost visionary calm.

In the midst of a precarious life transition, on the precipice of making some bad choices, Moishe said to me, "Tuvya, you are a winner." Those words of encouragement had a huge impact on me at the time. I came through that transition period, a better person by the grace of God and Moishe's timely affirmation.

Moishe was too young to be my father. I think only 15 years separated us. However, those caring, uplifting words of confidence gave the sort of fatherly support that a young man needed. It was an extraordinary and very personal moment. I know that God used Moishe to touch many of us with his grace.

But not all of Moishe's moments were so grace filled, as has been previously mentioned.

Tuvya also explained,

There's no way that he could have used the same leadership behaviors in the 1980s that he had employed with such an unruly group back in the early 1970s. Moishe did make some adjustments in his leadership style—at least he did with me. Some people said he was "over controlling," but I found him personally respectful. He was demanding and dissatisfied with mediocrity. He expected everyone in the ministry to strive for excellence. He often said, "It's better to do the right thing than a good thing."

Still, there were times when I considered his behavior to be unnecessary or over the top. It was usually in reaction to something he found unsatisfactory. I don't know whether those behaviors were from habit or if they were expressions of frustration. The reason didn't matter to me; I didn't want to excuse it and I usually found that he didn't either. I wasn't going to change the way he occasionally reacted. The best I could do was take responsibility for how I might respond.

Jhan Moskowitz added,

By the 80s we were [geographically] separated. Our relationship [Jhan's and the various branch leaders no longer in San Francisco] was on the telephone and at council meetings. We were a bunch of emerging leaders that Moishe had to figure out how to release, healthily. And I'm not sure he knew how. I think he worked at it but . . . that was a difficult time, the 80s.

When asked if there was a particular event or process that Jhan utilized to see his relationship with Moishe differently, he said,

Yes, I did. I was in England, 1983. I was in charge of the London witnessing campaign, "Messiah Has Come." And for the summer, I didn't talk to Moishe. We just didn't talk. I didn't report in once a week. And I really had to rely on my own leadership gifts. It was after that that I felt like, he can be my friend, and he can be my boss, but he's not my mentor anymore. The interesting thing is, that helped me stay [with Jews for Jesus].

You get to a certain place where you start defining yourself and trying to find out where that individual who is so significant in your life, where his influences kind of end, and yours start. And I think that summer was a real paradigm shift for me. It wasn't that I stopped learning from him, but he stopped being the dominant voice in my life.

I felt fortunate that circumstances and God and grace allowed me to be able to continue to be listening and loving [Moishe] and [at the same time] finding my own voice.

Some have suggested that Moishe tended to relate better to women. Susan Perlman said,

I actually do think he did better with women than with men. I think part of that is because Moishe was such a sensitive, verbal person. But I don't think that he was able to relate to women better than men in the mentoring role simply because they were women . . . he also had a high regard for women that a lot of women, particularly in evangelical circles don't feel [from other male leaders]. That was a very enabling thing that men didn't need from him. If I look at other Jewish missions and other missions back in those days, the idea of having women leading teams or being chief advisors was not very common. Moishe just looked at people. Their gender and their age weren't the issue. If they had something to contribute, he gave them opportunities. And I think that he had a lot of brainy women around . . . because he gave them opportunities that they weren't getting elsewhere.

In terms of the mentoring relationship she had with Moishe, Susan recalled,

In a sense it was very much a matter of situational mentoring. Moishe would go on visits to Jewish people [who didn't believe in Jesus] and he would take me along and I would observe how he would interact. And then after the visit was over, we would talk about it; we'd analyze it. He'd say, "What did you learn?"

Moishe was always throwing out aphorisms and taught me through those as well. Things like "Susan, in life you're going to have to choose whether you want to get something done or get credit for it." Or "there are good choices and then there is the best choice to make in a situation."

Some of how he mentored me I don't even know if he was aware of. But I would see how he treated people and cared for them and especially how he related to younger people. When Moishe had opportunities [he could have kept] for himself, I observed him giving those to others to do and helping them to do them in a successful way.

Susan also responded to the question of whether she reached a certain point when she felt that that mentoring period was drawing to an end, and whether it was a difficult transition:

> Yeah, that is definitely true. I continued to learn things from Moishe, but I don't see it in the same way as my early role with him. The transition. . . . was difficult all around. When he was mentoring me, he almost had a father role in my life and there came a point where I felt like, 'Okay, [now] he's more of an older brother than a father.' I wanted to maintain the proper respect but I [no longer felt] that I was the student he was the teacher in every situation.
>
> And yet, he had other staff that were close to him throughout that period of time, younger staff that he continued to mentor. I think Moishe always liked that role of being a mentor. He always needed people to mentor.

One person whom Moishe mentored in the 1980s was David Brickner, Avi and Leah Brickner's son and middle child. That relationship, which proved to be crucial for the older man as well as the younger man, was fated to become more than a little complex.

TWENTY-EIGHT

*We are not preaching ourselves, but Christ. And whether or not we do
well does not depend on how well we serve Jews for Jesus,
but on how well we serve Christ.*

—MOISHE ROSEN

Moishe wasn't afraid, but he was definitely concerned. As usual, he'd tried to think of everything that could go wrong and how he would respond. They might not allow him onto the plane. Worse, they might allow him to leave the country, then arrest him on some crazy charge and hold him for investigation for who knew how long. He'd prayed about it and felt now was finally the time for him to make his first trip to Israel. After all, the Liberated Wailing Wall, Tuvya, and others known to be Jews for Jesus had already been there.

So far, Jews for Jesus had only had occasional "in and out" evangelistic forays. If Moishe was allowed in, he'd return with a study group of missiologists who'd help Jews for Jesus formulate a consistent approach to taking the gospel to Israel. The group would include the president of Biola College as well as the head of the missions department of Dallas Theological Seminary. "Everyone on staff was proud that Moishe was a staunch supporter of Israel. In the 1970s he had even encouraged some of the Jews for Jesus donors to start their own ministry called "Christians for Israel."

"So there he was at JFK in the line to be processed. At last it was his turn. He handed his passport to the pert Israeli officer, a young woman with a vivacious smile. She studied his passport, which demonstrated that he had been abroad numerous times, though never to Israel. "You have the name of a famous apostate," she observed, still smiling.

Moishe smiled back and gave a one-word affirmation.

"Are you connected with Jews for Jesus?" she asked.

Moishe replied blandly, "You might say so."

She nodded and said, "You know, I have the power to keep you from coming home." By "home," she meant Israel, recognizing the almost universal connection that Jewish people felt with the land.

Moishe, his voice still amicable, looked the young woman in the eye and said, "Yes, I know that you do. But let me tell you what would happen." He showed her a list of telephone numbers that he would call, including those of the Associated Press and the *New York Times*. He added, "And they'd be ready to hear from me because you'd have created an international incident."

The security agent didn't blink. She merely said, "Well, I didn't say I would do it, did I?" With a smile, she waved Moishe through.

He trudged to the gate, the ubiquitous black leather briefcase in hand. Waiting to board he noticed that about half the passengers were Hasidim, (a sect of Orthodox Jews) while the rest seemed to be various tourists. Then locating his seat he found himself settled in amidst a sea of beards and black coats.

Why'd they put me in the Hasidic section? he wondered drowsily after he found his seat. *Oh, yeah, Perlman decided I should get kosher meals when I travel. She thinks they're healthier. Well, I guess it makes sense for the airline to seat all the kosher people together.*

As they waited for takeoff, the man to Moishe's left decided to strike up a conversation:

"I see you're Jewsh." He pronounced the word as though there were no "i."

Moishe nodded, not certain what the man could see of his Jewishness, other than the fact that he'd been seated in the obviously Jewish section.

"So, where are you from?" the man continued.

"I'm from the West Coast—San Francisco."

"Oh, I have an uncle in the movie business."

Moishe nodded but said nothing. The plane had taken off. He was dead tired. The man obviously wanted to make conversation. *He can see by my clothes that I'm no Hasid and probably hopes he can recruit me for Chabad* (the outgoing Hasidic organization whose "missionary" zeal—to bring other Jews into what they felt was a proper Jewish lifestyle—rivaled that of Jews for Jesus).

"So, what do you do for a living?"

Moishe shook his head. "You wouldn't want to know." He'd often used that line to pique curiosity, but this time, he was actually hoping the man would take it at face value and leave him alone. He was ready for a nap.

After a moment's reflection, the man spoke up again: "You know, if you're a diamond smuggler, that's not against Jewish law. I wouldn't hold it against you."

Moishe shook his head. "No. I'm not a smuggler."

"So, what then? What could be so bad?"

The mission leader sighed. "Did you ever hear about Jews for Jesus?"

"Oh, yes, we know all about them," his inquisitive neighbor replied. "Let me tell you, the head of Jews for Jesus isn't even a Jew. He's Italian. Our rabbi told us all about it."

Moishe couldn't help smiling as he shook his head. "I promise you, the rabbi doesn't know all about it." He reached for his passport and wordlessly handed it to his seat mate, whose eyes got bigger, *almost like you'd see in a cartoon*, Moishe thought.

The man whispered to a fellow traveler, and within moments, there was a commotion as many people changed seats. Soon all the women and children were on the outer edges of the section, and the largest and sturdiest-looking men were closer to Moishe.

The man said, "We have to know something. We have to know that you're a real Jew."

Moishe shook his head. "No, you don't."

"Wouldn't I go to hell if I believed that you were going there, and you weren't?"

"No, you'd go to hell because of your sins, just like everyone else who hasn't received the atonement God offers."

"Just one thing" the other said. "You know what this is?" And he pulled out his *tefillim.**

"Yes," Moishe answered wearily, and pulling his briefcase out from under the seat in front of him, he produced his own tefillim. He began wrapping the leather straps around his arm in the prescribed manner. *I'm sure I'm making mistakes*, he thought, and no doubt he was. Having learned the ritual as a child, he had not practiced it for many years—nor was he in the habit of carrying tefillim with him.

The man's eyes opened even wider than before as he watched. Then he said, "Anybody could learn that."

---

* Scriptures inscribed on parchment, encased in small leather boxes to be strapped on the arm and forehead for prayer.

Moishe was quick to agree and soon dozed off.

His fellow passengers were left to ponder if there was really anything so offensive about this man, other than the sound of extremely loud snoring.

———

Moishe's first visit to Israel passed without incident, though certain people seemed to keep him company wherever he went. He did appreciate being spared the unpleasant scene experienced by the Liberated Wailing Wall and the New Jerusalem Players in 1984 when they arrived in Israel for the second to last stop on their world tour. That team had been led by David Brickner, one of the up-and-coming new leaders whom Moishe had begun to mentor. David recalled,

> We were met at the gate by people who presented us with a bouquet of dead flowers and pronounced, "Welcome, missionaries, we are praying for a speedy death." They had gotten our itineraries and knew everywhere that we were going to be.
>
> What was far more discouraging was that the believers we were supposed to work with there didn't want us to wear our Jews for Jesus T-shirts or use the tracts that we were prepared to hand out. . . .
>
> Moishe made some suggestions to me about how to approach [one of the established leaders who was requiring these restrictions] but told me if I couldn't get anywhere, to call him.
>
> It didn't take long for me to see that I wasn't getting anywhere, so I called Moishe. A minute later I told [said leader] that Moishe Rosen was hoping to speak to him; he got on the phone with Moishe, and when he got off, he said, "Okay, you can wear your T-shirts and you can hand out whatever literature you want."

Moishe could make things happen. In this case being so open did make for a very eventful tour as the antimissionaries actively opposed the group. But the group was willing to take the heat for the sake of the many Israelis who were curious and even interested in what they had to say. As is usually the case, the hostility of those trying to silence the group only increased the sympathy and interest of the others.

David called his boss from the airport as they prepared to leave Israel. "We've gotten through the toughest part of the tour," he informed Moishe.

"Don't be so sure," Moishe replied. "You've still got South Africa."

David later recalled, "I thought, *South Africa? What's the big deal about South Africa?*" In fact, there were riots everywhere they went, and they needed police protection. "[The antimissionaries there] made Israel look like a cakewalk. So that was a very prescient moment. It was almost eerie, the way Moishe seemed able to predict how things would be." After the tour, David brought the Liberated Wailing Wall back to San Francisco. '

No doubt Moishe took an interest in David primarily because of who and what David was, but that interest also had a foundation in Moishe's friendship with the young man's parents, Avi and Leah Brickner.*

Not until he was a student at Boston University did David become serious about the beliefs and values his parents had taught him. The Jews for Jesus Boston branch played an important role in challenging and encouraging him, and eventually he felt that he could best fulfill his destiny by serving with Jews for Jesus. He remained involved with the ministry throughout the rest of his time in college and beyond, and through various leadership roles, was mentored by Moishe.

David recalled,

> I always had a very loving and a respectful relationship with Moishe, but I never felt like what he said came from Mount Sinai. And [when I saw him make what I regarded as mistakes] I felt like "Okay, I'm never gonna be as smart as Moishe or have the mind he's got, but I do understand some things that I am that he is not." And it made me feel good about our relationship.

In some ways, David was more fully formed than most of the first generation of Jews for Jesus had been at his age. He already had the spiritual framework and upbringing that Moishe, to some extent, had provided for many of the core volunteers and early staff. Perhaps that had some bearing on why David, who considered Moishe to be his mentor and one of the most influential people in his life, didn't experience the kind of transition in his relationship with Moishe that some of the others did in the 1980s.

Once Moishe made up his mind to do or say something, it was difficult to get him to change course. Difficult, but not impossible.

---

* This was also true of David's older sister, Martha, and her husband, Loren, both of whom served with Jews for Jesus for many years.

Jhan recalled, "I remember it was in the middle eighties in a council meeting in Chicago when Susan and Mitch and I really pushed Moishe to go international. An opportunity in England was opening up, some of us really believed God was paving the way, and Moishe never wanted to go international. His maximum was one hundred twenty missionaries. That was it; that was all he felt he could manage." But eventually, Moishe relented, and Jews for Jesus incorporated several international branches during his tenure as executive director, including South Africa, Russia, the UK, and France.

Moishe preferred to help and encourage missionaries "across the pond" to stay with their own mission agencies rather than come under the auspices of Jews for Jesus. This was certainly the case with a young Jewish believer named Richard Harvey, whom he met in the late 1970s in London, and mentored in the 1980s. He eventually brought Richard on staff but only after realizing that he would not otherwise remain in the field of Jewish evangelism.

Richard recalled how he first met Moishe at a conference at London Bible College (now London School of Theology) where there were about 20 young Jewish believers in Jesus. "I remember clearly what he said to us. He spoke about what was happening in the USA, and said, 'You may think you are a small number, but God can do great things through you.' I remember this big man with a booming voice and his American accent. But it was the content of what he said, a prophetic word to me as a young believer, that impressed me."

In the years to follow, when Moishe flew to Israel or South Africa, he often had a layover in London, and frequently invited Richard to join him for a meal. Richard recalled,

> Even though I was working with another mission at the time, he [Moishe] never tried to recruit me. Rather he mentored me, listening to my issues and concerns, teaching me about Jewish mission history, sharing his own perspectives, philosophies, joys, and trials. I remember him in the UK just after his father had died; he was grieving, but he shared of himself and his feelings.
>
> I got from Moishe that "almost-family" bond. . . . He became a sort of spiritual father . . . who knew the ways of Jewish mission and could teach me so much about evangelism, media, leadership, character.
>
> In media, I saw a master at work. In humour, I saw a zany prophetic edge, in strategy, I saw a military cunning. Often when he would phone from San Francisco I would take copious notes during the conversation. I would

come downstairs with my head buzzing with new ideas and a smile on my face, and my wife Monica would say: "You've been on the phone to Moishe, haven't you?" It wasn't hard to tell.

That is not to say that Richard Harvey's experiences with Moishe were all positive. Richard was on staff with Jews for Jesus from 1990-1997. As the London branch leader supervised by Moishe, he experienced the same difficulties mentioned in previous chapters. Having acknowledged those difficulties, Harvey concluded,

> [These negatives] never, never outweighed the sense of being with someone who was not only larger than life, but cared, loved, and was passionate about what they sincerely believed. I did not always agree with Moishe . . . but who cares? He was a genius, master strategist, and rare eccentric who could bring a new perspective.

Richard Harvey spoke of Moishe as a man who filled the role of "one of the most encouraging people in my life."

> Moishe was a tremendous support to Monica and me when we arrived in San Francisco having just suffered the loss of a near full-term pregnancy. He was able to share with me his suffering through a similar experience. And, when my back was so bad I could only lie down on the floor at the international LCJE meeting at All Nations, he would lie down on the floor next to me!

Years later Harvey authored a book on messianic Jewish theology* and expressed concern that "although I found eight or nine types [of messianic Jewish theology], there is one type that is missing, which is 'Jews for Jesus/Moishe Rosen' messianic Jewish theology." He went on to say:

> I don't think it is correct to sum up his [Moishe's] theology as "Conservative Baptist with a dispensationalist edge"—this may be accurate from one

---

* Harvey's PhD is from the University of Wales (Lampeter). His dissertation was published as *Mapping Messianic Jewish Theology: A Constructive Approach* (Carlisle, UK: Paternoster/Authentic Media, 2009).

perspective (official, church-based)—but I think there is a lot more depth and subtlety to his position. Unfortunately, it does not seem to have been formulated systematically. I think [Moishe] has had a pivotal influence in causing other messianic Jews . . . to formulate their own positions, often in reaction to or imitation of Moishe's unsystematic and implicit theological system.

Moishe's theological positions probably did have more depth and subtlety than some might think. Over the years, I had many discussions with my father about spiritual and philosophical matters. It was probably in the last year or two of his life that I expressed to him that as time went by, it grew easier for me to hold certain matters in tension, in large part because of an expanded awareness of many biblical realities as mysteries, now known only in part, leaving room for some amount of wondering and/or respectful differences of opinion. He nodded and said that he'd had similar thoughts.

To codify or categorize a system that would go beyond the basics of the gospel would have been counterproductive to Moishe's determination to remain single-minded in his efforts. Moishe was a dreamer, but he was also extremely practical and dead set on avoiding distractions from the cause to which he had dedicated himself. He staked his life on the belief that God had called him to communicate the gospel to his people. He spent his life pointing out that Jesus is the only solution offered by God to breach the gap between his holiness and sinful human beings, be they Jewish or Gentile. Moishe identified with particular theological leanings to a certain extent, but resisted being defined by any detailed and systematic description of theology.

Moishe also concerned himself with preserving the right to proclaim the gospel freely in public venues. In 1981 he was arrested for handing out broadside tracts at the Portland airport. The charge was violating a port ordinance "requiring advance registration by those desiring to exercise First Amendment rights at the terminal." Although the ordinance was upheld by the district court, the Ninth Circuit ruled it unconstitutional. It was a precedent-setting case.

In 1986 Moishe hired a young Jewish believer in Jesus, Jay Sekulow, to serve as the organization's general legal counsel. Jay had answered the invitation to follow Jesus at a Liberated Wailing Wall concert. Moishe wanted him to try a case in which Jews for Jesus missionaries had been arrested for handing out tracts at the Los Angeles International Airport. Sekulow had to get special permission to argue the case before the Supreme Court of the United States in 1987 because of his age (he was only thirty years old). Nevertheless, he won.

When Jay formed his own ministry, Christian Advocates Serving Evangelism, Moishe encouraged him to buy a property not far from the Supreme Court: "Because you'll be coming back here often." At the time, Sekulow did not take Moishe's suggestion seriously. Later in his career,* after trying multiple cases before the Supreme Court, he recognized that Moishe's suggestion had been somewhat prophetic.**

Moishe had been adamant that Jews for Jesus fight to maintain the right of free speech at a time when few Christians were willing to file the lawsuits necessary to protest actions that would quash those rights. He recognized that it was not only fascists and totalitarian governments that threatened to deprive people of those rights, but bureaucrats, desk jockeys, and a growing number of uptight citizens who were already developing a somewhat Orwellian notion of tolerance. He wanted Jews for Jesus to be the first to meet a challenge to free speech and to keep the way paved not only for themselves, but also for others.

Throughout the 1980s, Moishe had seen his persistence in pressing the right to free speech pay off. Other struggles remained an uphill battle. His weight spiked and his energy began to lag. At one council meeting, he told the senior staff that while it was important to the ministry for him to travel and speak, he wasn't sure how to balance a travel schedule with his health needs. The staff suggested he always have an assistant while traveling.

He also knew he needed help with his weight, though that was a far more sensitive subject. Meals had always meant more than mere sustenance to him. Sharing good food meant fun and fellowship. In 1986 Moishe went to the Cooper Clinic (of Kenneth Cooper "Father of Aerobics" fame) for a thorough health check and recommendations on weight loss. He was so impressed by the consultation that he wanted the senior staff to have opportunities to be examined by the Cooper Clinic as well.

During Moishe's tenure as executive director, this was a benefit that Jews for Jesus career missionaries received regularly at three-to-five-year intervals. More than one staff member discovered a medical condition that, if left untreated, could have had very serious consequences.

---

* Sekulow eventually became known for his role as chief counsel for the American Center for Law and Justice.

** He bought the property and in 2010 named it the Moishe Rosen House in memory of Moishe.

Nevertheless, he didn't always follow his own path to good health. Although he lost a significant amount of weight, most of it returned, and Moishe faced a sobering reality: a crisis in his health could leave Jews for Jesus in a quandary over the selection of his successor.

Moishe thought through a painstaking plan by which the next executive director ought to be nominated not by him, but by the senior missionaries. He then secured the understanding of the board that they would accept a nomination so long as it came from a unanimous vote of the Jews for Jesus council. The strategy for selecting the next executive director became an official board document, and Moishe was satisfied that a chapter of history he had witnessed at the ABMJ* would not be repeated.

---

* Regarding selection of Joseph Hoffman Cohn's successor.

TWENTY-NINE

The quality of your life is shaped by what you really believe,
not just what you say you believe.
—MOISHE ROSEN

A clear, cool night had settled over Hertfordshire, England, and almost all was peaceful on Chalk Hill. Almost, but not quite all: a couple of visitors had made their way to the residential neighborhood to protest the presence of the missionary music team, the Liberated Wailing Wall, at Bushey Baptist Church. The two young visitors, both wearing yarmulkes, had arrived late, possibly expecting to slip in unnoticed. However, they never made it past the lobby because as they entered, Richard Harvey immediately recognized them. Moishe was there, too, in town for a meeting of the European Board of Jews for Jesus. He was prone to intermittent back spasms and found it difficult to sit in pews for long, so he had settled into one of the more comfortable chairs in the church lobby.

Moishe knew that several church members had brought Jewish friends to hear the Liberated Wailing Wall, but he sensed that these two had not come to enjoy the concert. He could imagine that one young man observant enough to wear a yarmulke might come out of curiosity, but two? Few Orthodox Jews would feel comfortable being seen by their friends in a Baptist church, he reckoned. With some effort, he rose from his chair to meet them.

Richard rose simultaneously. "Hullo, Daniel. Hullo, Andrew," he said amiably.

"You know these guys?" Moishe kept his voice neutral as he eyed them.

Richard said, "I can't say I know them, but I know who they are. I see them most every week at Speaker's Corner, don't I?" He continued speaking to Moishe but was watching the two men. "They're antimissionaries, Moishe, hecklers, as you'd call them."

As though to verify this, Moishe demanded in his most sonorous voice, "Have you come here to worship Jesus?"

One snorted in contempt as the other said derisively, "Of course not! We're *real* Jews. We've come to make sure you don't deceive—"

"You're not welcome here," Moishe announced bluntly.

The intruders protested that they had a legal right to be there.

"I know what the law says." Moishe moved closer to them. "Call the police," he instructed Richard.

"Right, Moishe," and off Richard went to find a phone.

A barely audible gasp escaped from a church member who had been chatting with Moishe, Richard, and Susan—all of whom he had just met for the first time. Mark Greene, also a Jewish believer in Jesus, was on staff at London Bible College,* a school closely affiliated with the church. At Richard's request, he had spoken to the pastor about inviting the team to come to Bushey Baptist. And it had been quite a plum for the team to find a welcome at this vibrant and highly respected church.

Mark was not prepared to hear a missionary ask people to *leave* a church. Shocking! *And had that Harvey bloke actually gone to call the police?*

Mark's shock turned to fascination as he watched Moishe trundle the two out the door without laying a hand on them. With each step the hefty American took, the young men had to back up to avoid being bumped by his sizeable abdomen, which preceded the rest of him by at least ten inches. Before long, two frustrated and somewhat bewildered protesters found themselves outside the doors, which were now blocked by the outsized mission leader.

Soon the police arrived. They listened to the antimissionaries' accusations, then heard from Richard, who explained the type of adversarial relationship they'd had with him, and his reasons for supposing they had come to disrupt the meeting.

"That's rubbish," the more vocal of the two insisted. "We have every right to be here."

"Actually, you don't," one of the bobbies said calmly. "This isn't Speaker's Corner, is it?"

The other added, "If they don't want to grant you access to their meeting, they don't have to. That's perfectly legal.'"

Dejected but still determined, the two stopped just outside the church's property.

Mark wondered aloud at how Moishe had handled the situation; having unbelievers removed from the church seemed rather an odd way of conducting missionary work, after all.

---

* Now called London School of Theology.

Moishe took a chair next to Mark and said earnestly. "I appreciate your wanting to share the gospel in this or any situation," he said, "and your heart for evangelism is why we've invited you to the board meeting tomorrow. But you have to understand that these men did not come to hear the gospel. They were not interested. They came with a position and a purpose, and that purpose was to disrupt.* Some Jewish people came tonight to hear what we had to say. These guys wanted to prevent that from happening. They're wolves. And a shepherd doesn't let the wolves meet the sheep."

As Mark listened, his skepticism began to melt away.

The hour passed quickly enough, and as the notes of the final song faded, the pastor returned to the platform to make final remarks. Mark Greene slipped back to the lobby in time to hear Moishe ask Richard, "Are our friends still out there?"

Richard checked and found that they were.

Moishe did not seem surprised. "Here's what we'll do. You and Susan go out and begin engaging them in conversation. Keep them occupied as people leave. If they're busy arguing with you, they won't buttonhole anyone who came to hear the group. Got it?"

Richard and Susan grinned. Mark, once again observing the mission leader's tactics, was impressed. "Brilliant!" he said as he, too, smiled approvingly, and he promised Moishe that he would be at the board meeting the next day.

———

Years later as Mark Greene recounted the story, he said of Moishe's strategy: "It was countercultural, but it was biblical. It was a tremendously smart, biblical response, just like Paul [when he said], 'I'm a citizen of Rome.' He was using the law [to his advantage]." Mark not only attended the board meeting, but became a member, and soon afterward, the chairman of the board of Jews for Jesus in the UK.

Moishe was a master at using the law to his advantage, but he also learned to use other people's procedures to his advantage, as the following story shows.

Moishe was an early advocate of desktop computers, but when at one point the organization had seven of the latest and supposedly greatest computers at the headquarters office, Moishe recalled,

---

* In fact, this happened at another church during the group's London tour—one of the antimissionaries co-opted a meeting partway through—proof that Moishe's concerns at Bushey Baptist Church were not unfounded.

Unlike the earlier models, they were subject to continual breakdowns. The repairman would come out and the same machine might freeze up the next day. And since all but one of these machines was subject to the same problem, I asked [the company] to replace them . . . but the dealer argued and the company just stonewalled us. I filed a lawsuit.

When it was apparent that we were getting nowhere, I personally bought a hundred and seventy five shares of stock—it was priced low enough at the time. The next time we got together for one of these negotiating stints, I made a point of saying, "Now I understand that stockholders can come to the board of directors meeting, is that right? And if they ask in advance, they'll be given a certain amount of time to speak . . . I bought 175 shares of [your] stock."

But then I found out that you had to have more stock to attend the meeting and I bought another 225 shares. Then I told the attorneys that I intended to come to the next stockholders' meeting and express my displeasure with the way they chose to treat their customers. Within 48 hours, [the company] and the dealers settled the case and we had seven of their latest desktop computers to replace the "lemons."

I completely forgot to sell the stock afterwards. One day I realized I had 400 shares that were worth almost ten times what I'd paid. But that is the story of my life; if I ever made any money, it was by mistake.

In describing his role during that era, Moishe said,

From about 1980 through 1995, I was chiefly working as a strategist, trying to discern the best places to spend my energy and the energy of Jews for Jesus. [But] by the nineties, my chief role was that of a fireman. I had pretty much taught the staff all that I could teach them in doing the work, and a lot of my new work was putting out fires, making things work according to their principles and practices.

Moishe's reflections on his "fireman" role in the 1990s mainly pertained to his work within Jews for Jesus. Yet he still liked to help other people get things started and encouraged numerous groups and individuals in their own ministries. He took an especially active interest in creative people who were longing to tell others about Jesus. It didn't matter that they were not part of the Jews for Jesus staff; in fact, Moishe tended to be more generous with those who he thought could do better by remaining separate and distinct from Jews for Jesus.

That was certainly the case with Sally Klein O'Connor and her husband, Michael. Michael wrote brilliant lyrics, and his singer/songwriter wife, a Jewish believer in Jesus, sang with power, passion, and a vulnerability that was truly unique. Moishe first heard Sally sing in autumn 1989 at a Jews for Jesus conference; she had been invited to perform a song that she and Michael had written called "Improbable People for Impossible Tasks." The crowd was bowled over by the song's calypso beat, humor, and biblical message. Sally recalled,

> The following day I was "summoned." I had never met Moishe before, [though] I had heard little bits and pieces about him from friends who were on staff with Jews for Jesus. . . . I had no idea that I stood on the precipice of tremendous change in my life. He never said hello or introduced himself, but just got straight to the point. He liked the song very much and wanted to know if I had ever recorded an album.
>
> He could not have known how burned out I was on that subject . . . I could still taste the bitterness of years of rejection as a singer and songwriter. I tried to answer politely: "No."

He told her that she should do an album and offered her the funds to make the recording.

She said,

> Two weeks later, true to his word, a check arrived for $1,500. In the memo Moishe had notated "for album." I tacked it above my piano and just stared at it for two weeks. I couldn't believe it was real. My dad finally told me to deposit it.
>
> Moishe insisted on a deadline . . . the truth was, without a deadline we might never have finished that first album. I wondered how Moishe knew.

Moishe also suggested that Sally come to San Francisco with her husband and daughter for a concert. They were well received, and a generous "pass the plate" offering was given to them, since there had been no charge for the concert. Moishe surprised Michael and Sally by announcing to the audience that the couple was recording an album—and that they could take pre-orders for the album that very night.

Later that evening, Moishe took Sally aside and talked about her and Michael starting their own ministry. He envisioned them traveling across the country, reaching people with their music. After the couple returned to Southern California, Moishe called Sally, continuing to encourage her to step out in faith and use her God-given gifts. And six months later, Improbable People Ministries was born.

Some of Sally's good friends from Jews for Jesus later left the organization and spoke to her of how they had been hurt by Moishe. A deeply compassionate person, she commented, "I cannot ignore what has been said to me. But neither can I forget the integrity Moishe showed to us in all of his dealings with and for us. The longer I stay in ministry, the more clearly I see we don't understand everything that is going on."

Commenting on the degree of hurt and anger that some former staff members expressed, Moishe said,

> What I've noticed is when people leave a ministry, which, like marriage, has a high degree of commitment, that if they're dismissed they tend to try to get along with the ministry afterward. But if they leave of their own accord, inevitably, eventually they turn against that ministry. It's as though they need to justify the separation. . . .
>
> I hope that I am not a person who holds grudges—I don't want to be. And if somebody's angry at me, I don't necessarily think that they are wrong to be angry at me. Sometimes I'm angry at me.

In fifty-four years of knowing Moishe, I never saw him as a person who held grudges, but I did see him adamant in his mistrust once a person showed himself or herself to be less than trustworthy in his eyes. He was sometimes quite vocal in expressing that mistrust. He seemed to feel obligated to point it out so that others would not be taken in, not realizing that he was alienating some people who might not want to hear about the matter. And in the few instances where he expressed not merely distrust but actual dislike for an individual, his feelings came through in a way that generated dislike in return.

Research for this book provided unique opportunities to discuss some of these issues. I told him that I had observed in him a tendency to polarize his views of certain people, which didn't seem to allow for "gray areas" where a person might not be as good or as bad as he thought. He paused, looking thoughtful, then replied with an eye opening insight: "Eventually, most people become heroes and villains in my mind. There are not too many villains, but a person who had villain-[like] traits becomes a villain. And a person who has heroic traits [becomes a hero]. It's a tendency to filter things out and assign [what seems like a dominant] quality to them. That's always been a problem."

Moishe did not see himself as a hero or a villain—but he made provisions to guard against his human failings, just as he tried to guard against the failings of others. He said:

> I've always found that I had to protect the organization against myself, and I set up different safeguards to do that.* But I also found that I had to set up the safeguards in the organization to protect the organization and its purposes from staff who [could be tempted to] change things for their own benefit at the expense of getting the task done.

Just as Moishe's views of certain people tended to become polarized, many people's views of him tended toward the same polarization.

Moishe continued to speak his mind bluntly and without regard to what others wanted to hear. He sometimes joked that he was an equal opportunity offender, but he always saw himself as a combination of the boy pointing out that the emperor had no clothes and what he called "a natural born agitator."

One arena in which he was considered an agitator was that of messianic congregations, that is, local bodies of Jewish Jesus-believers who chose to have a community of worship that reflected their Jewish upbringing. In fact, Moishe was a great proponent of messianic congregations; he deeply appreciated Jewish liturgy and worship services where Jewish visitors could recognize that believing in Jesus did not mean a rejection of all things Jewish.

At the same time, Moishe was deeply concerned that certain distinctions be maintained. For example, he never liked the use of the term *rabbi* for the leaders of messianic congregations. To him, leaders of messianic congregations implied by use of the term that they had the same credentials as rabbis who had received ordination from mainstream Jewish institutions.

---

* For example, Moishe exempted himself from signing ministry checks. He also put in place a committee of board members to review any appeal letters he wrote, and he would not send them without the committee's approval.

Moreover it bothered Moishe to see any believer in Jesus attaching importance to honorific titles.* Some of the messianic rabbis, like former staff member Loren Jacobs, understood Moishe's point of view and never let it become an
issue. Others thought that Moishe was undermining their qualifications and
their efforts, or casting aspersions on their motives.

Moishe supported messianic congregations and leaders who wanted his
support, giving seed money to new congregations and offering their leaders
moral support by phone, written correspondence, and sometimes through personal visits. He made it clear that Jews for Jesus policy was to refer people to
healthy, Bible-believing congregations close to where they lived so that they
could easily become part of that community of believers. If there was a good
messianic congregation, nearby, so much the better—but often the distance
factor meant referring them to mainstream churches. If there was a good
church within five miles of the person, Moishe didn't feel it was sensible to
ignore that church in favor of a messianic congregation many miles away. Nor
would he recommend people to any congregation, messianic or mainstream,
no matter how conveniently located, if that particular congregation embraced
doctrines that he felt were contrary to Bible teachings.

Moishe never doubted that a day would come when the trickle of Jewish
believers in Jesus would become a flood—he looked for it as a fulfillment of
biblical prophecy that would transcend all earthly strategies and human ideas
of how things should be done. He was convinced that when the time came,
it would be something so obviously of God that no one would be tempted to
believe it was because he or she had found "the right way" or "the key" to changing people's hearts and minds.

"You can't turn off what the Holy Spirit is turning on," Moishe used to tell
people, to assure them that they need not fear sharing their faith, even if they
didn't feel they had exactly the right words to say. It was always up to God to
bring a person to that place of faith, and God could use individuals who were
willing to tell of the hope they'd found in Jesus. How much more would that
be true when, as end times prophecies indicate, the Jewish people would turn
to Y'shua en masse.

Some messianic congregations did not wish to partner with Moishe or
with Jews for Jesus, which was certainly their prerogative; however it is most

---

* He had long since dropped the term "Reverend" that his own education and ordination entitled
him to use.

unfortunate that some have characterized disagreements or disappointments they had with Moishe as being proof of Moishe's relationship (or lack thereof) with the entire movement.*

Though the health issues that began surfacing in the 1980s were unrelenting,** Moishe continued to travel quite a bit in the 1990s. He loved to see new places, as did Ceil, who accompanied Moishe on trips taken with the Jews for Jesus board of directors, some of whom she came to regard as dear friends. The board usually met in San Francisco, but every three or four years they arranged to meet at one of the branches, particularly once the ministry became international. Thus in 1990 they traveled to Johannesburg, South Africa. In the Rosens' personal annual letter (sent out each December) Ceil wrote,

> The day we flew into Johannesburg, riots had broken out in the black township of Soweto where Moishe was first scheduled to speak. He had chosen to speak there in order to make a personal statement against apartheid and for Christian unity. We drove to Soweto that Sunday morning, even though it was rumored that a riot was "scheduled" for 2:30 that afternoon. The church service, which, unlike most American services, normally lasted for about four hours had to be cut short because of the threatened riots.

Moishe's sense of wonder was apparant as he later described the music and the service. There was a sense of admiration, and though Moishe would have been the last person to sit through a four-hour service of any kind, he was deeply impressed by the worship he experienced in South Africa.

Moishe also loved to share the experience of travel with others, and in 1992 he was invited to address a conference of the Norwegian Church Ministry to Israel. My mother had been included in the invitation, but Moishe also arranged for me, his daughter, to speak and to help with the outdoor evangelism the Norwegian Ministry was conducting.

There were very few times that I felt I received special privileges because of who my father was, but that time in Norway was one of them. He really had to

---

* This is understandable if those who felt at odds with Moishe viewed themselves, their theology, and their practices as representative of the entire movement—and it appears that some have chosen to view themselves and the movement in that way.

** In 1992 progression of his adult onset Type II diabetes necessitated daily insulin injections, and that same year arthritis required surgery on his right knee. He also suffered from copious nosebleeds resulting from a deviated septum.

twist my arm to go, but once there, I enjoyed it beyond anything I could have imagined. The stunning scenery and the beauty and hospitality of the people made every moment worth remembering. But aside from the incredible aesthetic experience, I remember how deeply impressed I was with him especially when we were invited to "an informal garden party."

First, Moishe insisted on my asking our host, Helge Aarflot,* how we should dress for the occasion. I thought this strange, since "informal" seemed to imply casual attire.

He shook his head and said, "You don't know that. They might mean something very different by informal than you or I would mean." He was right. Helge assured me that for the men "a sports jacket and tie would be fine," and the women could wear "simple dresses." I was so grateful Moishe had asked—I probably would have come in jeans.

We arrived at our host's home, met his beautiful wife and children, and were quickly shown into a lovely garden where tables, chairs, and a picture-perfect meal awaited. For dessert, there was an amazing tiered cake, covered with marzipan, and beautifully decorated, almost like a wedding cake. We had never been to a party quite like this.

Before the cake was cut, Ole Kvarme (mentioned in chapter 28) clinked a fork or spoon against his water glass, and with all eyes turned to him, he cleared his throat and began to speak. He recounted the history of Jewish missions in Europe, told where and when he had met Moishe and affirmed Moishe and the ministry of Jews for Jesus most eloquently. He then gave strong assurances of his pleasure in the relationship and his hopes for continued friendship and opportunities to serve the Lord together in years to come.

Following this speech, Helge Aarflot made another, and it became quite clear that there was a certain form, a certain etiquette to these "impromptu" speeches. Before I knew it, it became quite clear that it was my father's turn to address the group.

I knew that he was an exceptional public speaker, and I'd rarely seen him at a loss for words. Still, he had a style that was very much his own, and this situation seemed to call for a very specific approach. And it became obvious that he had carefully observed that approach.

With truly impressive ease, he followed the pattern that had been laid

---

* President of the Norwegian Israel Mission at the time.

out, and gave an extemporaneous speech that reflected every social grace that had been shown to us, and yet was still uniquely and sincerely Moishe. As he finished, our Norwegian friends smiled and nodded with satisfaction, and I was so proud. I thought I knew his range pretty well, but that informal garden party—besides being a wonderful experience in and of itself—showed me a whole other side of Moishe.

In 1993, Jews for Jesus celebrated its twentieth year as a ministry. The U.S. and Canadian board of directors hosted an elegant dinner for Moishe, our family, and many of the senior leaders of Jews for Jesus. Ceil recalled, "The board also gave a very generous gift to the Jews for Jesus Library in Moishe's honor. He much preferred that to any personal gift they might have chosen. He leaned over to me just before the presentation and joked, 'If they give me a gold watch, it's all over!'"

Ironically, that was the year that Moishe knew it was almost time for him to step aside as executive director of Jews for Jesus. He later recalled,

> Sometime in 1993, in that area of intuition where God speaks to me, he let me know that soon he was going to be telling me to step down. Now in 1993, I was still strong; I was sixty-one years old, could travel well, and my thinking capacity was good. But the voice-that-wasn't-exactly-a-voice was like the voice that had first called me to the ministry and had later called me to San Francisco—and I knew that it would be confirmed.

By 1994, Moishe was convinced that the time was drawing nearer, and by 1995, he felt he had his confirmation. He formally announced to the staff that he planned to step down from his position in 1996.

THIRTY

If you want to teach people not to listen to you,
state the obvious over and over again.

—MOISHE ROSEN

Moishe was perspiring profusely as he and grandson Asher lugged the last
heavy suitcase across the threshold of the Maui condo they would call home
for the next week.* *Spacious, neat—and very nicely decorated,* Moishe thought.

It was June 1997. Asher had graduated from high school in May, his sister,
Bethany, had turned fifteen on June 7, and June 8 marked Lyn and Alan's
twenty-third wedding anniversary. With so much to celebrate, it was the perfect time for the two families to enjoy a special vacation together in Hawaii—
something they had never done before.

In fact, Moishe and Ceil had never taken a two-week trip unless it included
a ministry speaking tour—which accounted for their previous visits to Hawaii.
As executive director, Moishe had always felt it would be inappropriate to be
away from Jews for Jesus for that long unless he was doing something ministry
related. Now that he was no longer executive director, he was seeing things a little
differently.

Still, it did not occur to him to take such a vacation until he and Ceil received
an unexpected windfall—the ministry leadership recalled that the couple had
spent five thousand dollars of their own money to pay for the first Liberated
Wailing Wall album in the early 70s. Just recently, and with a great deal of appreciation, it had been repaid.**

I never expected to see that money again, Moishe had thought, *but this is the
perfect time to gather the whole family together before the grandchildren grow up
and go their separate ways.*

---

* The previous week they had been in Oahu.

** I suspect that the board of directors and senior leadership wanted to present Moishe with a signifi-
cant gift as a gesture of thanks for his many years of leadership when he stepped down from his position.
Moishe would have seen an expensive gift as an unworthy use of ministry funds. The repayment of this
sum, however, was welcome not only as a windfall, but as a demonstration that others remembered what
he had sacrificed, especially early on.

He'd called Lyn to ask, "Where would you like to go for a family vacation? Think of somewhere you haven't been yet."

In a heartbeat Lyn replied, "Hawaii!"

Moishe was enthusiastic. "Yes, we should all go to Hawaii! I'll pay for it if you'll plan it."

As for Moishe's other daughter:

I had been shocked at my father's announcement that we would vacation together for two whole weeks. "Who *are* you and what have you done with my father?" I'd been tempted to ask. At that time I was editing four Jews for Jesus publications and mentioned that two weeks away might be tricky given my various deadlines.

Moishe brushed off this concern somewhat impatiently, pointing out that I had a right to the two weeks. This too, seemed different than his attitude of old. However, he was willing to take the publication's schedule into account when fixing the specific dates, and with all of us on board, Lyn got to work. We all agreed that family members ought not feel obligated to do everything together. Those who wanted solitude could choose not to participate in a given activity.

Moishe wished he had used that "nonparticipation" option to decline a catamaran ride off of Waikiki Beach during the first week of his once-in-a-lifetime two-week family vacation.

"Aloha!" The man in the brightly colored shirt had greeted them enthusiastically as he handed Ceil, Lyn, and finally Moishe into the gently rocking boat. Asher and Bethany nimbly hopped in, completing the party. (Alan had opted for a quiet reading time in the hotel room and I had left early that morning for a day trip to Kuai.) Ceil and Lyn breathed in the salt air and sighed happily as they took their seats.

When the boat reached open water it began to bob higher then lower with each new wave. *It's a good thing I brought this,* Moishe thought miserably, as he opened a wadded up plastic bag he'd brought "in case." He bent his head over it, but the bag remained mockingly empty. Moishe lifted his head for a moment. "Well, I guess the anti-nausea pills are doing *half* their job," he told Ceil, in a feeble attempt at humor. She stroked his head as he bent over the bag once again, hoping her touch might comfort him. At 65 he showed no signs of balding, though his medium brown hair was well on its way to silver.

Thankfully, it was only an hour-long ride and when the boat docked, the bag was still empty. Asher helped his *zayda* stand up and stagger back onto terra firma. Moishe, still feeling ill, leaned on his grandson as he made his way back to the hotel with the rest of his family. The two blocks seemed like two miles.

Everyone except Moishe was hungry for lunch. "I may never eat again," he groaned, as he headed for bed.

At Ceil's suggestion, she and the others piled onto a bus and headed for a nearby shopping mall. "There's a really good take-out restaurant there. They serve authentic Hawaiian dishes."

When they arrived at the mall, she knew just what she wanted to order. "But I better call Dad first, to see how he's doing," she said. "There's a Jewish deli over there—I can bring back some nice clear chicken broth if he thinks he can handle it."

She soon had him on the line. "So, how are you feeling?"

"A lot better. By the time you get back with the food, I'll be ready to eat something."

"You want some chicken soup? Maybe a matzo ball if it isn't too greasy?" Ceil offered.

"Nah, chicken soup is for sick people." Moishe was sounding much more himself. "You're at the Hawaiian place, aren't you? How about some lau-laus? And get some rice, some lomi salmon . . ."

Ceil smiled, much relieved. He was back to his usual self.

———

Vacation or no, Moishe preached at a supporting church during that trip and took the family to meet one of his donors, who prepared a memorable meal of homemade sushi. Ceil was happy to participate in those activities; she had previously met and enjoyed the people Moishe wanted to see. But he also rose early each morning to write thank-you postcards to ministry supporters. *Plus* he spent time each day on his laptop computer, checking his e-mail. Ceil sighed, sometimes in irritation and sometimes in resignation to the fact that her husband would never, ever completely set aside his work.

The fact was, Moishe felt a personal interest and warmth toward those he thanked, and he enjoyed expressing his appreciation. Moreover he had a deep need to remain connected to the ministry he'd founded. He was still on staff, still a member of the board of directors, but he often felt disconnected and depressed now that he was no longer part of the hub of the director's office.

One of the most extraordinary things about Moishe was his willingness to give up leadership of the ministry he loved so well without any apparent pressure or even any apparent reason. The board had appointed him to his position for life. Considering that it was his life's work, and that his identity was so integrally entwined with leading Jews for Jesus, the general expectation was that the founding executive director would remain as chief until a crisis in health or a decline in mental acuity rendered him unable to continue.

Moishe, however, knew that God had told him it was time. It never occurred to him to ignore what he considered a clear directive from the Chief of All Things. It was an act of obedience.

It is true that Moishe had begun to feel that it would be better to have a leader with more energy than he had—but his health had actually improved by 1996. It is also true that he felt he was getting bogged down in administrative details. Although that concern played a part in the timing, it was not what motivated him. As he saw it,

> Once I believed God had told me I would be stepping down, I waited for the confirmation that was to tell me when. And I felt that the confirmation came in the fact that I could not get done certain things that an executive director should be able to get done if he was in charge of the organization. Ordinary things, like getting a sprinkler system installed in one of our buildings—I seemed to be hitting a stone wall.
>
> I was also concerned that we were not recruiting new missionaries. But none of these negatives had me stepping down. I didn't feel incompetent to lead, and I don't feel incompetent today. It was just a belief that that's what God wanted.

When it came to the nomination of his successor, Moishe had never said a word to indicate a preference. He often expressed satisfaction that several people in the organization would be competent to take over his position. And he had always encouraged the senior leaders to aspire to it. He'd told them frankly, "You ought to want my job." He wanted the next executive director to love the work as much as he did.

When in 1995 Moishe formally announced at a council meeting his intent to step down in 1996, the staff took very seriously the mandate to prayerfully select his successor. There was something so right about knowing that the next executive director for this group of strong-willed leaders was going to be ushered in by a unanimous vote of the council.

At the last council meeting where Moishe would preside as executive director, everyone present was struck with the reality that in mere months, the group would be discussing and voting on Moishe's successor. Moishe had outlined basic intentions about his future role: he intended to build a platform for the next executive director, to affirm and introduce that person through the ministry's publications and perhaps through key churches. He wanted to serve the next executive director in an advisory capacity. He also talked about writing, helping to train others, perhaps hosting a Bible study in his home, and witnessing on the Internet.

At the end of that council meeting, the group gathered around Moishe for prayer. David Brickner (who was serving on the council, as was I) recalled,

> We all came forward to pray for him, and something happened inside me that I was so completely unprepared for. I just—something deep, deep, *deep* within me emotionally just broke open. And I don't even know where it was coming from, but I was just weeping. As we were trying to pray, I couldn't say a word. And I'm thinking to myself, *What is going on?* But that was an indication of how deep my love for Moishe is.

David had absolutely no idea that the next time the Jews for Jesus Council gathered around someone to pray, it would be him—newly nominated to serve as Moishe's successor.

In the months and weeks leading up to that nomination, Moishe never tried to get a sense of how council members might be leaning. Yet a few days before the council meeting, he did ask if I knew who I would be voting for.

I told him that I had narrowed my short list to two people, and that between the two, I knew which I would probably vote for. "But," I told him, "I've committed myself to not being committed to any one person until we are actually voting. I don't know what God might do or what he might show us. And I want to do whatever I can to vote for the person he is choosing." Then I told him that as best as I could determine from my conversations with other council members, they felt the same way. Moishe nodded his approval.

The process that Moishe had designed allowed the council a full ten days of deliberation to reach a unanimous choice. If and only if they failed to do so within the allotted time, the task of choosing a successor would revert to the board. Moishe's system allowed for as many people on a beginning ballot as the senior staff might choose. The council would vote, and the lowest vote getter on the ballot would be dropped. The procedure would repeat until one name was left, and then a vote would be taken to see if the council would unanimously nominate that candidate. If not, the entire procedure would begin again.

When the time came, seven people were listed on the initial ballot, four of whom were voting members of the council. At some point, at least three and possibly four people would have to vote for someone other than themselves in order to reach a unanimous decision. What Moishe didn't foresee, and what no one had dreamed possible, was that once the voting began, it would take less than half a day to come to a unanimous decision.

Moishe had been on standby to address the group once a unanimous vote was reached. For participants in the meeting, it was a heady experience. There was a sense of awe that it had all happened so quickly, and the consensus seemed to be that God had given a powerful answer to prayer by uniting the council and working through them to make known his choice of Moishe's successor.

As Moishe entered the room, everyone made way for him to take his usual (now former) position at the head of the long table. There was a heightened sense of anticipation as he paused to catch his breath. What would he say to put the capstone on this amazing experience?

He smiled briefly and nodded to the group. He acknowledged that the choice had been made and expressed mild surprise that the position had fallen to David. The surprise was neither approving nor disapproving. He then gave a succinct talk that was fairly generic, inasmuch as it had been prepared to apply to the group, irrespective of the person selected. Moishe affirmed the process by which the decision had been made and his belief that God had worked through it. He went on to say that the strength of the organization had never been in just one person.

When I talked to him about it years later, Moishe admitted that he'd thought it likely that one of the older, founding leaders would have been chosen, but he never placed a value on that. It had merely seemed most likely to him. In fact, it had seemed more likely to David as well, which was why he had voted for one of those founding leaders and not himself in the first few ballots. So any surprise was not to be taken personally. Moishe had not been part of the process, and in retrospect, it must have been very difficult for him to address the group from a position of noninvolvement.

It didn't occur to us then, but Moishe had probably been in a slight state of shock when he addressed the group. Perhaps it might be more accurate to say that he was emotionally dazed. He'd designed the process to curtail his influence, recognizing that the group had to commit themselves fully and of their own accord to following the next leader. Then he'd initiated that process at a certain point in time, believing it was in obedience to God. But now there was no going back, and he had to deal with the reality that someone else really was going to lead the ministry that he had always led.

To my knowledge, Moishe had not spent a great deal of time reflecting on what it would be like when he was no longer the leader of Jews for Jesus. If he had known how hard it would be, actually handing over the reins of power, he might not have been able to do it—a fact he readily admitted in later years.

While Moishe apparently had not prepared himself internally for this monumental change, he did make preparations for his successor. David recalled,

[Moishe] already knew that he wanted to see a consecration service at Tiferet Israel, which was the messianic congregation where I was a member at the time.

And he also wanted to have a ministry-wide installation party/banquet. He had a certain amount of money he wanted to spend, and he wanted one of the board members to preside over the installation, along with her husband. He'd obviously thought quite a bit about how to memorialize the transition so that others would feel the importance and value of it. I appreciated that about Moishe.

In fact, David wrote about Moishe's part in the consecration service in an article for the Jews for Jesus newsletter:

Many who took part in the service offered me sobering admonitions.

Moishe took his turn, saying he didn't have a mantle to give me except his parking place at headquarters, the executive office, and the staff. But he did want to bestow a symbol of authority, and he felt it should be something that had belonged to him during his tenure as executive director. We waited in suspense as Moishe described how he had pondered what he might give. He felt it should not only help me face my new responsibilities but, if the Lord tarried, he wanted something that would someday also help my successor. Finally, he reached into his pocket and pulled out something that someone had given him long ago—a shiny, gold-plated yo-yo.

He proceeded to explain that while a yo-yo is a fun toy, it also illustrates some key principles. For example, the yo-yo can only function when it is in the hand of its master. In order for a yo-yo to work, it must be in motion. Sometimes that motion is downward, but the harder the yo-yo goes down, the quicker it comes back up into the palm of the master's hand.

In his inimitable manner, Moishe had used his trademark timing and humor to make some serious points without any sanctimonious stylings. Once again, it was "practical piety."

Though Moishe hadn't thought through all the ramifications and possible consequences of his choice to step down, he knew that it would be challenging for him to stop thinking and acting as the executive director. He therefore had apprehensions about remaining in San Francisco and thought it might be best to put some distance between himself and the headquarters office.

He told Ceil his concerns and suggested they consider moving to San Diego. They decided to remain in San Francisco, and later wondered, together and separately, if that had been a mistake. Yet it is questionable whether a geographical move would have addressed the depth of the difficulties that Moishe faced as a founding executive director handing over leadership to another.

Moishe wanted to be a help and support to David, and David had made a commitment that, as he put it, "any seat Moishe sat in would be a seat of honor." The two of them did far more to uphold one another than many others in their positions might have done. Still, each found the ability to help and be helped by one another less than what they'd hoped for in their new roles.

When Moishe would visit David for regular appointments at the office, he frequently arrived early or stayed later to wander through various departments. He had always done so when he was executive director, to assess how things were going. While no longer in charge, Moishe was still interested to see how things were going, and his "rounds" sometimes resulted in problem-solving initiatives that were no longer his to take. At times the new executive director agreed with these initiatives but at times they caused tension.

Meanwhile, Moishe had his own inner tensions to manage. He'd never intended to retire completely, and yet to his dismay, people outside the ministry often asked him how his retirement was going. He came up with a plan whereby he felt he could better serve the ministry while regaining some of the challenge and excitement that seemed to be lacking in his present situation.

Accordingly, Moishe came to one of his regular appointments with David and informed him that he wanted to turn things around in the department responsible for recruiting new missionaries. He wanted to head up that department, and as David recalled, he wanted to do so from the headquarters office.

David had not doubted Moishe's competence to oversee the department (known as minister-at-large), but he hadn't wanted to undermine the relatively new department head who, he felt, needed a chance to succeed at the task. Nor was David comfortable with a change that would have Moishe working daily from the headquarters office again.

On one level, Moishe was truly content not to run the mission any longer. He not only felt that he had obeyed God in stepping down, but a great weight of responsibility had been lifted from him. On another level, however, he still believed he knew how to do things better than anyone else. David wanted to avail himself of Moishe's wisdom and often asked him for advice—but quickly found that Moishe's idea of advice was different from his.

Perhaps former subordinates might have asked for Moishe's opinion or perspective rather than "advice" with more satisfactory results. When asked for advice, Moishe didn't take it as a request for a possible way to solve a problem. He took it as an invitation to impart information about the best (or sometimes, to his mind, the right) course of action. If that course was not followed, he took it as a sign of disrespect or rejection. This dynamic was not peculiar to his relationship with David; in general, many of Moishe's suggestions sounded a lot more like instructions.

Moishe was happy and magnanimous when his advice helped solve a problem or set a worthwhile project in motion, which happened frequently. However, on occasions when his advice was not taken, he had difficulty letting go. He also had a tendency to express his differences and disappointment to others, so that he sometimes fell short of his best intentions of affirming his successor. It was sad for mutual friends and colleagues to see his relationship with David become, on some levels, less than each had hoped or expected.

In addition to Moishe's periodic difficulty in "letting go" there were fundamental differences between him and his successor (whose nature was to be enthusiastic and upbeat), not in values, but in personalities. Past chapters recount Moishe's low grade depression, and his habit of preparing for the worst-case scenario. This was ingrained in his leadership style, as was his tendency to be skeptical of anyone he thought was overly optimistic or too expansive in their vision. These tendencies did not serve to ease the very natural tensions of transition that still would have existed between himself and his successor even under the most ideal circumstances.

Yet all was not gloomy for Moishe, nor was he shunted to the side after stepping down. One month after the council nominated David, Moishe had elective surgery and received a new stainless steel knee joint. His improved health that year enabled him to travel, speak, and consult on behalf of the ministry within the United States and abroad.

Early the following year (1997), Moishe trained new missionary candidates, who came to his home for lectures. He and Ceil also finished a book they had begun the year before titled *Witnessing to Jews*. It started as a rewrite of their previously published *Share the New Life with a Jew*, but the project grew as Moishe saw where the book could include further insights. The updated language made the book more readable, and the many additions rendered it a fairly comprehensive work on Jewish evangelism. He was also acknowledged as a contributor to the *Nelson Study Bible*, published by Thomas Nelson in 1997.

One of his primary interests was opening channels for the ministry to use the Internet as a "place" to witness. He entered the realm of chat rooms and acknowledged that while it was still important for Jews for Jesus to be visible out on street corners in major cities, the Internet was, in many ways, the new marketplace for public discourse. Following the family vacation in Hawaii, he began a new dimension of his work: summer interns.

Moishe taught from experience, and he deeply believed what he imparted to the interns and to the many others whose paths crossed his. Though some aspects of his post-executive-director years were more successful than others, he never stopped looking for ways to spend himself. He was always eager to invest in others, and he hoped they would benefit from what he had to give.

THIRTY-ONE

Our love cannot preserve itself
Nor our rightness last
O Lord, love us and we shall be
loved and love
Keep us right till we are
right with you.

—MOISHE ROSEN

O h, how we danced on the night we were wed. We vowed our true love, though a word wasn't said . . ."

Moishe smiled as he steered his wife onto the dance floor. He was comfortable, if not dapper, in his new size seventy custom-tailored navy blue suit. Originally he planned to wear one of his ubiquitous black wool preacher's suits, but Ceil was planning to wear blue, and as she pointed out, "Black and blue might not look so nice together on the dance floor or in the photographs."

"My wife always has to have everything color coordinated," Moishe had joked with the tailor. "Even me." Ceil was relieved that he'd agreed to a less severe color and fabric for this happy occasion. And even though she felt a bit self-conscious in front of so many friends and family members, it was nice to be in her husband's arms as the schmaltzy, romantic "Anniversary Song" emanated throughout the Crystal Ballroom of the Marine's Memorial Club in downtown San Francisco. It was August 27, 2000. They had been married for 50 years.

Much as the couple loved the nostalgic song, the lyrics, written four years before their own nuptials, did not quite apply. Moishe and Ceil had *not* danced on the night they were wed. They had been unable to afford a ballroom reception, let alone a dance band, and unlike tonight's festivities, there were no DJ's to be had in 1950. Regardless of its humble beginnings, Moishe and Ceil's marriage had lasted fifty years, and that was worth celebrating.

Lyn and I took care of all preparations and arrangements for the event. I was in charge of creating and mailing invitations, so I asked my father for his brother Don's address in Denver.

"He won't come," Dad said flatly. "I *would* like him to come. But I don't think he will."

Over the years the brothers had not found many occasions to stay in touch. Sometimes they phoned each other on birthdays or holidays, but the calls seemed few and far between.

Lyn and I began to pray that our father's brother would come to the party, and I wrote a special note on his invitation: "We want you to know this is not a perfunctory invitation. We would truly love to see you if you are able to come." I didn't realize that my uncle, who had been divorced for some time, was now seeing someone. But his daughter Jodi discreetly contacted Lyn and said that her father would be more likely to come if his date was also welcome. She certainly was most welcome! We were thrilled when Don wrote "yes" on the response card and came to the party, along with Jan, his wife-to-be.

Several relatives on Mom's side came from the Boston area, as well as a nephew and his wife from the Bay Area. Moishe's cousin Donald and wife, Ginni, came from Denver. This made Moishe particularly happy because he and Donald had been close friends in their youth. In addition to family members, many friends came from all over the country: one flew up from Los Angeles, while others, like one couple from St. Louis, traveled many more miles for the event. Leslie and Harry Wright donated their photography skills as an anniversary gift.

The party was a landmark event—not only because fifty years of marriage had become somewhat rare in twenty-first-century society, but because it seemed to signal a change in the relationship between Moishe and his brother. In the following years, they found more occasions to call each other and seemed to include each other more in their lives. Lyn and I saw this as an answer to our prayers.

———

The last decade of Moishe's life was characterized by a mixture of all the best and the worst that senior citizenry may offer. One highlight of the year 2000 was the new chapter in his relationship with his granddaughter, Bethany. She chose to attend San Francisco State University and settled in with her savi (grandmother) and zayda (grandfather), who were absolutely delighted to have her in the house. They hadn't lived in the same city with her since she was a very little girl, and now they would have the privilege of really getting to know her. Her presence added a wonderful new dimension to the first half of the last decade of Moishe's life.

After a year or so, Moishe began to think a great deal about his grandson, Asher, in Austin, Texas. Though bright and very computer savvy, Asher had opted not to go to college. He seemed to have no difficulty finding work, but Moishe was concerned that without further education, he might have a rather limited future. Moishe was also concerned that Asher was the only family member who lived so far from any other family member. The more Moishe thought about it, the more reasons he found to invite Asher to San Francisco.

Asher, three years older than his sister, had had a bit more time to get to know his grandfather before the Bonds left San Francisco. He recalled his first memory of his zayda:

> I remember him picking me up and hugging me and he had whiskers that made my face itch—I had never experienced whiskers before. My dad had a beard but that was softer. Zayda's whiskers were very abrasive. But he was very friendly so the whiskers kind of caught me off guard. He seemed like a really soft person so when you got to the whiskers, it was a shock.

In some ways, Asher's recollection is an interesting metaphor. Many others would agree that Moishe had a softness as well as an abrasiveness that went beyond his physical attributes.

Regarding Moishe's invitation to come to San Francisco, Asher said,

> At first he was trying to sell me on it, and I told him, "Well, you know I'm already kind of settled in here in Austin and happy with my life how it is." But when he said, "I need you to come," I thought about it and I realized, if he needs me, I'll go.

So it was that in 2002, when Bethany was nearly midway through her studies at SF State, Asher joined the household. He enrolled in City College, and Moishe really did rely on his help.

Diabetes and circulatory problems had caused Moishe's calves and feet to turn dark brown, almost black. His fragile skin blistered easily if bumped or scraped, especially when he traveled. One of the few things that could help was the daily use of extremely tight-fitting, knee-high compression stockings.

Moishe was too heavy to bend over and pull them on himself, and Ceil didn't have the strength or agility to get them on smoothly, without leaving painful creases. Asher became quite good at it. Moishe also relied on him often for companionship as well as his wealth of technological skills and knowledge. Their relationship was complex, caring, and occasionally frustrating.

For Moishe, the opportunity to bond with both his grandchildren over a period of several years was an unexpected and deeply gratifying pleasure. Bethany had lived with her grandparents for a couple of years before Asher came, and Asher remained after Bethany graduated and moved on to graduate school in Illinois. Moishe had ample time to get to know them individually, and they him.

Bethany recalled,

> Sometimes Zayda would ask me to go with him when he was speaking at a church. One time he asked me to go with him to the East Bay, and he sweetened the deal by promising to stop for sushi on the way back. The restaurant was fairly empty when we walked in, but soon two women were seated close to us.
>
> They were talking about chorus or music in general, and Zayda turned to them and mentioned how his wife loved music, sang in the San Francisco Choral Society, etc. To which we were immediately met with glares from the two ladies who then turned away to continue their conversation.
>
> He didn't allow the response to shut him down. While he attempted again to speak with one of them, the other turned to me disapprovingly, and said, "Who is *he* to *you*?"
>
> I was taken aback, but tried not to show it as I answered, "He's my grandfather." She immediately softened, and from there the conversation was pleasant.
>
> On the way home, we were discussing the whole occurrence. Zayda didn't bear the women any ill will for what they had first thought. He actually had a sense of [their moral indignation] being right, since they did not realize I was his granddaughter. I don't know how many people would have reacted the way he did. He didn't bear grudges and he often understood what others thought or felt.

Although Moishe was quick to engage with others, he was one of those rare people who didn't often feel lonely if there was no one around. Yet he really needed interaction to fully enjoy a meal, a movie, or even a good book, which he always passed on to others. He also needed other people to energize his creative processes.

David Brickner continued having regular appointments with him, more often than not at Moishe's home. Moishe also depended on Susan Perlman to keep him in the loop concerning what was happening throughout Jews for Jesus. Various staff, especially David, Susan, and I, often asked for his input on one project or another and found his ideas immensely helpful.

As long as his health allowed, Moishe attended board meetings, and though he absented himself from council meetings, he sought to maintain relationships with missionary staff. When the quarterly meetings of the Jews for Jesus council came to San Francisco, the whole group typically met at his house for pizza or Chinese food before beginning their deliberations the following morning. Still, Moishe often felt understimulated and, at times, underutilized.

I don't think Moishe ever entirely understood or accepted his post-executive-director role, even though he continued to make contributions. He worked toward what he hoped would eventually become a cyber branch of Jews for Jesus. While his travel had become more restricted due to his size and circulation problems, the world of the Internet allowed him to be in touch with people regardless of geographic location.

One of the people Moishe "met" this way was Jan Spence, who eventually became a co-laborer (trained volunteer) with Jews for Jesus. Jan had been using AOL for a few years when she noticed a Jews for Jesus chat room and decided to stop in. Moishe, under the screen name Mity Mo* asked her if she was a Gentile, and when Jan responded that she was a Jewish believer in Jesus, he sent her a private message, asking how she had come to believe. So began their friendship. Jan recalled,

> A few days later I found out that Moishe Rosen was the founder of Jews for Jesus, although it was already clear that he was regarded as the leader of the room. Even though it was an environment which allowed for very brief one line correspondence, Moishe [was] clearly a person who liked and cared about people. Periodically a curious Jewish person would come into the room. If I started to chat with the person, Moishe would send [me] a private

---

* Dad had a habit of joking with his name. While some thought the screen name was a bit grandiose for a ministry, Dad had mischievously taken on a nickname that to him, was a take off on "mighty mouse."

message offering encouragement. Other times antimissionaries would come into the room and Moishe would send a private message, explaining what an antimissionary was, how to tell, and how to handle the situation. Not only was he dedicated to sharing the gospel, but was also dedicated to helping others learn how to share the gospel and be effective.

While Moishe saw himself primarily as an encourager (and was seen by many others in that role) he still occasionally expressed himself in ways that could discourage people. But he could also be very good with apologies when he realized the need for them.

One occasion concerned a Jews for Jesus Rosh Hashanah service—including music, liturgy, and more—which a staff member had worked hard to organize. However, Moishe felt that the service had been marred by the announcement portion and I overheard him mention this rather bluntly immediately after the service to the person who was in charge of the service. I had an opportunity to discuss it with him, and a few days later he sent me a copy of his apology to that staff member:

> Dear (name withheld):
>
> After I left on Friday night, I felt I had really wronged you. I had hoped my criticism would be helpful but as is often the case I chose the wrong place, wrong time, and wrong tone for what I wanted to convey.
>
> I do want you to know that I thought your contribution to the service was excellent, except for the announcements. I should have waited to tell you what I felt needed improvement till later.
>
> Please forgive me for embarrassing you in front of your friends who should have every reason to appreciate their association with you.
>
> Moishe
>
> P.S. If you want to know how to make effective announcements I would be happy to tell you what I know.

Like most people, Moishe could usually identify weaknesses more easily in others than he could in himself.

Having had the privilege of serving a four-year term as the Jews for Jesus staff representative to its board of directors, I attended board meetings where many people tend to display both strengths and weaknesses, and Moishe was not the only strong personality from whom there was an occasional outburst. Once when he commented on a particular person's loud and derisive comments I smiled and said, "You and [said person] have a lot in common. You both express yourselves . . . forcefully."

However, there was one board meeting when Moishe had an outburst that deeply troubled me, even though it related to an issue on which he and I were in agreement. I carefully detailed my concerns to him in a letter. When I came to his house for dinner that week, he mentioned having read my letter. "I'm not going to apologize," he said casually. "I don't see anything to apologize for." My heart sank, but I did not argue the point and he apparently continued to mull it over on his own. Before the next meeting some three months later, Moishe wrote an eloquent and heartfelt apology, not only to the person whom he had spoken against, but to all the board members who had witnessed the incident.

Moishe taught by example, and that included how to give an honest and meaningful apology, a skill that, while often overlooked, truly is a measure of greatness.

Moishe also showed by example that it is never too late to learn and grow. For the most part, his attitude toward change was to embrace it when he could see how it was both useful and in keeping with his principles as well as his goals. However, he had little tolerance for what he viewed as "change for the sake of change" and even less tolerance for change that he believed contributed to slippage and/or was contrary to principle-based policies and procedures. But sometimes what he saw as slippage was a difference in procedures that was simply in keeping with the changing times and culture. He actually came to realize this later in life.

Moishe continued to work from home with a full-time administrative assistant. It was not the easiest position in which to thrive. On the one hand, an assistant had the privilege of quality one-on-one time with Moishe, something that most of his assistants found rewarding in and of itself. On the other hand, the Rosen home was somewhat isolated from the rest of Jews for Jesus and from the headquarters community, and the position did not seem to allow for upward mobility in the organization. This was probably especially difficult for younger people, and Moishe lost a couple of assistants sooner than he'd expected.

He felt the loss of both assistants keenly, but both times, Leslie Wright came all the way from Columbia to help during the interim when Moishe was between assistants. The continuity of having a friend from some of his earliest days in ministry was very heartening for Moishe, and Leslie became like a member of the family. Even when her services were no longer needed as an administrative assistant, Moishe kept in touch with her. It came as a terrible shock when, in 2005, Leslie was crossing the street just a block away from her own home and was hit by an oncoming vehicle. Her death deeply grieved Moishe.

As Moishe aged, grief over friends who passed became all too frequent. At times he seemed to wonder why he was still around when others he knew were gone—but this was particularly so when they were younger than he was.

At one point, the teenage son of a friend required a heart transplant. The boy's father had undergone the same surgery years earlier, and apparently the heart problem was hereditary. Moishe and Ceil had spent a great deal of time with the husband, his wife, and their twin boys, and Moishe had great affection for the entire family. His response to the news that one of the boys was so gravely ill was unforgettable. In a private moment, he told me with tears in his eyes, "I wish it could be me instead."

THIRTY-TWO

Death can be a friendly nap when you know you'll awake
to see your best Forever Friend, Jesus.
—MOISHE ROSEN

The phone rang at 4:00 p.m., interrupting the clatter of my computer keyboard. Reaching for the phone, I inwardly grumbled, *I hope it's not going to be a long call.* I was rushing to finish the day's work, anxious to get over to the hospital where my father had been admitted the previous night.

I could hear my mother on the other end, talking to someone else; I greeted her without waiting for a hello.

"Ruth? You might want to leave work early and come over to the hospital now."

"What's wrong?" Cold fear washed over me, leaving me numb.

"We have the result of the CAT scan and it's not good." Mom paused briefly. "The scan showed lesions on some of Dad's bones."

"Tell her the doctors said it's cancer," I heard Dad coaching from the background. Instead of repeating the news, Mom handed him the phone.

"It's cancer that's spread to my bones," he announced. It felt like a dream, the kind where you're underwater, struggling in slow motion to surface. I managed to say, "I just need to talk to David for a moment, and then I'll be right over."

Seconds later, I repeated the news to David Brickner, his administrative assistant, Steve Wertheim, and Susan Perlman, all of whom were not only colleagues but longtime friends.

David asked, "Can we pray before you go?"

I nodded.

At the hospital, Dad repeated the news, sounding matter of fact about his impending death. He needed more tests before the doctors would give a prognosis—but when you hear the words *carcinoma* and *metastasized* in the same sentence, followed by sentences with the phrase "palliative care," it's natural to surmise that the end is near.

This was particularly true for my father, who from his earliest adult years

283

believed that his end was near. Despite his fantastically fertile imagination, he never seemed able to picture himself living a long life. When I was in my twenties and Dad was in his forties, he made a point of saying, "Ruth, when I die, I want you to tell people that I lived a good, full life. Tell them not to mourn for me because I will be with the Lord." He was not ill at the time.

"Stop talking like that," my mother scolded. "Can't you see you're upsetting her?" She knew that I had a more than normal fear of death—not my own, but theirs.

I'll never forget the look of surprised hurt on my father's face. "But I need her to understand," he said. "It's no tragedy."

I thought I saw something beyond hurt in his eyes. It looked like fear—not of death, but that I would not understand when it was his time to go. It was startling.

"Don't worry, Dad," I reassured him. "I will pass on your message when the time comes. But I don't want to think about your not being around just now, okay? You know, just because you'll be with God doesn't mean we won't miss you."

He looked relieved. It was one of the few times I remember feeling that my father needed something from me. He needed me to face his death well.

Which brings us to February 12, 2007. As I sat beside him on the bed, he was quite calm, and my mother seemed surprisingly peaceful as well, though I know that on another level she was not. The news that a loved one has metastasized cancer is frightening, no matter what you believe about the afterlife.

It had been close to a year since Dad's good friend Zola Levitt had died of cancer. Dad missed Zola and thought of him often. Though they had their differences, in many ways they were kindred spirits. On the day of his own diagnosis, Dad pointed to Zola as a man of God who accepted death matter of factly and was determined to finish putting things in order before being called home. He wanted to follow Zola's example.

"The worst thing that could happen would be for my family to turn my death into a tragedy," Dad said, giving voice to that same concern he'd expressed some three decades earlier.

I hugged him. "We need to take one day at a time. Let's wait and see. No one has to say good-bye to anyone today." He nodded his agreement.

Dad called Lyn, and I could hear her ask if she could pray with him and he gladly assented.

Then I took the cell phone, went out in the hall, and talked with Lyn. When I came back into the room, my father was on the telephone with Bethany, telling her what I had been telling myself and my sister: "Now is when we find out if we really mean the things we say we believe."

There was a tremendous sense of love in the hospital room. I stared and stared at my father, shifting my gaze only occasionally to see my mother looking at him with similar intensity. I was trying to memorize every detail, every expression of his face, wondering how much longer he would be with us, wondering when there would only be photographs to look at when I wanted to see him. Mom was probably doing the same.

Before long it was past 6 o clock. Though my father's appetite was a fraction of what it had been prior to the pain, he wanted something to eat and was determined that Ceil, her friend Gwen and I should have dinner. He wanted sushi. And not just any sushi, but from a particular place he liked—in a part of town some 20 minutes away where parking was typically difficult.

Before I left the office, David had said to let him know if there was anything he could do, and I knew he meant it. I stepped into the hall and phoned him—and before long he arrived, bearing a huge platter of sushi.

David stayed for quite some time. Somehow the subject of honor came into the conversation and Dad said, "Do you know how you honor a person?" We waited for the answer. "You listen. That's how you honor a person."

His words were not lost on us. We sat and listened to him for quite a while, occasionally, but not often, interjecting questions or comments. While the talk was serious, the mood in the hospital room was not overly somber or grim. Many smiles were exchanged and bits of laughter broke out now and again.

When David left, Moishe looked content. "I enjoyed that," he said. And to further express his satisfaction he said, "I felt listened to."

I left around 11:00 p.m. The hospital provided a small cot for my mother so that she could spend the night in Dad's room. After receiving the day's news, the two of them were not about to be separated.

———

A couple of days later the picture of my dad's health was pulled into better focus, though it remained somewhat fuzzy. We learned that Moishe's prostate cancer was still treatable, though it had metastasized. Most patients were known to live for years with proper treatment.

Uncertainty lingered because we knew that Moishe was not "most people" and might not be numbered among "most patients" who respond well to treatment. He'd already had three completely unrelated near-death experiences. First he'd contracted septisemia from an infection in the prosthesis after his first knee replacement. I was out of town* when Ceil saw the angry red streaks on his leg called an ambulance, and then called Steve and Janie-sue Wertheim to wait with her. His mind clouded with fever, Dad was refusing to go to the hospital and became quite agitated when the paramedics attempted to move him. His size prevented even a team of men from taking him anywhere he did not want to go. Janie-sue stepped in, spoke calmly, quietly, and firmly to him and to the amazement of all, he responded with immediate compliance. Moishe later credited the Wertheims with saving his life that day.

Moishe also had nearly fatal congestive heart failure brought on, we discovered, by sleep apnea. Finally, he almost died from internal bleeding and severe anemia. The symptoms of this were hard to detect until, as Moishe later described it, "I was so weak that I felt like I could go [die] if I wanted to . . . and it wasn't a frightening feeling, but a choice. I decided I didn't want to go yet." His doctor later confirmed. "You were about as close to being dead as a person can be." The crisis had resulted from an aspirin-based over-the-counter pain medication taken with a prescribed blood thinner.

With each recovery Moishe continued to work, play, and live a fuller life than many who enjoyed better health could boast. When he opted to have his other knee replaced, it was a show of optimism for a better quality of life. However, this time no one was surprised when a post-operative infection set in and a second surgery was necessary to clean it out. When granddaughter Bethany visited Moishe in the hospital, he said, "Come here where I can see you better. Your smile is like medicine to me." She stood there and smiled at him for a while, and he smiled back. After a couple of minutes he joked, "Okay, that's enough. I don't want to overdose."

He could usually maintain a sense of humor for the first day or two of a hospital stay. Once when David came to visit him after a surgery, Moishe wondered aloud when someone would finally bring him a meal. "Well," David pointed out, "Jesus is the bread of life." "Yes," Moishe smiled. "And the Holy Spirit is the butter."**

Then in November 2006, Dad began suffering from abdominal pain and

---

* I was with Susan Perlman who had a speaking engagement a couple of hours away when my mom called to say that they were at the hospital.

** This was an allusion to the biblical symbolism of oil representing God's Spirit.

was scheduled for gall bladder surgery. Out came the gall bladder and several stones. The surgeon said it was no wonder Moishe been in so much agony. But on top of a stressful post-op infection that took weeks of intravenous antibiotics, the pain was not resolved; it became more acute and landed him in the ER. Hence the CAT scan that revealed the metastasized cancer.

When we learned more about his condition, Moishe seemed slightly disappointed to discover that his death was not impending. And when he came home, there were some very apparent as well as subtle changes. Morphine was prescribed to manage the pain that was, presumably, referred from the spine where tumors had taken hold. This drastically diminished his ability to taste food. Pound after pound melted away, ironically improving some of his other health issues.

Other changes were emotional and probably connected with the first tier of treatment—hormone therapy. Moishe seemed more in touch with his feelings. If he became irritable, he wondered aloud why something small should cause him to overreact. He often commented on my mother's dedication and hard work in caring for him, and often expressed appreciation, saying how much the love of his family meant to him. He worried about less fortunate people who had to endure terminal illness alone.

One evening he surprised me by apologizing for not having paid more attention to me when I was a child. When I assured him that I had never felt a lack in that area, he insisted on being allowed to tell me that he should have done more, as he'd done with my sister.

In late March of 2007, we got reports that Moishe's PSA count had dropped significantly, and he no longer needed the serious pain medication. The cancer was backing off and my parents celebrated their seventy-fifth birthdays with real gratitude that year.

Moishe was relatively free of pain for nearly a year. I'd even forget from time to time that he had cancer. I don't think that my mother ever forgot. She spent a lot more time with him in his office, just being there, even though his furniture was not geared for her small size.

Herb Links, mentioned in chapter 26, flew out for a visit and when he returned to Philadelphia, he maintained his friendship with Dad on a new level. Every night, with very few exceptions, he called Dad. He'd read a Bible verse, chat for a while, then pray for him. Sometimes they'd talk about mundane things . . . Herb bought expensive tickets to hear a musician and the man only performed one song. Sometimes Herb would ask for Dad's advice or opinion about a sermon he was preparing. But he always called, a true friend with a real minister's heart. I was often there when Dad's phone rang, usually around the same time each night, and whenever he'd answer, Mom and I (and anyone else who happed to be there) would all call out "Hello, Herb!"

Another relationship that seemed to grow stronger during Dad's illness was his friendship with Paul Liberman, editor of *The Messianic Times* in Southern California. Following are portions of a letter that Paul wrote to him in 2007:

> We have not many fathers among us. At present, who is more of a father to our Movement than you? It isn't merely age or length of time in the Body. There is a sense of integrity that comes through. Perceiving and expressing truth seems to be of great importance to you. Sometimes, people don't have ears to hear real reasons, as distinguished from the fig leaves we all wear.
>
> When I ponder, who can understand me, you keep coming to mind. . . . Your analysis has always been good, both in mundane and spiritual matters. If you ever want to speak into my life, I will be all ears.
>
> Sometimes, people are caught off guard by your piercing through human rationalizations. Being confronted with truth can make some angry, as they feel personally impugned, rather than helped. To me you simply quest after truth. I also admire the integrity upon which Jews for Jesus was founded and has continued.

Dad's answer was swift, appreciative, and lengthy. The following part responding to Paul's overtures of friendship gives insight into what friendship meant to him:

> I appreciate your affirmation a lot. But friendship is like marriage: it's a commitment which requires work and patience. You are among the few that I decided I would like to have as a friend. I'm talking about over a lifetime— maybe twenty people . . .
>
> To me, there is a healthy relationship that I would call less than a friend. . . . I don't know what to call the other category, but it's a category of persons that I feel I want to be good for them; I want to be able to affirm them; I want to be able to uphold them and to give them something. I have had hundreds and hundreds of these over a lifetime. . . .
>
> Let me say that when it comes to friends, you can probably find some that are a lot more enjoyable than me. But I try to be committed.

Dad sent many letters during his last few years, and also wrote some documents that he hoped would be published after his death. One document was as follows:

> I always thought of myself as being a rather ordinary person who was called by an extraordinary God. That was proved true by my successes in life. It seemed that by following His direction I was the right man at the right place at the right time to say "yes." . . .
>
> I never set myself forth to be admired, and I didn't want to be an example. I thought that there were better examples. I liked myself; I enjoyed myself; I made myself comfortable. None of these seemed wrong to me, because it seemed what other people were striving for. Yet, deep down, I always knew that God would reward those who stood for Him [in a place of discomfort]. . . .
>
> I enjoyed people more than they probably enjoyed me. . . . It was easy enough for me to like people, even to love them, but it was difficult for me to admire those who wanted to be admired. Those that I admired best were . . . hard workers, soft-spoken, and people who didn't continually think on what they deserved.
>
> If there's anything to be said about myself—I knew the value of God's grace: that I always got better than what I deserved, that I always achieved more than I expected.

Moishe kept writing for as long as he could. Eventually, bouts of pain made it difficult for him and Ceil to make plans, but Moishe continued to endure and didn't lose his desire to minister to others. He often spoke of his death, and while he could sometimes be morose about his limitations, he did his best to remain positive about his expectations.

An oncologist friend (Jack Sternberg, one of the Jews for Jesus board members) suggested that low-level radiation to the spine might greatly alleviate Moishe's pain. The cancer had doubtless damaged his vertebrae, which could wreak havoc with the nerves and refer pain to various parts of his body. A local radiation therapist corroborated the suggestion.

In one of Dad's e-mails to Dr. Jack, he wrote,

> I go in for my third radiation treatment today. Until last night I could say positively that I had less pain but then I had another episode. Nevertheless, I am optimistic; last night's episode of pain was less severe. . . . I was able to preach twice yesterday. Peter Sandberg who helps me said that my energy was good. . . .

I think you have helped me have a better quality of life. I wish you lived close 25 years ago. We could have had a lot of fun together. I would have enjoyed helping you sharpen your witness and your public ministry of teaching. I would have liked going fishing with you as long as you left the boat to smoke your required cigar. You wouldn't mind taking a walk on the water would you?

Moishe finished his radiation treatments, but signs indicated that the cancer was progressing again. Another hormone therapy was employed and worked, but not for long. It seemed like we were out of options. Moishe had a new oncologist who hesitated to recommend chemotherapy because of his other health concerns. From a previous conversation, the rest of the family believed that Dad did not want to subject himself to chemotherapy so we did not press him.

Thank God for our friend Dr. Jack, who explained, as Dad's own oncologist apparently had not, that many advances had been made and that unlike the old days, the chemotherapy for prostate cancer had relatively mild side effects. "My oncologist told me not to expect to celebrate Thanksgiving this year," Dad had told Jack.

"If you get started on taxetere," Jack said, "You'll be around for Thanksgiving. Trust me."

Jack was right. The chemo, begun in June, was no picnic, but it wasn't nearly as bad as Moishe feared, and was well worth it. It looked as though it would be a Happy Thanksgiving after all. Then in October 2009, a bowel obstruction sent Moishe back to the hospital for emergency surgery. The two-week hospital stay and subsequent recovery kept him off the chemo for about six weeks.

Nevertheless, Moishe did enjoy that Thanksgiving and even mugged for the camera, holding up a turkey drumstick with an expression that was meant to look voracious, though he only ate a few bites. In fact, from the time he came back from the hospital, Moishe never really regained his strength, and needed someone with nursing skills available to attend him 24/7.

Many old friends came by to see him over the following months, and Moishe made a tremendous effort to rally for these visits, no matter how poorly he was feeling. In February 1010 Darwin Dunham came to visit for several days. After so many years it was great to see him and to hear him say, once again, how profoundly Moishe had influenced him. We traded funny stories and a few minutes later, I looked at Dad, sitting in his chair, so frail, covered in his blanket. He was smiling. Well, that was no surprise. As sick as he was, when he wasn't in pain he smiled a great deal. I'd like to think it wasn't just the morphine. It was kind of an angelic, almost ethereal smile, and sometimes he'd do it in his sleep.

But this smile was different, somehow earthier. And he said to me, "I see so much of my own humor when you talk." I guess any child hopes that her parents will see things in her that will continue when they are gone, and a sense of humor is not the least of them.

Due to the seriousness of his illness, I'd requested that my annual speaking tour for the spring of 2010 be kept local. I still had nights out of town—never more than a few hours drive away—but was checking in daily by phone.

One evening I phoned my parents shortly before I was to speak. Typically I'd have waited until morning, but Moishe had been scheduled to have chemo that day, and I was eager to find out how it had gone. It hadn't. Clearly there was more to discuss, so after the service I called my parents from the motel. My mother broke the news: "The chemo isn't working anymore. The doctor said there is no point continuing the treatments." It was as though I was hearing his cancer diagnosis all over again, but now there were no more barriers between my father and the progressing cancer.

Do I ask people to pray for a miracle? I wondered. Then, in that place of intuition where God spoke, not only to my father, but sometimes to me, I knew that he really was going to die, that his time was coming and it would be soon. He had been spared for a little more than three years, and in March he managed to keep one more speaking engagement. We were very proud of him, and from all accounts, the congregation and pastor were moved by his message.

In April, Lyn flew out to be with us for Mom and Dad's 78th birthdays. She recalled,

Many people sent birthday cards but Mom's friend Gwen hand delivered her card. Dad decided to read it himself (his assistant Peter had been reading most of the cards to him) and then he told me to read Acts 2:20, which he thought Gwen had written on the card. I looked it up and read it:

> The sun shall be turned into darkness,
> And the moon into blood,
> Before the coming of the great and awesome day of the Lord.

It seemed so inappropriate that I couldn't help laughing, along with Mother and Gwen. Then I thought perhaps Gwen had meant to write Acts 2:21, so I read that verse too:

> *And it shall come to pass*
> *That whoever calls on the name of the Lord*
> *Shall be saved.*

That seemed to fit the situation a whole lot better, but Gwen said that she had not referred to either scripture in her card! Mom looked at what Gwen *had* written and saw that what Dad interpreted as "Acts 2:20" was actually "April 2010."

It was pretty funny, but points to something so typical of Moishe. He was always quick to turn to the Bible. It's not surprising that, with his failing eyesight, he mistook Gwen's handwritten date for a Bible verse.

It was hard for Lyn to leave, not knowing if she would see Moishe again. He loved having her visit but told her, "I don't want you to come back just to watch me die." But she wanted desperately to see him at least once more, and would return with Alan when the time came.

Soon after Lyn left, Dad entered a home hospice program. Thanks to the experienced staff, Lyn and Alan knew exactly when to fly out to be able to see Dad while he was still somewhat lucid. It turned out to be just a few weeks after Lyn's April visit. Bethany and her fiancé, Gary, had just finished their final year of veterinary school and were able to visit before returning to Illinois for the graduation ceremony. The joy of having the whole family together was tempered with the knowledge that the next time we would all be gathered was going to be for Moishe's funeral.

At times when he was awake, we all crowded around his bed, even the dog. At other times, a couple of us would stay with him while the others took a break in the large nearby den, remembering better times, and recording memories for this book.

Alan had the following to say about his father-in-law:[*]

Who is Moishe? He's the little boy in the story—the little boy in Hans Christian Andersen's "The Emperor's New Clothes." The little boy who is

---

[*] Early in Lyn and Alan's marriage, Moishe had told Alan, "You're not just my son-in-law; you're my son."

willing to either state the obvious when others are pretending, or the little boy who sees something that others have missed. . . .

Some decided to make a career of proving that Moishe was wrong . . . and may still be shadow-boxing Moishe to this day.

Still, there's a whole generation of men and women who have been mentored by Moishe directly or indirectly, who have embraced a lot of his philosophy—have tested it in their own arenas, and found it to be true. . . .

Who is Moishe? The kind of guy who gets a congregation physically marching around the sanctuary in a circle to the song "Marching to Zion." Why? Not because Moishe needed to lead; but because people needed a way to register their commitment. It's good for them to provide a way they can identify with something.

When Dad was really ill, he depended on Asher more and more. Sometimes when he'd wake up at one or two in the morning either in pain or else feeling the loneliness that creeps into the process of dying, he would call on Asher (knowing that Ceil, who spent almost all day every day with him, had difficulty sleeping.) Asher recalled,

> The most important thing he showed me was how, in the worst of his pain, he would always cry out to the Lord. And that was very inspiring to me. I had seen him in different situations where he stood up for what he believed in, but even through his worst struggles with cancer and the most painful situations he always cried out to the Lord . . . it showed me that even in the worst situations, I can still have that freedom.

At 2:30 p.m. on May 19, I was on an errand when I received the phone call from Barbara, Moishe's CNA. She urged me to come immediately to my parents' house. I was there within thirty minutes. The hospice nurse had arrived and stayed long enough to tell us that Dad would not be with us the next day. Standing quietly in the background was Lucy Ogden, the parish nurse from Moishe and Ceil's church. She had come for a visit that morning and had spent hours helping Barbara. When Mom suggested she go home, Lucy had told Mom very firmly, "I'm not going anywhere." Later that day, we were all extremely grateful for her foresight.*

---

* Having Peter and Barbara there was important, but Lucy was God's answer to our prayers that we would have "official medical help" at home when the moment came.

We planned to be up with him all night, but he did not keep us waiting. He died peacefully at 7:30 p.m., with Mom, Asher, and me each laying a hand on his fragile body, telling him that Jesus was waiting for him, ready to say, "Well done, good and faithful servant."

Dave Garrett, Susan Perlman, and David Brickner were there on the spot, continuing to act on Moishe's behalf, making calls and seeing to it that everyone was informed. Susan had already put together a press release that would go out the following day. The content of the press release (it was picked up by more than a dozen newspapers) saw to it that one of Moishe's longtime wishes was fulfilled: that even in his death, he would preach the gospel.

At one point, David and Susan took a break from their calling to come and tell us, "Do you know what day it was today? Moishe went before the sun went down. It was Shavuot."

I gasped. I could hardly believe it. I'd been too preoccupied to realize what day it was—Shavuot, the Jewish Feast of Pentecost! It is also a special time in church history; according to the second chapter of Acts, Jesus' promise to send his Spirit to empower his disciples to preach the gospel was fulfilled on Shavuot. Not only that, but Dad had made his first public profession of faith in Jesus on Pentecost Sunday. There is never a happy day to be parted from someone you love, but for us, there could be no more meaningful date to see him go.

When at last the people from the mortuary came, a new flood of tears sprang from my eyes, and I sobbed, "I . . . can't . . . watch them . . . take him away."

My nephew put his arm around me and said, "It's okay. *They're* not taking him away. God already took him a few hours ago."

He was right; what made Moishe Rosen a real person had not died, but had been called home to his Maker. Not only would he live on in our memories, but he was actually more alive now than ever, and one day, we would see him again.

Moishe was a man with a mission, called to controversy; a man with a beautiful soul and feet of clay. Now that his race was at an end, I could imagine him on the other side of that finish line, cheering on his family and friends, just as it says in Hebrews 12:1–2:

> We also, since we are surrounded by so great a cloud of witnesses, let us lay
> aside every weight, and the sin which so easily ensnares us, and let us run

with endurance the race that is set before us, looking unto Jesus, the author and finisher of our faith, who for the joy that was set before Him, endured the cross, despising the shame, and has sat down at the right hand of the throne of God.

CEIL'S POSTSCRIPT

How do you say good-bye to a husband you've loved and lived with for almost sixty years? My cowlicked, lanky young sweetheart and I were barely out of childhood when we started our new lives together—forever, whatever that meant to an eighteen-year-old. I don't think either of us fully understood what marriage involved, but we were convinced we could meet any challenge together.

The challenges came, and sometimes we survived only by God's grace. There was the melding of two headstrong personalities into a cohesive family unit. There were worrisome threats, like possible military conscription and financial uncertainty of temporary unemployment. There were heartbreaks— renunciation by family, friends, and community that followed our commitment to Y'shua (Jesus) as Savior, and perhaps most devastating, the loss of our precious unborn son.

The good things were also challenges: Moishe's call to missionary service and the subsequent successes that often stretched him to the limit of his capabilities; the delightful challenges of parenting two wonderful daughters, and new opportunities to establish bonds with family members we barely knew.

Different as we were, God "grew" us both through all those experiences. I always said that Moishe was the nice one. Even before we experienced the changing power of God's Spirit working in us, Moishe was patient, kind, and caring. He was unselfish and generous, sometimes to a fault.

As for household duties, Moishe loved to cook, but avoided cleanup. He didn't mind mowing lawns or gardening, but as to carpentry, painting, and other house chores, his willingness far outweighed his skills. More a student than a craftsman, he was inquisitive and could even enjoy reading the dictionary. He liked people in general, often watching strangers, conjecturing who they might be or what they did for a living. He studied a variety of subjects he found interesting. He memorized large portions of the Bible. Despite a slight stammer that he fought and usually overcame, he loved to preach. Conversely, he found it hard to sit in church and listen to someone else. Nevertheless, he made it a point to attend worship when he was not scheduled to speak.

He loved giving gifts and, having bought an intended surprise for someone, would usually have a hard time not presenting it early. He was so eager, he just couldn't wait! In general, he was good hearted, a great encourager, always supportive of people's talents, dreams, and aspirations.

He had a strict code of ethics and acted on principle rather than convenience both in leadership and in personal matters. He always respected my feelings, but occasionally attempted to steer my attitudes and behaviors when they differed from his. While we often argued over minor differences, we agreed quickly on life's larger issues. We trusted each other implicitly because we had promised never to lie to each other.

Because we married so young, Moishe did more than shape my life. Aside from my commitment to God, in many ways, for such a long time, Moishe *was* my life. When he became so sick that he needed a separate bedroom, I left him every evening with a kiss and "See you in the morning."

Toward the end, I was never sure I would see him the next morning. I would have liked to say those words to him as he took his last breath, but it happened so fast. I barely had time to say I knew Jesus was calling him home and would tell him, "Well done, good and faithful servant." I have said that farewell to Moishe often since then, and every time I miss him. When I see him again, it will be a great and glorious time, indeed the dawn of a new day. This, then, is the echo of my heart: Good-bye, my love. See you in the morning!

EPILOGUE

I complain, therefore I am.
—RUTH ROSEN, for MOISHE

Large amounts of morphine slow you down—not just your body, but your mind. For someone as bright as Moishe, an impaired thought process was particularly frustrating. Yet he maintained a sense of humor even through the final months of his illness.

"I was complaining to myself about my mind today," he told our family one night at dinner. "You know, how it's not working like it used to. And then I thought, *Hey, if I can complain about my mind . . .* " He trailed off, running out of energy and words at the same time.

"If you can complain about your mind, then you still have the ability to think critically?" I suggested.

"Yes," he nodded and smiled, glad to be understood.

"Sort of a twist on Descartes," I continued. "I complain, therefore I am." He laughed, and I was happy that he liked the joke.

It's funny, but it's true. One of Moishe's strengths was his tremendous critical facility. Being critical for the sake of being critical is useless, but the ability to see and say what is wrong is necessary if one wants to make things right.

This is not only true practically and professionally; it is a spiritual truth, and it remains at the core of the gospel. If one cannot discern the problem of sin, one cannot recognize the need for forgiveness. Months after Dad died, I was still looking through bits and pieces of his writings, one of which said, "Crime is an action against society. Sin is an attitude against God. We're all sinners. Trust me."

If one cannot recognize the presence of sin, how it affects us and why we need forgiveness, it is not possible to receive the good news of full reconciliation. Some people are so focused on the appearance of their own rightness that they spend all their effort to convince themselves and others of how right they are. Others do the harder work of *becoming* right, which begins with admitting that they are wrong and reaching for the hand that can lift them and help them to be right.

When Moishe heard the gospel, he knew that the part about him being a sinner was true. Over time, he came to believe the rest of the gospel was also true, though it made him an outcast from the community he loved. And in his new community, the community of believers in Jesus, he continued to see and say what he thought about what was right as well as what was wrong.

A preacher once said, "Your greatest weakness is an unguarded strength." If it is true that one's greatest weakness is an unguarded strength, perhaps it is also true that all human strengths have fault lines—fissures where pressure can build and things that seem firm are shaken.

My father was a brilliantly insightful man and, on most occasions, a compassionate man. But he was not an empathetic man. He often knew how others felt, usually because they told him in verbal or nonverbal ways, intentionally or unintentionally. He was a keen observer with uncanny intuition. He could sense when he had seen symptoms of certain feelings before, and that helped him intuit how people would feel or respond in a situation. He often sympathized with others. But he was too much himself to be truly empathetic. That, too, was a great strength that carried with it inherent weakness.

My father could not have been the decisive and cutting-edge leader that he was had he been less himself, setting aside his feelings or perspectives as a truly empathetic person sometimes does. Yet he might have had some different expectations, different behaviors, some perhaps for the better, had he been prone to step outside himself to imagine how others felt or perceived things.

Moishe knew it was important that his biography be quite clear that he was flawed. He wanted the world to know that God does not need people to attain a level of perfection to be used for his purposes. Those who knew and loved Moishe the most were very much aware of his shortcomings. I hope anyone who knew him only through his writing and through brief encounters will not love him less for having learned about some of his failings.

A robust personality often includes traits or behaviors that seem to contradict one another. Some may say this is inconsistent, and perhaps on some level it is. But it is also the mark of a very full life, packed with many experiences and many circumstances and many opportunities to succeed or fail at living out one's principles.

My father would be the first to tell you that what you think of him makes little, if any, difference. It's what you think of Jesus that really matters. So while this book is not meant to force beliefs on anyone, please excuse this one burst of gospel fervor: if you don't know Jesus and will consider him with an open mind and heart, I believe God will bless you beyond anything you have ever dreamed possible.

Moishe never considered himself God's gift to Jewish evangelism. Rather, he considered Jewish evangelism to be a gift from God, entrusted to him.

We can spend our brief lives any way we choose, but we can spend them only once. It's important to recognize value, in ourselves, in others, and in whatever work God calls us to do. That's something I learned from my father.

APPENDIX A

WHY WITNESS TO THE JEWISH PEOPLE?
BY MOISHE ROSEN

Until recently, evangelical Christians didn't have to think twice about Jewish evangelism. Evangelical churches realized the urgent need to present the gospel to all people so that others might gain God's forgiveness and eternity in heaven. It was understood that "all people" included Jewish people.

Now there is considerable deviation from the understanding that Jesus is the only way to salvation. Nowhere is this seen more clearly than in the attitudes of many churches toward Jewish evangelism. Some question whether or not the Jewish people need the gospel at all. Others say that Jews need Jesus, but they challenge just about any method of evangelism that doesn't begin with a Jewish person approaching a Christian to know more about Christ. Usually there has not been firsthand observation of the methods that are challenged or rejected.*

Why has Jewish evangelism become so controversial? Two reasons present themselves. One is the all too human tendency to choose the easy path. It's easy to go with the flow—to evangelize those who are down and out, who have no cultural barriers to prevent them from hearing our message. Jewish people are among the people groups missiologists have described as "gospel resistant." Jews who feel a need to resist Jesus tend to see him as a threat to the survival of the Jewish community. They do not realize that our survival does not depend on submitting to the religion of Judaism, but to the God of Abraham, Isaac, and Jacob. Anyone who wishes to take the path of least resistance will avoid witnessing to Jews.

The other reason is that many Christians—whether or not they realize or

---

* In a book titled *Rules for Radicals*, Saul Alinsky says that in dealing with opponents, if you can't attack their ethics, disparage their methodology. This is what we expect of antimissionaries because they see us missionary-evangelists as their opponents. However, it is most discouraging when Christians hear and repeat portions of the antimissionary propaganda or otherwise draw negative conclusions without checking with their own brothers and sisters in Christ to see if it is true.

admit it—want to be "politically correct." Maybe the second is just part of the first.

Most describe their inactivity in noble or compassionate terms. One says, "I don't target Jews. I preach the gospel to everyone who comes to my meetings." Another says, "Yes, Jews need the gospel, but they are so hurt by the Holocaust and other persecutions that we have no right to speak at this time."

Christians need to recognize that it takes courage to witness to someone who just might be offended, angry, or argumentative. It takes courage to broach the subject to someone who may not only reject your message, but reject you for telling it. A person who is not willing to do that sometimes finds it easier to come to terms with their own choices by putting down those who *are* willing to be rejected when they ought to be praying for and encouraging them for doing the difficult thing.

Some who want to be politically correct say, "The Jews have their own religion, an ancient and noble religion that predates Christianity." Yes, the Jewish people do have their own religion, and originally it was based entirely on Scripture.

Yet if the Jewish religion were sufficient in itself, why would the all-wise, all-knowing Son of God tell a religious Jew like Nicodemus, "You must be born again"? Why did God decide that Y'shua (Jesus) should be born to a Jewish mother in a Jewish place in accordance with the Jewish prophets? If the Jews didn't need Jesus, wouldn't it have been better just to have him born in Norway, Karachi, or Papua, New Guinea, to those who did need him?

But God demonstrated—not only through Scripture, but also by the Incarnation at Bethlehem—that if anyone needs Jesus, the Jewish people do. Jewish evangelism is important to God because he cares for the Jewish people and wants them to be reconciled to him. It's not that one person's religion is superior to another's. Religion is not enough without the reality of the Redeemer.

It is incumbent on the church to continue to evangelize Jewish people because like everyone else, without Christ, they are lost. Furthermore, Jewish evangelism is almost as important to the church as it is to those unbelieving Jews who need salvation!

The church proves its confidence in the validity of Jesus by earnestly endeavoring to tell all people about the gospel, regardless of what non-Christian religion they possess. If Christians decline to contend for the faith by remaining mute because of someone's religious background, we have basically assented to the world's supposition that biblical Christianity is merely another man-made religion.

Seeing the gospel of Christ as "our religion" is a trap! Those who don't know Christ quite naturally say that we are arrogant to suppose that "our religion" is The Truth. No Christian wants to be arrogant, and many shrivel at the accusation. But let's not confuse confidence and arrogance. We would be arrogant if we had invented the Bible, if we forged a "myth" that Christ was born in accord with the Jewish prophets to be the Jewish Messiah who would do miracles, die for our sins, and rise again. But Christianity is not a Gentile invention nor is it a Jewish myth. It is the truth of God, the Creator of the universe.

I have said it before before, and I will continue to say it: Bringing the gospel to the Jewish people is perhaps the most significant issue on which the church will prove its character, conviction, and commitment to evangelism in general.

APPENDIX B

MOISHE'S LETTER

Moishe asked to have this letter posted on the Jews for Jesus Web site after he died. Many of his obituaries quoted from it and thus fulfilled his desire to preach the gospel, even in death.

Dear friends,

If you are reading this, it means that I have gone on to my reward. As I write this, I can only think of what the Scriptures say and that is, "Eye has not seen, ear has not heard, neither have entered into the heart of man the things that God has prepared for those who love him" (1 Corinthians 2:9). Well, I have a big curiosity and by now, I know.

I don't suppose that I will be writing you any new material, but there are a few articles in the works that might still come through.

As I go, I feel that I have left a number of things undone. I think everyone must feel that way. There were words of appreciation that I looked for an occasion to express, but they didn't come. There were words of regret that I would have expressed to others. And there were words of encouragement that I had for all who were believers.

I'd like to encourage you to stay with Jews for Jesus. I was the Executive Director until 1996. Many things have changed. Some of them definitely for the better and others that I can't say were for the worse, but things that I would not have thought to do. Nevertheless the core of what Jews for Jesus stands for is still central.

As I go, one of the things that concerns me deeply is how much misunderstanding there is among believers. I never thought I would live to see the day when those who know the Lord and are born again were supporting the efforts of rabbis who, frankly, not only don't know Christ, but don't want to know Him.

To be an honest ministry, it can only come from the Holy Spirit; and the Holy Spirit can only indwell those who have the new birth and are born again. Therefore, I would urge you to think very seriously before you support any "ministry" that involves Jewish people and doesn't actually bring the gospel to the Jews.

Likewise, I am concerned over something else that I never thought that I would see or hear and that is, Jews who have become believers in Jesus and have important positions in ministry yet feel that their primary purpose is to promote Jewishness and Judaism to the Jews.

I hope I can count on you to show love and respect for the Jewish people, but Jewishness never saved anybody. Judaism never saved anybody no matter how sincere. Romans 10:9–10 makes it clear that we must believe in our hearts and confess with our mouths the Lord Jesus in order to be saved. There are no shortcuts. There is no easy way. Within Judaism today, there is no salvation because Christ has no place within Judaism.

Aside from these concerns, I want to say that I feel as I have always felt that we stand on the edge of a breakthrough in Jewish evangelism. Just a little more. Just another push. Just another soul—and we will have reached critical mass where we begin generating that energy that the whole world might know the Lord.

I would also encourage you to be faithful to those Bible-teaching, Bible-preaching churches that give spiritual food. More than ever, the church needs faithful members who can be an example to the young people coming in. Maybe there are some features about your church that keep you from being enthusiastic—look around and see if there might be a better church for you. If there is, join it and enjoy it. If your church is doing a lot right, then stay where you're planted.

I don't expect that Jews for Jesus will be undergoing any turmoil because of my demise. For many years, the leadership has been in competent hands, but this is a time when there needs to be some encouragement. The executive director and the staff need to hear that you intend to continue standing with us.

Anything done for Christ will last. Anything you do to help and encourage Jews for Jesus at this time will have lasting effects on all of us. So instead of saying "good bye," I'll just say, "until then—I'll see you in the sky."

MOISHE

ACKNOWLEDGMENTS

I'm thankful to every single family member and friend who took time to contribute to this biography: without your insights and memories, this project would have been impossible. There are too many to name, but I especially need to thank:

Moishe Rosen: Dad, I doubt you're reading book acknowledgments in heaven, but I still want to say that telling the story of your life has been one of the greatest experiences of mine.

Ceil Rosen: Mom, your "first eyes" input was invaluable. And your perseverance and enthusiasm as we teamed up in a project that meant as much to you as it did to me—what an unforgettable experience! It's a privilege to be your daughter.

David Brickner: You are not only "the boss" but a dear friend. I had no idea what I was asking for when I wanted to write this book, but your response encouraged me to dig in. You not only gave permission* but your eyes lit up over the prospect. The value that you saw in recording Moishe's life story, as well as your confidence that I was right for the job, means more than I can say.

Susan Perlman: Again, you're not only my boss, but a dear friend. Thank you for helping me pick up momentum with this book in 2008, and for patiently allowing me to take far more time to write a much longer book than I originally anticipated—even though you knew that no publisher would actually print the full manuscript! You let me do what I felt I needed to do, and I am grateful.

Thanks also to:

Tracy McElhone nee Stiffler, who transcribed hours of tapes from my interviews with Moishe and painstakingly indexed them.

---

* I work as a full-time writer and editor with Jews for Jesus, so the permission was not to write the book, but to do so under the auspices of—and as a large part of my work with—this ministry.

Josh Cohen, my trusty intern in 2007 who did a great job reading through and organizing countless documents for this project.

Bill Proctor, who authored the *Jews for Jesus* book in 1974; from which I adapted for the opening of chapter 22 of this book. He also mentored me when I was his intern in 1977, built my confidence then, and in subsequent years, and gave me the benefit of his expertise when it came to putting together the proposal to "pitch" this book.

Byron Spradlin who made the first contact with Thomas Nelson and wowed us all by saying they wanted to see the book proposal—and in fact the whole manuscript—before I had the nerve to approach them.

Joel Miller at Thomas Nelson, whose enthusiasm for the manuscript was so encouraging, and who actually succeeded in the unenviable task of paring the enormously long manuscript I handed him down to a manageable length.

Heather Skelton, at Thomas Nelson, who pulled together so many details to prepare this book for print.

The many, many friends who kept the writing and publishing of this book in your prayers. You may not know what a difference you made, but I sure do!

Always and most of all, to the One who is the Author and Finisher of faith and of everything else; I hope this book brings honor to him.